Praise for

The Jazz Age President

"Presidents are ranked wrong. In *The Jazz Age President: Defending Warren G. Harding*, Ryan Walters mounts a case that Harding deserves to move up—and supplies the evidence to make that case strong. No historian of the 1920s makes the case for Harding after Walters."

—**Amity Shlaes,** bestselling author of *Coolidge*

"He cut taxes and regulations, got the economy roaring, put America first after years of wearisome globalist utopianism, and for all his efforts was derided as unfit for the job. Ryan Walters's *The Jazz Age President: Defending Warren Harding* is a long overdue defense of the man who was Trump before Trump, a criminally underrated and unjustly maligned president who in a just, America-first ranking would be regarded as one of America's greatest presidents. This book is a timely and much needed salvo in the ongoing war to wrest American history back from the socialist ideologues who have dominated it for too long."

—**Robert Spencer,** author of *Rating America's Presidents*

"Warren Harding is perpetually labeled as one of the 'bad presidents,' as a bumbling idiot who couldn't write a speech, or as a philandering playboy with literal closet affairs, but as Ryan Walters expertly shows, this is unjust. Rather than one of the worst presidents, Harding should be regarded as a man who believed in the original intent of the presidency and who was able to stave off one of the worst economic crises of the twentieth century by doing nothing. You'll have a new appreciation for Wobbly Warren after reading this book."

—**Brion McClanahan,** author of numerous books on American history, including *The Founding Fathers Guide to the Constitution* and *9 Presidents Who Screwed Up America and Four Who Tried to Save Her*

THE JAZZ AGE PRESIDENT

THE JAZZ AGE PRESIDENT

Defending Warren G. Harding

Ryan S. Walters

REGNERY
HISTORY
Washington, D.C.

Regnery History™ is a trademark of Salem Communications Holding
Corporation
Regnery® is a registered trademark and its colophon is a trademark of Salem
Communications Holding Corporation

Cataloging-in-Publication data on file with the Library of Congress

ISBN: 978-1-62157-884-0
eISBN: 978-1-68451-280-5
Library of Congress Control Number: 2021946364

Published in the United States by
Regnery History, an Imprint of
Regnery Publishing
A Division of Salem Media Group
Washington, D.C.
www.RegneryHistory.com

Manufactured in the United States of America

10 9 8 7 6 5 4 3 2 1

Books are available in quantity for promotional or premium use. For information on discounts and terms, please visit our website: www.Regnery.com.

CONTENTS

WHY DEFEND WARREN G. HARDING?

"Harding is reckoned a rock-bottom Failure by the experts, and this view is so commonly held that for an historian to argue otherwise is heresy."

—*Thomas Bailey*

Tell someone you are writing a book about President Warren G. Harding, and you will get quizzical, even skeptical looks. "Why write a book on him? Wasn't he a really bad president?" is a typical response. Or, "Didn't his wife poison him?" That's another one I've heard. My answer is: Why not? Warren Gamaliel Harding, more than any other American president, has been named the worst chief executive in our history. He is the butt of many political jokes, all of them bad. But the "conventional wisdom" on the twenty-ninth president is incorrect. Simply put, Warren Harding deserves defenders to counter what has been a smear campaign against him for nearly a century. I am one of his defenders, few as there are.

As a student of history, I was always familiar with Harding but, like most everyone else, only vaguely so. Back in the 1990s, I was an enthusiastic backer of Patrick J. Buchanan, whose Harding-style "America First" campaign drew me to support his presidential candidacies in 1992, 1996, and 2000. I remember watching coverage of the 1996 campaign on CNN. One conservative commentator, defending Buchanan, referred to Bill Clinton as "the Democrats' Warren Harding." Such comparisons never sat well with me even then, but not because the comparison was unfair to Clinton; it was unfair to Warren Harding. But if you had asked me to defend Harding at the time, I would have been very short on ammunition. From careful study over the subsequent years, I've found out that most of the tales about President Harding are in the realm of myth, not fact.

A Marion, Ohio, newspaper editor, Warren Gamaliel Harding won election to the presidency in 1920 and served nearly two and a half years before dying in office in August 1923. He had previously served in the Ohio state senate from 1900 to 1904 and had then gone on to serve a two-year term as lieutenant governor. After losing the 1910 election for governor, Harding rebounded in 1914 and won a seat in the U.S. Senate, where he served until his election as president. His political career was just fifteen years, certainly not the satisfaction of his life's ambition, and they were years filled with heaps of scorn and ridicule.

The more I learned of the jokes, the rumors, and the lies, the more determined I was to right the wrong. The more I studied Harding, the more I admired him. The more I looked into his personality, the more I liked what I found. Harding was staunchly conservative and in favor of "America First." Coming from humble origins, he was a people person who liked to spend time with average, everyday, ordinary folks, not politicians or stuffy academic types. He loved animals, particularly dogs, and had no tolerance for those who treated them cruelly. Harding came out of small-town America, and he believed it was the heart and soul of the country—a belief rare among presidents.

In many ways, Harding was the personification of the Jazz Age, the name pinned on the decade of the 1920s by F. Scott Fitzgerald. More popularly known as the "roaring twenties," it was unlike any period in American history. By 1920, for the first time in history, more Americans lived in urban areas than in the countryside, helping push a second industrial revolution that, along with old-fashioned laissez-faire economics, made the economy roar. People were bursting with optimism about the future. No other decade can match the energy of Harding's era.

The Jazz Age was a transformative period for America, when the old values of the Victorian era were giving way to a new outlook on life. But not everyone looked on the changes with approving eyes. There were those who clung to the morals of the old times that were clearly slipping away. These Victorians characterized this age of a new, emerging America as a period of great moral disintegration, not one of robust dynamism. They believed that old-fashioned mores needed to stay rigidly in place to curb mankind's natural impulses. And very few of them would be enamored with President Harding. Victorians were prim, proper, prudish, and puritanical—everything Warren Harding was not, at least not in their wary eyes. Despite prevailing opinion, though, Harding was not a moral degenerate; he simply radiated vigor, vitality, and vivaciousness, just like the era in which he served as president. In contrast to Woodrow Wilson and the academic world from which he came, Harding was energetic and had a magnetism that attracted people to him. That same force would stamp the decade with the robustness for which it is known.

Despite his kind, caring, and fun-loving ways, as well as his fierce dedication to America and the American people, Warren Harding is the most maligned president in American history, needlessly wronged by historians, scholars, and political commentators who may acknowledge his kindheartedness but have been merciless with his record as president, as well as loose with the facts of his personal life.

In this book I will tackle eight major myths regarding Warren Harding and his era, the roaring twenties. First, his detractors say he was not intelligent—even dumb, certainly not fit for the presidency (a fact he himself readily admitted). Second, while in the U.S. Senate, before he became president, he was a man of no accomplishments, a backbencher. Third, as a "dark horse" candidate, he was nominated in a "smoke-filled room" by a select group of powerful senators who chose him because he was pliable and could be easily led. Fourth, while president, he allowed his cronies, known as the "Ohio Gang," to loot the public treasury, a plan that was put in place during the nominating process, well before the presidential election in November 1920. Fifth, during his tenure in the White House, some 882 days, he had no great achievements. Sixth, a notorious womanizer all his life, Harding had relations with mistresses in a closet just off the Oval Office. Seventh, he died in a mysterious way, possibly by poisoning, either by his wife or by his own hand. Eighth, and finally, Harding and his era of excess led directly to the Great Depression of the 1930s. This book will answer and correct each one of these legends.

My goal in writing this book is to produce a work for the general public. Judging by surveys and polls, much of the population knows very little of the real Warren Harding. So rather than do what others have done and write a massive five-hundred-page academic treatise covering every aspect of Harding's life and administration, my aim is to write a smaller, more concise political profile covering the major aspects of Harding and his presidency, defending him against his critics, and helping to educate those who may know little of the humble newspaperman from Marion, Ohio. In short, I'm interested in setting out what Warren G. Harding got right in both his life and his administration, to show that he was a much better president than advertised.

Defending President Warren Harding may be a daunting task, but it is of particular importance for conservatives in the present time because of Harding's similarity to former president Donald Trump. In 2016, Trump ran what amounted to a Harding campaign. Harding's "return to normalcy," Jared Cohen has written, "was basically the 1920s version of . . . 'make America great again.'" Both Harding and Trump campaigned on "America First" policies on trade, immigration, foreign policy, and putting the American people first. And, like President Harding, Trump was attacked—in similar ways and for similar reasons. The establishment despises those with such a viewpoint; it always has. So it's important for those who hold similar values to defend President Harding and the issues for which he stood.[1]

Hopefully, change is on the horizon. The Warren G. Harding Home and Memorial in Marion, Ohio, recently underwent a major renovation and expansion to fully restore it to its original likeness in 1920, when Harding ran his famous "front porch campaign." A new Warren Harding presidential center recently opened in Marion near the site of Harding's home. So interest in Harding and his presidency should certainly increase in the future and, with any luck, people will realize what they've been told about President Warren Harding does not reflect historical truth.

Over the decades there have been gentle pushes forward from those with open, honest minds who have looked at the evidence. John W. Dean's book on Harding for Arthur Schlesinger's American Presidents series has helped begin to turn the tide in recent years, but while there have been a few articles, columns, and book chapters, there have been few major book-length works aimed at restoring Harding's reputation. My undertaking, then, is to stand on the shoulders of those who have gone before me and take another step in the right direction, and to uncover why Warren Harding is so maligned by "mainstream scholars." Why do people say what they say about him? Where does it all come from?

But with all the good that may come from this book, there will also be some bad, as most assuredly I will get tagged with the dreaded label "historical revisionist," or worse. As Thomas Bailey observed in *Presidential Greatness*, "Harding is reckoned a rock-bottom Failure by the experts, and this view is so commonly held that for an historian to argue otherwise is heresy."[2] Presidential historian Michael Beschloss once told the *New York Times* in regards to Harding, "If you had to reach for a great revisionist mountain to climb, that would be it."[3] So in this book I shall be committing historical heresy, ascending the Everest of historical revisionism. But "revisionist history" is not really an accurate description of this book. The true revisionists are those scholars and journalists—some beginning while Harding was alive, others emerging soon after his death in 1923 and before his papers were made public in 1964—who are responsible for the campaign to smear and besmirch our twenty-ninth president and his legacy, causing his reputation to suffer and pushing him to the bottom of presidential rankings. I am simply trying to restore Harding to what he once was in the eyes of the American people: a beloved president. So if I am to be labeled by journalists and historians, I hope it will be as a historical protector and restorer.

THE MOST MALIGNED PRESIDENT IN AMERICAN HISTORY

*"No president has managed to sink in history's estimation
to a level below that of Warren Gamaliel Harding."*

—Robert W. Merry

The United States found itself in the midst of turmoil not seen since the days of civil war. The nation had endured a decades-long period of progressive reforms that changed the relationship between citizen and government. A war in a distant, foreign land saw the loss of over 100,000 soldiers, and new laws imprisoned those who dared to speak out against it. A horrific bout of a new strand of influenza took the lives of nearly 700,000 Americans, infecting as much as a quarter of the entire population and spreading fear across the country. An economic depression drove up both unemployment and the cost of living, and wartime taxes and government spending remained sky-high two years after the conflict had ended. A summer of discontent and violence disrupted domestic tranquility—a tumultuous period that included labor strikes, acts of terrorism, and the lynching of scores of citizens simply because of the color of their skin. And to make matters worse, the sitting president, who had been campaigning across the country to win support for an unpopular peace treaty in the midst of a nasty fight with the Senate, had suffered a debilitating stroke that remained hidden from the public for months, effectively bringing his administration to a screeching halt, leaving the nation a ship adrift at sea without a rudder.

The majority of the American people, already saturated by twenty years of change, had reached the breaking point and were more than ready for new leadership and a new direction. The recent international crusade had simply been too much. When the long-awaited national Election Day finally arrived, the people threw out the ruling party and selected a new president who pledged a return to more normal times. He vowed to make no new reforms—and to heal the nation of its economic and social disruptions. And he succeeded in a shorter period of time than anyone had thought possible. After he instituted a program of retrenchment, the economy rebounded rapidly, soon growing at a rate scarcely ever seen in the history of the country, while unemployment eventually fell to a level no one had thought possible. Much of the violence subsided as the new chief executive called for new laws and a new crackdown on vigilante justice to make American democracy as inclusive as it was boasted to be. Those who had suffered the loss of their liberty simply for having the audacity to exercise it were redeemed. For the most part, the nation was calm and at peace, even jubilant, for the next decade.

Surely an American president able to calm such turbulent national waters and achieve such extraordinary accomplishments should rightfully be regarded as one of the nation's greatest. But sadly that is not the case, for the American president whose remarkable achievements I have just outlined is none other than Warren Gamaliel Harding, the most maligned and slandered chief executive in U.S. history, the occupant of the White House who has, with little doubt, received more scorn and abuse than any other. Rather than being praised for his accomplishments, he is the butt of political jokes, frequently subjected to ridicule, and almost never missing from a "Worst Presidents" list. Historians have labeled him "Worst President Ever," "Dead Last," "Unfit," "Corrupt," "Immoral," "Incompetent," "Inept," "Shallow," "An Amiable Fool," and a "Notorious Womanizer." Many contemporaries were equally cruel. The Baltimore journalist H. L. Mencken once said of Harding, "No other such complete and dreadful nitwit is to be found in the pages of American history."[1] To Teddy Roosevelt's oldest child, Alice Roosevelt Longworth, he was simply a "slob."[2] To Rexford Tugwell, a member of FDR's esteemed "brain trust," he was "shady" and "demeaned" the White House.[3] In our modern era, Harding is used as a stick to beat other presidents. In 1981, Ralph Nader said of the new chief executive, "Ronald Reagan is the most ignorant President since Warren Harding."[4] Such is the historical reputation of the twenty-ninth president of the United States.

Despite his popularity as a newspaper editor and politician in Ohio, his popularity as president of the United States, and his likable, good-natured personality, the nation's scholars have always tended to judge Harding very harshly. To Nathan Miller, author of *Star-Spangled Men: America's Ten Worst Presidents*, Harding was "a prime example of incompetence, sloth, and feeble good nature in the White House."[5] University of Texas history professor Lewis L. Gould wrote that Harding's performance as president "fell well short of the high standards of his office."[6] Paula Fass's essay on Harding in *The American Presidency*, edited by Alan Brinkley and Davis Dyer, opens with this sentence: "The presidency of Warren G. Harding began in mediocrity and ended in corruption."[7] Historian Elaine Weiss calls him "quite the bumbler."[8] West Virginia University professor Robert E. DiClerico wrote that the nation's current presidential primary process has not "yielded a nominee whose overall level of competence was as deficient as Warren Harding's." In fact, he claimed, "Warren Harding proved to be the most inept president in this century."[9] Harding was the "most disgraced president in the country's history," in the judgment of William J. Ridings and Stuart B. McIver in their 1997 book *Rating the Presidents*.[10] He was "in far over his head." Such judgments of Harding are not exceptions; they are the rule.

Even Hollywood movies take shots at Harding and liberties with his legacy, most particularly his alleged womanizing. The 1994 film *Cobb*, a baseball movie based on the fanciful tales of reporter Al Stump, depicts a bawdy party scene, which viewers would most likely surmise was in the White House, complete with half-naked gals, booze, and poker.

Tommy Lee Jones, playing the part of Ty Cobb and narrating the film, praises Harding, who "had the best broads and threw the best damn parties," in contrast to his successor, Calvin Coolidge, "who wasn't any damn fun at all." Six years later, *Thirteen Days*, a film about the Kennedy White House during the Cuban missile crisis, managed to slip in a joke about Harding. As several of JFK's cabinet secretaries are being directed into the White House through a secret underground tunnel so as to avoid detection by the media, one remarks, "I hear ole Warren Harding used to get his girls in through here." Aside from the fact that known tunnels under the White House weren't built until World War II, these depictions are not accurate representations of the Harding presidency or the man's character.

A sleazy version of Harding was also featured in the first season of the HBO series *Boardwalk Empire*. His actual character, played by Malachy Cleary, appears in only one scene of one episode, where Harding, then the Republican nominee for president, is introduced by Harry Daugherty to the show's main character, the gangster "Nucky" Thompson. Harding's mistress, Nan Britton, along with baby Elizabeth, tries to enter the gathering. In the scene, Harding's popularity is accurately represented, though his morals and intelligence are not. In a later scene of the same episode, Nan Britton reads a steamy, amateurish poem Harding has written for her, then excuses herself to use the ladies' room. At that point "Nucky" comments, in reference to the poem's author, "That imbecile is going to be the next president of the United States."

While James Buchanan is sometimes awarded the title of "worst president," it is Warren Harding who has been subject to more mockery and who has finished last in a majority of presidential rankings. In fact, Harding finished dead last in every one of the six major polls of presidential historians from 1948 to 1996. "Warren G. Harding occupies an unenviable position in the pantheon of United States presidents," write Ridings and McIver. "He has been voted the worst chief executive in every presidential poll ever conducted." Ridings and McIver rank him last in their own poll, too. Only in recent years has the Harding star risen, and only very slightly. In a 2005 survey by the *Wall Street Journal*

Harding managed to move up one notch. In two C-SPAN surveys in 2000 and 2017, Harding managed to get off the bottom rung but remained in the "failure" category, up by only four spots.[11]

These low marks shouldn't surprise anyone, given Harding's reputation among scholars, writers, and teachers of history. Columnist Douglas Alan Cohn called him a "dupe." Harding, he wrote, "looked the role, but was otherwise not presidential, and his corruption-filled administration seemed to be the result of his devil-may-care, easygoing, can't say 'no' approach to life that carried over to governing."[12] David C. Whitney wrote that Harding's presidency "stands as a black mark in American history."[13] And Kenneth C. Davis described him as "indecisive," "lazy," "intellectually weak," and "incompetent." Harding's reputation is so bad that he is not even mentioned in the fifteen-part 1999 ABC News documentary *The Century: America's Time*. Nor is Calvin Coolidge—or the economic boom they created and presided over.[14]

As we passed the hundredth anniversary of his election to the presidency in 2020, Harding continued to receive heaps of abuse in the press. Just in the last few years, with the release of erotic letters Harding once wrote to a lover, numerous articles and one salacious book have appeared to sully his reputation further. The book, authored by Eleanor Herman, brims with scandalous tales about a sex life that "involved a rotating buffet of delectable young women."[15] But perhaps a headline on *Politico*'s website said it all: "America's Horniest President."[16] Harding, who in truth had perhaps two mistresses in his lifetime and none while in the White House, is depicted as being far worse than Democratic presidents who had women issues—it now seems as if FDR, JFK, LBJ, and Bill Clinton, all of whom had an abundance of dalliances, never existed. With such a vast amount of mistreatment piled on Harding by historians and journalists, it's easy to see why the public would have such an unbalanced view of him.

It is certainly within the realm of possibility that at least some of the negative opinion about President Harding is due to political differences. Harding's status as the consummate conservative president has obviously led to many of the assaults by historians who do not share his worldview.

Writing in 1966, Thomas Bailey, a scholar of the presidency and American foreign policy, noted that Harding is "generally downgraded by the experts, themselves largely Democrats who admire Wilson and the League of Nations which Harding spurned."[17] Robert Spencer, who ranked Harding as the ninth best president in his book *Rating America's Presidents*, agrees, writing, "Harding's presidency deserves an honest reassessment, but that is unlikely to happen given the fact that most historians today share Wilson's messianic globalism and visions of massive state control."[18]

In fact, polling has revealed that most of academia consists of liberal-leaning professors. Naturally, they often give bad marks to conservative presidents in comparison with those who supported expanding government. "Harding is an underrated president because he is being ranked by those who overrate the capabilities of the federal government," explains Professor Burton Folsom.[19] But in an interesting 1982 survey that divided the scholarly respondents into "conservative" and "liberal" categories, *both* groups picked Harding as the worst president,[20] which can only mean that the many false and sensationalist writings about Harding that emerged soon after his death in August 1923, as well as those still appearing in the media, are continuing to have an impact. As this book will demonstrate, the bulk of those lies, rumors, and smears directed at Harding, which later generations took as fact without any attempt at corroboration or balance, came from left-wing journalists and Democratic politicians.

For students of the modern presidency, presidential success seems to center on "the vision thing," as President George H. W. Bush described it. Progressive, forward-looking, idealistic presidents, such as Woodrow Wilson, certainly had it; Harding most certainly did not, his detractors continually tell us. Charles F. Faber and Richard B. Faber, in *The American Presidents Ranked by Performance*, assert that Harding "was not an inspirational leader" and "did not provide energetic and creative leadership" as president. He "did not have an organized plan laid out" for the accomplishment of a list of goals and "was not much concerned about long-range planning, being more interested in the present than in the future. . . . Lacking charisma, Harding did not inspire people. They followed him mainly because he and they wanted to go in the same direction."[21] According to the Miller Center at the University of Virginia, which studies the American presidency, "Most historians regard Harding as the worst President in the nation's history. In the end, it was not his corrupt friends, but rather, Harding's own lack of vision that was most responsible for the tarnished legacy."[22]

"Lack of vision." "The vision thing." It's the weapon used most often against conservative presidents, who are regularly denounced for a lack of action to implement an ambitious vision. As Gould has written, scholars deride Harding as a conservative who "failed to use the powers of the institution in the forceful manner of Franklin D. Roosevelt during the New Deal." Harding and his conservative successors are seen as "actual detriments to the forward progress of the president."[23] William E. Leuchtenburg, a scholar of Franklin D. Roosevelt, agreed, writing that with Harding and the Republicans of the 1920s, "the expansion of the presidency all but ground to a halt." Conservatives have no great and far-reaching vision, it is widely held in academia, so therefore they cannot and will not forcefully use the awesome powers of the presidency for the common good.[24]

It is true that a "conservative vision" for the nation can *almost* be considered an oxymoron. Conservatives such as Harding seek a restrained government that remains within its constitutional bounds and a presidency that resides within its clearly defined limitations, rather than a "grand vision" of "new powers" for a "new nation." But Harding did not actually suffer from a lack of vision; his vision was just not what his many progressive cynics wanted to see from their president. As Charles and Richard Faber have conceded, "Harding was no visionary, but he knew he wanted a nation of peace and prosperity and a world without war. This was a sufficient vision for his countrymen at the time."[25]

Harding's campaign promise to "return to normalcy" was not so much about returning the country to what it once was before the era of progressivism, a state of affairs more in line with the vision of the "founding fathers," a term not coined by Harding but certainly made more popular by him, as it was about a return to normal times, reestablishing order in what had become a very chaotic time. Harding did take the office of the presidency—which was never meant to be an active office constantly pushing unwanted and unnecessary change on the people, but more of an administrator overseeing the operations of the executive branch, most specifically foreign affairs—back in the direction the founders intended. In fact, when he campaigned for the presidency, Harding did not promise any major reforms. As he said in perhaps his most famous campaign speech in May 1920, "America's present need is not heroics, but healing; not nostrums, but normalcy; not revolution, but restoration. . . ." The country had experienced enough change during the Progressive Era. "The world," he said, "needs to be reminded that all human ills are not curable by legislation."[26]

When Harding took the presidential oath of office on March 4, 1921, America was in decline as it emerged from World War I. The economy was deteriorating, tumbling into what some economists have labeled "the Forgotten Depression." Unemployment, federal spending, the national debt, and the cost of living had all soared to levels not seen in a generation. Manufacturing production had declined significantly, as had overall economic growth. Farmers were hurting as much as industrial workers. To make matters worse, the new income tax, initially sold as a "tax the rich" scheme in 1913, now touched everyone, with some rates seeing a ten-fold increase by 1918. There were also a host of problems in U.S. foreign relations and the nation's social fabric.

The torrent of problems that faced the country was daunting, but even that fact is denied to diminish President Harding's accomplishments. Jeremy Rabkin of Cornell University has written, "No one ranks Warren G. Harding among our great presidents. His administration did not face the sorts of challenges that call for heroic leadership. Harding came to office when the Great War had already been won—and President Wilson's peace treaty had already been rejected by the Senate." Professor DiClerico has asserted along the same lines that "the judgement of history might have been more charitable" to Harding if there "had been some overriding achievement" in his administration.[27]

But this attitude doesn't accurately reflect reality. In addition to a shattered economy, the country seemed to be coming apart socially, with public disorder culminating in what was known as the "Red Summer" of racial violence in 1919, a period of race riots and lynchings perpetrated against African Americans across the country. A pervasive fear of Bolshevism had spread with the emergence of the Soviet Union two years earlier and an influx of immigrants from eastern Europe, heightened by anarchist violence, acts of terrorism, and labor unrest, also thought to be the work of communists. President Harding became a national healer, and it's this important aspect of his presidency that is not given its due by historians. He worked to heal the racial divisions in the country, calm an anxious public, and restore domestic tranquility. He also demonstrated forgiveness toward many anti-war "radicals" who had been jailed for standing in opposition to Wilson's War. As we will see, Harding's accomplishments as president are actually quite impressive.

As for the scandals that scholars converge on in their denunciations of the Harding presidency, they certainly tarnish Harding's record, but not as badly as many historians have tried to claim. There were three major scandals during the Harding years: scams in the Justice Department and the new Veterans Bureau and, of course, Teapot Dome. All of them concerned personal theft in one form or another, but not by Warren Harding. Harding, a man of great personal warmth, humor, and good will who unreservedly trusted his closest friends, must be held responsible for those he appointed to office. But there are notable differences between Harding's administration and those of other scandal-ridden presidents: Harding did not personally benefit from any of the schemes; much of the underhanded conduct remained undisclosed to Harding, and to the public until after his death in 1923; and when he found out about two of the scandals, he acted against those who had violated the public trust.

Despite the opinions of historians, scholars, and much of the general public today, the gracious and well-liked Warren Harding was popular with the people during his presidency. He won his election by the largest popular vote in American history up to that time, and when he died on August 2, 1923, two and a half years into his presidency, the outpouring of affection rose to a level not seen since the assassination of Lincoln.

While serving as president, Harding reopened the White House to visitors after it had been closed by Woodrow Wilson. A caring man who loved his "countrymen," he was quite a contrast to his stuffily arrogant, intellectual predecessor, whose pompous self-righteousness, as much as his devastating stroke, derailed his administration. President Wilson believed he was the smartest man in any room he entered, and he wanted everyone to know it. Harding once said of himself, in all humility, that he did not think he was fit for the presidency; Woodrow Wilson would have never made such a statement. And the facts tell a story different from what we might expect: the humble Harding, who was no intellectual, restored the nation to greatness—after Wilson, with all his academic prowess, had nearly wrecked it.

Given the truth about his administration, President Warren Harding deserves better than he has received from his detractors, including credit for calming national waters and righting the ship of state by rebuilding the economy and restoring domestic tranquility and setting the roaring twenties in motion. Although his own personal faults and the scandals in his administration, which he was not a part of, will deny him a spot on Mount Rushmore, he does not deserve to be ranked last or dismissed as a failure. And if his full story is told accurately, his star should rise considerably. Despite his own personal failings, Harding was a good man and a very good president.

In humility, though, I must admit that I am far from the first to figure this out. It may seem that hostile academics have a lock on scholarly opinion on Warren Harding, but some are beginning to push back against that consensus. Although finding optimistic appraisals of Warren Harding is a rarity, lately there has been a slight uptick in positive stories and assessments of his presidency. Concern over the state of today's economy and the skyrocketing national debt has caused a few scholars, mainly conservatives and libertarians, to take another look at the roaring twenties, a time of massive economic growth, budget surpluses, and a dwindling national debt, and rightfully conclude that Harding wasn't so bad after all, at least in his management of the economy.

Professor Robert F. Martin reached essentially the same conclusion that his colleagues had: although Harding's "lowly station in the pantheon of presidents is not unwarranted" because "he brought to the presidency limited vision, an undisciplined intellect, and little talent or inclination for strong leadership," Harding also possessed some good qualities. He "brought to the office commitment to the nation and to his job, sound political instincts, and fundamental, though flawed, decency." Harding's critics, he wrote, "have often exaggerated his weaknesses and underestimated his strengths."[28]

Steven F. Hayward, in *The Politically Incorrect Guide to the Presidents, Part Two: From Wilson to Obama*, assessed Harding very positively, giving him a "constitutional grade" of B+. "An unbiased assessment of Harding would conclude that, all in all, he was the kind of president the Founders had in mind—unassuming, not out to remake the nation or the world according to some fanciful 'vision,' working hard at administering the laws while showing Congress the proper deference when he recommended measures for their attention."[29]

In his book *Recarving Rushmore*, Ivan Eland ranks Harding number six, the second president listed in his "good" category. Harding, explains Eland, "generally set good economic policies," "advocated a very restrained foreign policy," "tried to heal the domestic wounds from World War I," and is "overly faulted" for the scandals of his administration.[30]

Robert W. Merry wrote in *Where They Stand*, "No president has managed to sink in history's estimation to a level below that of Warren Gamaliel Harding." Writing for *National Interest* in 2018, Merry concluded that such an opinion is wrong, as are most of the presidential surveys, which "identify Warren G. Harding of Ohio as the worst ever. This is ridiculous. Harding presided over very robust economic times. Not only that, but he inherited a devastating economic recession when he was elected in 1920 and quickly turned bad times into good times, including a 14 percent GDP growth rate in 1922. Labor and racial unrest declined markedly during his watch. He led the country into no troublesome wars."[31]

For American foreign policy critic Justin Raimondo, Harding is an American president worthy of study and emulation today precisely because he was not a "warmonger":

> Although derided by modern historians, who favor more dramatic figures such as the warmonger FDR, the crusading Wilson, and the authoritarian Lincoln, Harding presided over a period of peace and prosperity. He repaired our relations with Latin America, where Wilson's promiscuous interventions had alienated the natives, cut military spending, beat back the naval lobby, and energetically pursued disarmament initiatives. He rejected the meddlesome ambitions of the League of Nations, and kept the US focused on solving its problems on the home front rather than trying to export "democracy" to the farthest darkest corners of the globe.[32]

Conservative commentator, author, and three-time presidential candidate Patrick J. Buchanan, who, like Trump, ran on Harding's "America First" agenda, has praised Harding and questioned the presidential rankings and those who create them:

> Now consider one of the men whom all the raters judge a "failure" and among our worst presidents, Warren G. Harding.
>
> Harding served five months less than JFK, before dying in office in 1923. Yet his diplomatic and economic triumphs were of the first order. He negotiated the greatest disarmament treaty of the century, the Washington Naval Agreement, which gave the United States superiority in battleships and left us and Great Britain with capital-ship strength more than three times as great as Japan's. Even Tokyo conceded a U.S. diplomatic victory.
>
> With Treasury Secretary Andrew Mellon, Harding cut Wilson's wartime income tax rates, which had gone as high

as 63 percent, to 25 percent, ended the stagflation of the Wilson presidency and set off the greatest boom of the century, the Roaring Twenties. When Harding took his oath, unemployment was at 12 percent. When he died, 29 months later, it was at 3 percent. This is a failure?

Polls like these, he concludes, "[tell] us more about who has been doing the ranking" than they do about real history. Real history, in contrast, is the objective of this book.[33]

CHAPTER 1

THE LEAGUE

"I am quite convinced as the most bitter 'irreconcilable' that the country does not want the Versailles League."

—*Warren Harding*

The nation was overjoyed with the news: at 11:00 a.m. on November 11, 1918, the Armistice went into effect, halting the killing that had consumed Europe since the summer of 1914 and involved the United States for the previous seventeen months. The Great War was over. Ten million soldiers lay dead, along with eight million civilians. Twenty million were wounded, many severely so. There was scarcely a family in Europe untouched by the war; the entire continent, the homeland they knew so well, would be redrawn in the chaotic aftermath. Three of continental Europe's longest-standing and most powerful monarchies had been toppled. The German kaiser, the emperor of Austria-Hungary, and the Russian tsar were all gone, one way or another. The ancient Ottoman Empire, the long-suffering "sick man of Europe," had finally fallen as well.

The world that emerged after the guns fell silent and the smoke cleared was far different from the innocence that had prevailed in 1914. When war had come that summer, no one could have believed the ravages that awaited Europe, or the fact that America would eventually be drawn into the conflict. There had been no existential sense of dread in the minds of most people, in Europe or the United States, at the outbreak of the war. Most Americans had seen it as yet another European interfamily squabble, certainly nothing that would require the intervention of the New World, while most Europeans had thought it would be a short war, over perhaps by Christmas.

In those pre-war days, the general mindset on war was certainly different—different from our mindset today, no doubt, but also different from what it would be just four years later. A prevailing attitude in those antebellum days was that war was generally good, a healthy development when it came, even a cleansing process. War would strengthen a nation, not weaken it. Former U.S. president Theodore Roosevelt, a hero of the Spanish-American War of 1898, wanted America to enter the European conflict immediately in 1914 and tried his best to gain command of an army division in France in 1917 when the nation did finally declare war. Journalist Evan Thomas has branded him a "war lover," and he certainly was one. "All the great masterful races have been fighting races," declared Roosevelt at the Naval War College in 1897, "and the minute that a race loses the hard fighting virtues it has lost its proud right to stand as the equal to the best." The consequences of the full-scale industrialized war that broke out in the summer of 1914 destroyed that notion forever.[1]

What Americans came to know as World War I was not quite over on that day in November when the Armistice was announced. Unbeknownst to most American citizens at the time, U.S. forces were part of an international coalition fighting in Russia on one side of a civil war that pitted Bolshevik Communists, the Reds (soon to be called Soviets), against anti-Communist forces known as the Whites. Approximately eleven thousand U.S. troops did their part to try to stop the imposition of a Bolshevik government in Moscow, with American losses near three thousand by the time it was over—only to see Lenin's new regime emerge triumphant.

But that didn't matter to those jubilant in the streets in the fall of 1918. "The Armistice made everyone crazy," wrote historian Nell Irvin Painter. "It was like Mardi Gras all over the country." One contemporary writer noted that the area of Chicago known as "The Loop" resembled "a nuthouse on fire. The sidewalks were swollen with people, the streets were clogged, and autoists honked their horns, and motor men donged bells in vain. Tons of paper and confetti blizzarded from the upper stories of buildings and sundry noise-makers echoed an insistent racket. People sang, shouted until it seemed that their lungs would burst from their mouths." When Mary Roberts Rinehart, who had been a war correspondent in Belgium, returned home after the war, she was amazed at what she found. "I was gazing with a sort of terror at an America I hardly knew, a jazzed America, drinking, dancing, spending; developing a cult of ugliness and calling it modernity, and throwing aside the simplicities and charms of living in pursuit of a new god called Smartness."[2]

The elation was due partly to the fact that no one had believed the war would end so quickly, even with the participation of American troops. Soon after arriving in Paris, U.S. general "Black Jack" Pershing had warned the Allies that his soldiers would not be fully trained and operational until 1919. And many had believed the war would probably drag on until at least 1920—including Senator Warren G. Harding of Ohio, who agreed with the assessment that the country would probably need "an Army of five millions of men by January 1, 1920." He wrote, "Moreover, I have a pretty strong conviction, that under the present plan, we will have an Army that size if the war continues throughout the year." But now it was over. Still-green American doughboys, arriving by the thousands every day, had made the difference, providing much needed relief to worn out British and French troops and—with a million men on the field—helping to stop the last-ditch German offensive meant to win victory for the kaiser. They also played a vital role in the counter-offensive that pushed Allied forces toward Germany itself.[3]

The end of the war was the occasion for the festivities, but it was not the only thing that everyone was celebrating. Nearly a year before, a new virus that history has termed the "Spanish flu" had devastated troop encampments in Europe and then spread worldwide. The first known case in the United States, and perhaps the world, emerged at Fort Riley,

Kansas, in March 1918. Within a few days, more than 500 were sick. By the time it was over, half a billion people worldwide had contracted the bug and it had killed as many as 100 million, some 5 percent of the world's population, spreading as far north as the Arctic and to the remotest of the South Pacific islands. It is thought that more than a quarter of the entire populace of the United States was infected, with as many as 675,000 dead in influenza hospitals across the country. Under Woodrow Wilson, the federal government, then deeply entrenched in the war, had done nothing, but state and local governments had instituted severe restrictions and regulations, going so far as to keep the public from schools, theaters, churches, bars, and anywhere else people congregated in order to check the spread as best they could. But by the Armistice, the pandemic seemed to be subsiding, too. People were now free to congregate once again, and they were jubilant to be able to do so.[4]

Though America had not suffered the same devastation as Europe, the war had had an enormous effect on Americans across the country, regardless of their standing in life, and it had done so in a very short period of time. It wasn't just the 4.7 million who had served in the American Expeditionary Forces (AEF), the 117,000 dead, the 320,000 sick and wounded, and the millions who worked in war industries. It was also the hardships imposed on the people by their own government. The new income tax, instituted in 1913, had ballooned to catastrophically high rates, with the wealthy paying three-quarters of their income in taxes. And no class of American was immune. Even the poorest citizen paid a minimum of 4 percent to finance the war. The federal budget had grown more than 20-fold, while the national debt shot up to more than 25 times what it had been in 1914. The people also had to deal with the shortages, rationing, and inflation that always come with war.

The government had instituted a draft to press citizens into military service and cracked down on civil liberties with the passage of new laws designed to punish espionage and sedition. In shades of the Alien and Sedition Acts of 1798, any criticism of the federal government was swiftly and harshly punished. Despite the clear violation of the protections of the First Amendment, the Supreme Court would eventually uphold the government's actions because of a "clear and present danger" to the nation. With Wilson's crusade in Europe finally over in November 1918, Americans were ecstatic that life would be returning to normal very soon. The elation, though, would be short-lived.

With the Armistice in place and hostilities abated, the next phase would be to secure peace. President Wilson decided to do something no other American commander in chief had ever done. He traveled to France in December 1918 to personally represent the United States in the peace talks at the Palace of Versailles outside Paris.

The peace conference faced a monumental task. The assemblage had to deal with a war-ravaged continent, shattered economies, starving and displaced people, angry victims, fallen monarchies, colonial possessions, and hostile nationalities clamoring for independence, not to mention finding of fault and assigning reparations, which would itself be a massive undertaking led by the British economist John Maynard Keynes. The work lasted six months and produced a treaty that virtually ensured another war, as Pennsylvania senator Philander C. Knox, who had served as secretary of state under Wilson's predecessor, William Howard Taft, warned the president in a Senate speech that proved eerily prophetic. The treaty "does not spell peace but war—war more woeful and devastating than the one we have but now closed. The instrument before us is not the Treaty but the Truce of Versailles," he said.[5]

The Treaty of Versailles redrew the map of Europe, created nine new nations, placed the blame for the war on Germany, imposed harsh reparations payments, and created Wilson's signature League of Nations, a forerunner to the United Nations, crafted for the purpose of solving world disputes—or, as the *Wall Street Journal* called it, "Mr. Wilson's pet scheme to ameliorate everything and banish trouble from the world." That would be the main sticking point in the U.S. Senate, a body controlled by the Republican Party since the mid-term election in November 1918. Needing a vote of two-thirds of the members for ratification, the treaty met with stiff but not insurmountable opposition. A little finesse and goodwill from the White House, and the treaty would likely navigate the one treacherous obstacle in its path.[6]

The contention centered on Articles X and XI of the Covenant of the League of Nations, which introduced the new concept of global collective security:

> The Members of the League undertake to respect and pre-serve as against external aggression the territorial integrity and existing political independence of all Members of the League. In case of any such aggression or in case of any threat or danger of such aggression the Council shall advise upon the means by which this obligation shall be fulfilled.
>
> Any war or threat of war, whether immediately affecting any of the Members of the League or not, is hereby declared a matter of concern to the whole League, and the League shall take any action that may be deemed wise and effectual to safe-guard the peace of nations. In case any such emergency should arise the Secretary General shall on the request of any Member of the League forthwith summon a meeting of the Council.

For independence-minded senators, led by Henry Cabot Lodge of Massachusetts, these clauses were more than a little troubling; they represented a vital threat to the sovereignty of the United States. The treaty would obligate the nation to go to war to defend any member nation under threat and potentially call for the mobilization of American troops without the approval of Congress. This was an abdication of congressional prerogatives that Lodge and many other senators would not take lightly.

A prominent son of Massachusetts, Henry Cabot Lodge had served in the U.S. Senate since 1893, and before that in the state legislature and in the U.S. House. Best friends with Theodore Roosevelt until the latter's untimely passing in January 1919, Lodge was one of the leaders of the Republican Party and, unofficially at least, the Senate's majority leader after the GOP takeover of Congress in 1918. Lodge, wrote journalist Edward Lowry, "is a figure apart in the Senate, and, whether the other Senators acknowledge the fact or not, they do allow him a place of his own. He is one of the personalities. Strangers in the galleries always ask to have him pointed out. There is an atmosphere about him of tradition, of legend, myth."[7]

As chairman of the Senate Foreign Relations Committee, Lodge would get the treaty first; it had to pass through his committee before it could receive a floor vote. In a deliberate delaying tactic, Lodge spent a full two weeks publicly reading the treaty to the other members, even though it was in a bound volume for anyone to see. As an astute politician, Lodge knew that the longer he could delay the vote on the treaty in the Senate, the stronger the opposition would grow. The opposition was mainly over the proposed League of Nations, not the other provisions of the treaty. Eventually the Senate broke down into four different groups. The treaty, with the League intact as is, did have its proponents, mostly Democrats, numbering about forty members. Then there was the opposition. The "mild reservationists" were mainly Republicans who were generally in favor but wanted some slight modifications. The "strong reservationists," led by Lodge, sought major revisions, or they would not support the treaty. Finally there were the irreconcilables, who numbered only about fifteen members, but included such notables as William Borah of Idaho, Hiram Johnson of California, and Robert La Follette of Wisconsin. They vowed not to vote for the treaty under any circumstances.

Senator Harding, a proponent of "America First," favored the treaty, but, like Lodge, he had strong reservations about the League. He wrote that he wanted "to preserve all of the League proposal which we can accept with safety to the United States, in the hope that the conscience of the Nations may be directed to perfecting a safe plan of cooperation toward maintained peace. But there will be no surrender of things essentially and vitally American." Lodge, Harding, and the other members of the large "strong reservationist" camp argued that the treaty would be ratified easily if Wilson would simply permit some modifications so that decisions to go to war and to mobilize U.S. troops remained solely in the hands of Congress.[8]

But Woodrow Wilson, the high-minded moral idealist, was not a compromising man. A Southern Democrat born in Staunton, Virginia, in 1856, he had come of age in the South during the Reconstruction era, where he was instilled with the attitudes of most white Southerners of the time. He was highly educated, first at Davidson College in North Carolina and then in law school at the University of Virginia. After souring on a legal career, he earned a Ph.D. in government from Johns Hopkins University in Baltimore. A born academic, he was first a professor at Princeton, later its president, and then governor of New Jersey from 1911 to 1913 before he entered the White House.[9]

A deeply religious man, Wilson prayed on his knees twice a day, but along with his piousness went a rigid and uncompromising mindset. He was a moralist who saw the world in black and white, who believed in absolute right and absolute wrong—which had the effect of making him quite stubborn. He was used to getting his way and was known to end friendships if his companion did not agree with his position on a given issue. The Kansas journalist William Allen White noted this dark side of Wilson, writing that he would "break ruthlessly and irrevocably, without defense or explanation, any friendship which threatened his prestige." Wilson's Paris press secretary, the journalist Ray Stannard Baker, remarked that Wilson was "a good hater." King George V referred to him as "an odious man." He could be petty and vindictive. He was arrogant, self-righteous, and pompous. After his election in 1912, Wilson told an aide, "I wish it to be clearly understood that I owe you nothing. Remember that God ordained that I should be the next president of the United States. Neither you nor any other mortal could have prevented that." Presidential historian Thomas Bailey described him as an "intellectually arrogant reformer" who was "bent on rocking the boat of big business and browbeating Congress."[10]

The latter charge fit Woodrow Wilson perfectly. On the fight over the League, he vowed, "Anyone who opposes me in that, I'll crush!"

When told that without changes his proposal would likely be voted down, Wilson responded that there would be no changes. "The Senate must take its medicine," he said. The obstinate attitude was justified by the way Wilson saw himself: not so much as a constitutional president but more of a prime minister with complete mastery over Parliament. The mere thought of a meeting with Lodge to discuss changes that would ensure passage of the treaty was unthinkable to Wilson. Lodge should have realized very quickly that Wilson would be more than a little inflexible about his treaty. Wilson safeguarded the treaty like a mother hen hovering over her chicks. He took the unusual step of personally delivering the treaty to the Senate when he returned from Europe; when Lodge asked Wilson if he could take the treaty into the Senate chamber himself, the president quickly responded, "Not on your life." For Woodrow Wilson this was more than personal. Lodge developed contempt for the president. "I never expected to hate anyone in politics with the hatred I feel toward Wilson," he said.[11]

A bit of tact and compromise would most likely have guaranteed that the treaty would sail through the Senate, but Wilson remained dogged in his determination to see his handiwork enacted just as he had crafted it. In his work on the treaty, Wilson referred to himself as "the personal instrument of God." His grand reception in France, noted his secretary of state, Robert Lansing, had given him "an exalted opinion of his own power of accomplishment and of his individual responsibility to mankind."[12]

Despite Wilson's attitude, in an effort to work out a compromise, members of the Senate Foreign Relations Committee, including Senator Harding, met with the president in the White House to discuss the League in a conference on August 19, 1919. The main sticking point was America's obligations to the rest of the world. And at that meeting the former newspaperman got the better of the former college professor. Wilson contended that the obligation the United States had under the League was only "a moral obligation" and that "any decision of the Council would require our assent and . . . its action would be only in the war of advice." But Harding did not want American sovereignty to be surrendered "to the prejudices or necessities of the nations of the Old World." If the treaty imposed only a moral obligation and "each nation was to judge this obligation," then "the whole thing would amount to nothing." So what would the United States get out of joining the compact? The exchange exasperated Wilson, who often referred to opponents of his League as having "pygmy minds." At his next cabinet meeting, Wilson said that Harding "had a disturbingly dull mind, and that it seemed impossible to get any explanation to lodge in it." And Wilson's treasury secretary, David Houston, wrote that Harding had an "inability or unwillingness to understand the meaning of the Covenant which he had revealed when the President received the Foreign Affairs Committee in August, 1919. He . . . indulged in reckless assertions, such as that the League was utterly impotent, that it could not be a preventive of wars, and that Europe was abandoning the League." In fact, the senator from Ohio understood the treaty quite well.[13]

Gaining nothing with the Senate, in the fall of 1919 Wilson—in what can only be described as a proxy battle with Lodge and the opposition in the Senate—embarked on a country-wide speaking tour to gin up support for the treaty, well aware that an overwhelming majority of Americans agreed with Cabot Lodge and Warren Harding. It was a grueling twenty-two-day trip of over ten thousand miles. In September, in Pueblo, Colorado, a completely beleaguered president collapsed from exhaustion; on October 2, back in Washington, he suffered a debilitating, near-fatal stroke that paralyzed his body and rendered him unable to speak. For the next seven months, the nation, in the dark about its president's true condition, was without effective leadership.[14]

Edward Lowry, a journalist who wrote for magazines including the *New Republic*, called the situation "a clumsy, forbidding mystery." No one really knew what was going on in the White House throughout the rest of 1919 and into 1920. The building itself, closed to visitors, including members of Congress, became a very dark and dreary place. "An air of secrecy had come over things during the day," wrote Ike Hoover, a White

House usher for forty-two years. "Those on the outside, including family and employees, could learn nothing. The President lay stretched out on the large Lincoln bed. He looked as if he were dead. There was not a sign of life." First Lady Edith Galt Wilson, who had married the much-older president in December 1915, nearly seventeen months after the death of Wilson's first wife, kept her incapacitated husband hidden from view and, in actuality, served in his stead until he could regain at least some of his physical functions.[15]

Edith Wilson was now fully in charge of the White House; in that role, she has been called the nation's first female president. "Every effort was made to save him from coming in contact with people or considering anything except what seemed to Mrs. Wilson important," Ike Hoover explained. "Persons who could not be put off were received by her. Information she received would be passed on to the President, many times to be heard of no more. Some few persons gained access to him, but in such cases he was watched and prompted during the audience. . . . From the first day of his illness no one ever got close to the President again." And that's because Mrs. Wilson would not allow it. "I doubt whether she will ever tell the world just what happened," wrote Ike Hoover. "My own opinion is that he never really got much better from the very first day of his trouble." Senator Albert Fall of New Mexico, who was allowed to see the president briefly, described the situation as "petticoat government."[16]

Senator Harding knew very little but wrote to a friend about the mysterious situation. "I do not know that anyone in the Senate, outside of Senator Swanson, really knows the truth, and I am not even sure that he does. It is generally accepted here that in his hysterical anger at Pueblo, Colorado, the President brought on a slight brain lesion. The statement has been denied but it sticks in spite of the denial. Apparently he is making some progress toward partial recovery. My judgment is that he will never be wholly restored to health," he wrote. "In the early days he was both physically and mentally unfit for duty. Undoubtedly he has passed beyond the mental perturbation which gave those about him such great anxiety."[17]

Wilson's body was frail and weak, but his mind was still sharp, and his weakness did not equate to an easing of his stubbornness on the treaty. If anything, the president grew stiffer in his resolve to see the treaty pass with no modifications. In fact, he would rather see it voted down than ratified with Lodge's reservations. "I could not stand for those changes for a moment," he told one senator who was allowed to see him. For his opponents he had nothing but "utter contempt."[18]

By this point, Senator Warren Harding was a full-fledged opponent to Wilson's League. "I don't think there is anything in it for the United States of America," he wrote to his friend Frank Scobey, and, what's worse, he continued, "It does make us the financial backer of all the bankrupt nations of the earth and pledges us to their preservation and protection for all time to come. I have not said anything much about it in a public way but I have made up my mind privately that I intend to oppose it no matter what the political result may be. My own judgment is that in the long run this country will be very hostile to this venture into the unknown." He would soon make these feelings very public.[19]

On September 11, 1919, as Wilson lay in bed, unable to govern, Senator Harding took to the floor of the Senate to begin the long debate on the treaty, an honor that had Lodge's full backing. It would be the longest speech of Harding's Senate career, coming in at ten thousand words, and, according to Harding biographer John W. Dean, his "most significant." Describing himself as "jealous of the Republic's nationality," Harding ridiculed the Versailles Treaty creating Wilson's League as "this untouchable and unamendable and supposedly sacred document." In its present form, said Harding, the League "is one of peril to the Republic. To accept it unaltered would be a betrayal of America." And even if the treaty were ratified, as Wilson desired, and if "it makes for the promised peace, I still prefer, and the great majority of Americans still prefer, to be the keepers of our national conscience and let Europe pass upon its moral obligations while we righteously meet our own." And since the "preservation of American safety is the main thing," he told his fellow senators, he could not support the League without Lodge's reservations.

That made Harding what was called a "strong reservationist." Harding told his fellow senators that he "could no more support 'mild reservations' than I could support mild Americanism." Lodge's reservations were "strong and unmistakable," with "a purpose to protect America first." Harding's speech was well received: he was repeatedly interrupted by applause from the packed galleries, much to the aggravation of Vice President Thomas Marshall.[20]

In the end, a completely irrational Wilson, refusing even the slightest change to the text, saw the treaty voted down twice by the Senate, first in November 1919 and then again in March 1920. The United States never ratified the Treaty of Versailles, and America would never have a place at the table of the League of Nations. "I am quite convinced as the most bitter 'irreconcilable' that the country does not want the Versailles League," Harding wrote to Lodge. Yet even in his weakened physical condition, Wilson vowed to fight on in the name of his beloved League, counting on the people to side with him in the election of 1920, which he hoped would be a referendum on the League itself. As William Allen White observed, the fight was about more than the treaty and the League: "It was about Woodrow Wilson having his way."[21]

But the end of the League did not bring the end of trouble. Not only would the League proposal become a key issue for both parties during the 1920 presidential election, but the country would begin to come apart socially throughout the year 1919—one of the most horrific years in U.S. history.

CHAPTER 2

1919: THE YEAR OF UPHEAVAL

"It looks to me as though we are coming to a crisis in the conflict between the radical labor leaders and the capitalistic system under which we have developed this republic."

—Warren Harding

With Wilson's stroke, his absence from many of his official duties, and the gridlock over the treaty lasting for months in the Senate, very little was coming out of Washington. It was as if "our Government has gone out of business," noted journalist Ray Stannard Baker in December 1919. "The deadlock is so complete," the British ambassador Sir Auckland Geddes wrote to Prime Minister Lloyd George, "that one would almost be justified in saying that the United States had no government."[1] Longtime White House usher Ike Hoover, who saw it all up close inside the White House, said, "Everything in the way of business came to a standstill."[2]

And America needed strong, effective leadership during a crucial time of transition from war to peace. A divisive political fight and a president largely absent after his stroke, with his mind fixated solely on his cherished League, were the least of America's problems in 1919. As Wilson and the Senate fought over the League, there were major social disruptions across the country—communist agitation and a heightened fear of Bolshevism, anarchist violence and acts of terrorism, labor unrest, and race riots. To make matters worse, in the year's time from the end of war until the end of 1919, the government had discharged most of the American Expeditionary Forces, sending more than three million men back into civilian life in a twelve-month period. The integration of these veterans—and the millions of workers in war factories—into a peacetime economy necessitated an economic adjustment that would triple unemployment, while post-wartime inflation increased prices considerably, as a 1918 dollar had the purchasing power of just forty-five cents in 1913. The cost of living for average folks was double what it had been before the war, and all of this preceding a major economic depression the following year.[3]

A 1919 poem by the Irish poet William Butler Yeats, though it described post-war Europe and the struggles in Ireland, also captured the situation in America:

> Turning and turning in the widening gyre
> The falcon cannot hear the falconer;
> Things fall apart; the centre cannot hold;
> Mere anarchy is loosed upon the world,
> The blood-dimmed tide is loosed, and everywhere
> The ceremony of innocence is drowned;
> The best lack all conviction, while the worst
> Are full of passionate intensity.[4]

The nation seemed to be on the brink of an abyss, with anarchy in the streets fomented by passionate activists and innocence drowned in blood. Things did seem to be falling apart, and the center, the core of society itself, looked like it might crumble under the stress.

For Americans in 1919, all of this upheaval—labor strikes, racial violence, communism—was a "Bolshevist" assault on the United States by radicals. It mattered not that the groups involved were hardly linked with one another. Anarchists were not working with Bolsheviks, nor did many of the strikers belong to the communist movement, and foreign agents were not stirring up blacks across the country to rise up in defense of themselves and their families—but that's the way it was portrayed in the press, and that's the way most Americans viewed it.

Whether monolithic or not, the biggest threat, it seemed, was the communist menace, the terror that had overtaken Russia in 1917 and a fear that pervaded the United States, culminating in what is known as the first "Red Scare." Like Germany, Russia came out of World War I in bad shape. Aside from suffering the worst loss of life, at 1.7 million dead, Russia also lost a huge chunk of its territory, and with it a quarter of its population and abundant resources after the signing of the Treaty of Brest-Litovsk.

But that mattered little to the man now leading a new government in Moscow, Vladimir Lenin. Lenin and the new Soviet Union under the "Bolshevik" party—from the Russian word for majority—were intent on exporting communistic ideals to Europe and across the pond to America if possible, making use of those who were susceptible to communism, later derided as "useful idiots." It was no secret that one of the communists' main objectives was to spread communism worldwide. They did not believe in nationalism, national borders, or nation-states, but in internationalism, globalism, and one-world government under the red flag of communism. And their philosophy was spreading in anything but a peaceful manner. Marx had envisioned a worldwide workers' revolution that would overthrow the existing order and replace it with a worker's paradise. And in the early twentieth century, that dream at last seemed possible. China had experienced revolution in 1911 and 1912, and—of greater concern for the United States—Mexico, which had been plunged into revolt in 1910, was still in the grip of revolution in the fall of 1918, inspiring Americans to fear that uprisings in impoverished and weak countries could move in the direction of Marxism and that Bolshevism could be on America's doorstep in the southwest. A more worrisome threat, though, came soon after the end of war in Europe in 1918, when actual communist revolutions broke out in Germany and eastern Europe.

Germany was ripe for revolution in the fall of 1918, and revolts began breaking out even before the announcement of the Armistice. The

German army had been stopped in its tracks in 1918, and its members had begun melting away as the troops realized that there was no possibility of turning back the Allied tide. Even the German navy mutinied in October 1918, refusing to embark on "a death ride." The German war effort was over. And the civilian population at home was suffering terribly. The British blockade had starved the people nearly to death, with major shortages of essentials such as food and medicine. Desperate people will look for hope anywhere they can find it. And communism appealed to many. With the German army completely spent and all but disbanded, a new private militia group composed mainly of war veterans, the Freikorps, moved into Berlin and Munich and put down the revolts. But revolutionary violence would continue in Germany for many months.

If such a violent upheaval could happen in a modern, civilized nation like Germany, could it also spread to America? "Political conditions are undergoing a very vast change," Senator Harding wrote to a friend. "I feel very pessimistic myself about the Bolshevik movement in this country. Perhaps we shall not encounter it in its most destructive form but I do think it likely that we will have a very radical labor party." Just thirteen days after the Armistice, the *New York Times* reported that "every cable brings further news of the spread of the Red Terror through Europe. Every day the situation grows worse, until many people are ready to declare that the United States will be the next victim of this dangerous malady." Such news naturally frightened the public. In response, the mayor of New York banned the red flag of communism within a week of the end of hostilities in Europe and disallowed any "unlawful assemblages," ordering the police to disband them. Former soldiers took it upon themselves to break up "Bolshevik" meetings—with five hundred of them storming into a socialist meeting at Madison Square Garden, while others took out a Women's International League meeting the next evening, seriously injuring six people in the melee.[5]

Near the end of 1918, there was more violence. On December 30 at 10:45 p.m., a bomb exploded at the home of Ernest T. Trigg, president of the Philadelphia Chamber of Commerce. At 10:55 p.m., another bomb went off at the apartment of acting police superintendent William Mills. He was blown out of bed and hurled ten feet into a hallway but luckily received only minor injuries. Around the same time, a third bomb detonated at the home of Pennsylvania Supreme Court justice Robert von Moschzisker, tearing off the front of his house. No deaths resulted from these three blasts, nor was anyone seriously hurt. Pamphlets at one of the scenes pointed to anarchists, but no actual perpetrators were ever apprehended or convicted. Superintendent Mills blamed the attacks on communists, speaking of a "plot which the Bolsheviki are starting on a nationwide scale. I think that they started in Philadelphia, and that outbreaks may be expected any day and in any part of the country."[6]

Was this threat real or imagined? William Allen White, a Kansas journalist, called it "a silly terror of Bolshevism in the hearts of the American people." The influential writer H. L. Mencken of Baltimore called it "a safe and sane bugaboo."[7] White may have been a long distance away from the action and thus able to afford a more abstract view of the situation, but Mencken was near the heart of it. A born pessimist—particularly about democracy, the politicians who ran it, and the people who voted to support it—Mencken often referred to the folks as "boobs," and once wrote that the "average citizen of a democracy is a goose-stepping ignoramus and poltroon." Not wanting to play favorites, he also thought the "average democratic politician, of whatever party, is a scoundrel and a swine." In Mencken's view, "the whole aim of practical politics is to keep the populace alarmed (and hence clamorous to be led to safety) by menacing it with an endless series of hobgoblins, most of them imaginary." Mencken put the fear of Bolshevism in that category. But surely it is not unreasonable for people to fear for their safety when bombs are exploding around them.[8]

In April 1919 that seemed to be the case, as more chaos reigned, with no fewer than thirty-six package bombs mailed to prominent Americans across the country. Fortunately, because of a postage error, only one was actually delivered and detonated. On the twenty-eighth of that month, a package arrived at the office of Mayor Ole Hanson in Seattle, but because he was out of town, it sat on his desk until someone noticed a fluid leaking from it—likely because of damage sustained in transit. The package was turned over to authorities and found to be a bomb. The next day a similar package arrived at the home of Thomas W. Hardwick, a former U.S. senator living in Atlanta. The bomb exploded, severing the hands of Hardwick's maid and burning Hardwick's wife.[9]

At that point, fortunately, Providence intervened. Reading about the Hardwick bomb in the newspaper, a postal clerk in Harlem remembered that he had set aside sixteen similar packages for insufficient postage. He called the authorities and, when they arrived, all sixteen packages were determined to be bombs. That same day, government agents found eighteen others bound for prominent citizens. Several were high-level targets: Attorney General A. Mitchell Palmer, Commissioner General of Immigration Anthony Caminetti, Secretary of Labor William Wilson, Supreme Court justice Oliver Wendell Holmes Jr., John D. Rockefeller, J. P. Morgan Jr., New York City mayor John F. Hylan, and at least three U.S. senators, one member of the House, and a number of governors, mayors, government officials, and newspaper editors. It was obvious that these bombs were set to do their intended damage on May Day 1919. One headline read, "Reds Planned May Day Murders." What else were Americans to think? Bolshevism, wrote Ann Hagedorn, "was sweeping the nation like a hot wind. . . . The mere mention of it aroused curiosity and intrigue as well as hatred and fear."[10]

A few days later, on May Day 1919, the day the mail bombs had likely been set to detonate, there was unrest in several American cities over the celebration of labor and workers' rights. In Boston, a parade of socialists carrying the red flag of communism marched without permits, and when the police tried to stop the march, a riot ensued. One police officer was fatally stabbed, and three others were injured, along with one civilian. In New York City, veterans of the Great War entered the Russian People's House, collected all the radical books, pamphlets, and magazines, and burned them, then forced those gathered inside to sing the national anthem. The same day, at the offices of the New York *Call*, a socialist daily newspaper, about 400 soldiers destroyed the office furniture and forced everyone out into the street, injuring 17 people in the process. The worst violence, though, happened in Cleveland, where a massive socialist parade, again featuring the red flag of communism, was met with violent resistance in which 20 socialists were injured. At least three other riots also broke out in the city, injuring 20 more and taking the life of one. Cleveland police arrested 106 socialists. Numerous newspapers across the country cast all blame on the radicals, viewing the incidents as "dress rehearsals" for a future Bolshevik revolution in America.[11]

About a month later, in June, more bombs exploded in American cities at the homes of prominent citizens. Eight devices set to go off at roughly the same time in seven different cities rocked the nation on the night of June 2. In Cleveland, the home of the mayor was bombed. A state legislator in Newtonville, Massachusetts, was targeted. In Pittsburgh, Pennsylvania, a federal judge and a city police inspector were marks. Paterson, New Jersey, New York City, and Philadelphia also saw bombs that night. Two people were killed.[12]

But the most prominent target was A. Mitchell Palmer, the U.S. attorney general, who lived at 2132 R Street in Washington, D.C., across the street from Assistant Secretary of the Navy Franklin D. Roosevelt, and who had also been a target of the May Day mail bombs. A Pennsylvania Quaker, Palmer was a pacifist who had served three terms in Congress and been offered the post of secretary of war by Woodrow Wilson in 1913 but declined, citing his Quaker pacifist ways. "The more I think of it, the more impossible it becomes. I am a Quaker. As a Quaker war secretary, I should consider myself a living illustration of a horrible incongruity," he said. In 1915 he did consent to serve a stint in the Justice Department as alien property custodian before Wilson offered him the attorney general position in March 1919.[13]

On the night of June 2, Palmer sat in his living room reading the newspaper. With his wife and daughter already in bed, the attorney general switched off the lights and walked up the stairs to his bedroom.

As he was preparing for bed, he "heard a crash downstairs as if some-thing had been thrown against the front door," as he later told a reporter for the *New York Times*. "It was followed immediately by an explosion which blew in the front of the house." Had he and his family still been downstairs in the living room at the time of the blast, all three would likely have been killed.[14]

The explosion was so large that it damaged neighboring homes, including the Roosevelts' across the street. The houses on each side of the Palmers' had their front doors blown in. Windows in a number of residences were shattered. Yet the only fatality was the bomber, who, it was later determined, must have tripped on the stone walkway from the front door of the Palmer house and been unable to escape his own handi-work. The scene was truly grisly. "The pavement in front of the [Palmer] house was marred with glass and leaves—the front wall looked as if it might fetch loose at any moment," wrote Alice Roosevelt Longworth, who was visiting her cousins, Franklin and Eleanor. "A leg lay in the path to the house next to theirs, another leg farther up the street. A head was on the roof of yet another house. As we walked across it was difficult to avoid stepping on bloody hunks of human being. The man had been torn apart, fairly blown to butcher's meat." Part of the bomber's torso had even crashed through the window of the nearby home of a diplomat from Norway. There were also anarchist pamphlets, entitled *Plain Words*, strewn all over the ground, along with enough of the terrorist's remains to identify him as a recent immigrant from Italy.[15]

After some initial hesitation, Attorney General Palmer, seeing a "blaze of revolution" sweeping the country "like a prairie fire," acted. In what became known as the "Palmer Raids," the attorney general, along with a young graduate from George Washington University School of Law, J. Edgar Hoover, whom Palmer had named head of the General Intelligence Unit, raided dozens of known radical establishments in dozens of cities across the country, arresting more than six thousand suspected agitators, whether there was proof of their guilt or not. These raids came in two separate operations, one in November 1919 and another in January 1920. Soon after, with the Department of Justice working in conjunction with the Labor Department, a deportation process began. Less than a thousand radicals were actually deported by the government, but two of the leading anarchists, Emma Goldman and Alexander Berkman, were among them.[16]

Palmer and Hoover have been criticized for a lack of respect for legal due process and Fourth Amendment protections for the accused, many of whom, especially those who refused to talk, were severely beaten. But at the time, the public was unconcerned; the raids were celebrated as necessary for public safety. "2,000 REDS ARRESTED IN 56 CITIES THROUGHOUT THE NATION," blared a *New York World* headline. "There is no time to waste on hair-splitting over infringement of liberty," opined the *Washington Post*.[17]

Although some in the government complained of such methods, others heartily approved, including many members of Congress, and some wanted even harsher measures. One Tennessee senator wanted every native-born radical exiled to a colony on the island of Guam. A minister called for the deportation of all Bolsheviks "in ships of stone with sails of lead, with the wrath of God for a breeze and with hell for their first port." Army chief of staff Leonard Wood agreed. The evangelist Billy Sunday did not; he sought firing squads in order to "save space on our ships." These attitudes reflected the thinking prevalent in the general public. In Indiana, a citizen named Frank Petroni shot and killed a man who publicly shouted, "To hell with the United States!" He was acquitted by a jury in two minutes. With the Palmer Raids, the reign of radical terror that gripped the nation in 1919 stopped. As Eric Burns has written, the raids "were successful, to a degree, in discouraging similar behavior in the future." By 1920, the Red Scare would essentially be over.[18]

Though Senator Harding did not agree with the harshest suggestions of his colleagues and other prominent Americans, he supported the Palmer Raids and the deportations. As a conservative, he had no love for radicals or radicalism, and certainly not for Bolshevism. "It would be the blindness of folly to ignore the activities in our own country which are aimed to destroy our economic system, and to commit us to the colossal tragedy which has both destroyed all freedom and made Russia impotent," he said in a speech in 1920. "Our policy is not of repression, but we make appeal to American intelligence and patriotism, when the republic is menaced from within, just as we trusted American patriotism when our rights were threatened from without." But these policies were only necessary because of the present exigent circumstances, he believed; the government should not hold such powers during more normal times. "We do hold to the right to crush sedition, to stifle a menacing contempt for law, to stamp out a peril to the safety of the republic or its people, when emergency calls, because security and the majesty of the law are the first essentials of liberty. He who threatens destruction of the government by force or flaunts his contempt for lawful authority ceases to be a loyal citizen and forfeits his rights to the freedom of the republic."[19]

And if the bombs and raids were not enough, the summer of 1919 became the "Red Summer," a long period of racial violence across the country in which an untold amount of blood, much of it African American, was spilled. James Weldon Johnson, the field secretary for the NAACP, is credited with coining the name "Red Summer" to describe the immense bloodshed. Many white Americans at the time, though, would have called the summer of 1919 "Red" for a different reason: the Bolshevik advance into the West. One prominent official who held that view was President Wilson, contending that "the American Negro returning from abroad would be our greatest medium in conveying bolshevism to America." The ideal of equality "has gone to their heads," he said. In the bombings and the Palmer Raids, writes Cameron McWhirter, "the phenomena known as the Red Scare and the Red Summer became enmeshed."[20]

The catalyst for the racial disorder, at least in the North, was "the Great Migration" of blacks from the South to the North. Black Americans had participated in the Great War, with many serving on the front lines in France. The American participation in the war "to make the world safe for democracy" struck many as more than a bit hypocritical. How could America claim to want to spread democracy around the world, yet deny it to a large population of Americans at home? For Senator Harding, the whole thing smacked of insincerity. "It has all been such an astonishing fraud, that it wearies one to think of it. Of course, I have always felt if we had been making war for democracy's sake, we would have gotten into it from the beginning," he wrote in a private letter in January 1919.[21]

While many blacks wanted to fight for their civil rights at home in the South, others chose to move to better political and cultural climates—or at least that was their hope. The South had been no safe haven for black Americans since Reconstruction, that much is true. The Great Migration of blacks from the South to the North began during the war, as war industries faced a shortage of labor. Many African Americans believed that if they pulled up stakes and moved northward, abandoning their native region where they faced poverty, segregation, and harsh treatment, they would be received hospitably and welcomed in factories across the North. By the end of 1919, a million blacks had migrated to major northern cities, greatly expanding the black populations in Detroit, Milwaukee, New York, and Chicago, many of which had had very few black residents before the war. Eventually, by 1970, as many as six million black people had moved from the South to the North. But the beginning of the Great Migration in 1919 was met with mob violence and eventually the reemergence of the Ku Klux Klan in the 1920s, most of whose members resided in northern, not southern, states.[22]

The Red Summer of 1919 was one of the worst periods of racial violence in American history, including what amounted to a full-fledged race war, with more than three dozen separate race riots. John Hope Franklin called it the "greatest period of interracial strife the nation has ever witnessed." Scores of blacks were lynched. Hundreds more were killed in what can only be described as pitched battles between whites and blacks. Thousands were injured. Tens of thousands became refugees with no home and nowhere to go. Black businesses were destroyed. This violence and blood-shed was not confined to the South, long the scapegoat of American racial problems; it also struck Chicago and other major cities in the North, Midwest, and West. There was violence in Washington, D.C.; Omaha, Nebraska; Wilmington, Delaware; and in Arizona, California, and Kentucky, as well as across the old Confederacy.[23]

In the "Windy City," in the hottest part of the summer, white and black Americans fought an eight-day battle in the streets that claimed the lives of thirty-eight people—fifteen of them white and twenty-three of them black. More than five hundred people were injured, and at least a thousand were rendered homeless and indigent. Journalist Frederick Lewis Allen wrote, "Chicago was virtually in a state of civil war; there were mobbings of Negroes, beatings, stabbings, gang raids through the Negro district, shootings by Negroes in defense, and wanton destruction of houses and property." How did it all begin? A seventeen-year-old black boy was swimming in a part of Lake Michigan that whites believed was their domain. After they pelted him with stones, the boy drowned. This set off a fight between the races that eventually spilled out of control. Only Governor Frank Lowden's use of militia troops brought it to an end on August 3.[24]

Individual lynchings were no less horrific. One black man in Arkansas met the lynch mob's noose because he refused to work for thirty-five cents a day. The mob literally nailed a sign to the dead man's head that read, "This is how we treat lazy n*ggers." In Omaha, Nebraska—hardly the deep South—a black man named William Brown was jailed for the alleged rape of a white girl. A mob soon formed outside the courthouse, where the jail was located, bent on lynching Brown. When the mayor attempted to block the mob, he was strung up from a light pole before police intervened to free him. He was then transported to the hospital to have his injuries treated. Authorities tried to use fire hoses to stop the mob, but the throng simply cut the hoses. They then set the jail on fire, causing the prisoners to flee. Federal troops had to be called in. But before they arrived, Brown was lynched. He was shot hundreds of times, and his body was burned, dragged through the streets, and hung from a pole for all to see, including the arriving troops. It was a grisly warning.[25]

Without doubt the worst lynching occurred in the small southern town of Ellisville, Mississippi. On June 9, Ruth Meeks, a white woman, claimed that John Hartfield, a black man, had raped her. In the Deep South at this time, such an allegation was taken more than seriously; it generally sent white men into a frenzy. Hartfield was hunted down, captured, shot and wounded, and had his fingers cut off. He was then hanged from the town's "hanging tree," and his body was riddled with a reported two thousand bullets, then cut down and burned. To make matters even worse, the event was publicized ahead of time, complete with a notice in newspapers around the South and as far away as New York. "John Hartfield Will Be Lynched by Ellisville Mob at 5 O'Clock This Afternoon," read the headline in one New Orleans paper. Thousands of citizens came to watch the spectacle, which took place in the middle of town.[26]

The NAACP tried to get Mississippi governor Theodore G. Bilbo to intervene and stop the lynching, but he refused, saying he was "utterly powerless" to do anything. "The Negro has confessed, says he is ready to die," noted Bilbo, "and nobody can keep the inevitable from happening." It was "practically impossible" to stop "the lynching of Negro rapists." There were insufficient men in the state militia to do any good, he said, and in any case sending in the militia "would doubtless result in the death of hundreds of persons." In fact, the governor was not actually powerless; he just chose not to do anything because he agreed with the lynchers. Bilbo, who in 1947 would be blocked from taking a seat in the U.S. Senate for another term after proposing a $2 billion appropriations bill to ship blacks to Africa, held virulent racist beliefs. "This is a white man's country," he said during the Hartfield episode, "with a white man's civilization and any dream on the part of the Negro race to share social and political equality will be shattered in the end." And he meant "shattered" literally. The federal government under Wilson lifted not a finger to intervene.[27]

And with the bombs, the raids, and the lynchings came the labor strikes. What would become the first "general strike" in American history began in Seattle on January 21 as a strike by 35,000 shipyard workers who wanted shorter hours and higher wages. It spread until the entire city was eventually at a standstill. Sixty thousand workers from 110 unions walked off the job on February 6. General strikes have cascading effects. Schools were closed, streetcars no longer ran, business activity ceased, and citizens bought up necessities in a panic. The mayor, Ole Hanson, beefed up security forces to maintain law and order, and within five days it was over. In all, there were some 3,600 labor strikes throughout the year of 1919, involving more than 4 million workers, including a major strike in the steel industry. Some of the strikes turned violent. Two workers were killed in clashes between strikers and scabs in Pennsylvania, and a labor riot in Gary, Indiana, required the use of federal troops to quell the unrest. To many, Harding's prediction of a "radical labor party" seemed to be coming true.[28]

Perhaps the worst strike came in the fall. It was not the biggest, but it had the potential to be the worst in terms of public safety. Two days before Harding's Senate speech on the League, on September 9, 1919, just nine months into the first term of Massachusetts governor Calvin Coolidge, the bulk of the police force in Boston, 1,117 of 1,544 officers, went out on strike. By the early afternoon, bands of thugs were smashing store windows and looting. Gangs were attacking and robbing pedestrians on the street. Governor Coolidge responded by sending in 5,000 national guardsmen and condemning the strikers as "traitors." Coolidge threw down the gauntlet in a statement that made him a national hero: "There is no right to strike against the public safety by any body, any where, any time."[29] The Boston police strike only heightened the public's fear of the Bolshevist threat. The press was certainly taking the lead in pushing that narrative. "Bolshevism in the United States is no longer a specter," opined the Philadelphia *Public Ledger*. "Boston in chaos reveals its sinister substance."[30]

And just as 1919 drew to a close and it looked as if things might be improving, that maybe the Palmer Raids would get control of the violence associated with anarchists and Bolsheviks, and that perhaps the labor unrest might be dying down, another problem emerged. As the nation geared up for what was likely to be a contentious presidential election, a new difficulty emerged that would touch almost every single person in America.

Coming out of the "great storm" of war in Europe at the end of 1918, Washington braced for the inevitable economic downturn that always came when the guns fell silent—as the prevailing conventional wisdom held that converting a wartime economy back to peacetime production always brought economic readjustment. In January 1919, two months after the Armistice, an official with the American Federation of Labor predicted "bread lines in every industrial center before May 1" if the government didn't step in to avert a depression. But the government did nothing, aside from scaling back the military machine, and in 1919, strangely enough, the economy actually boomed, driven mainly by consumption. Wartime inflation, though, continued unabated. Prices had risen 11 percent in 1916, 17 percent in 1917, and nearly 19 percent in 1918. That was expected during the war years, but 1919 saw prices rise another 14 percent. How did this affect the average American? A good pair of shoes that cost three dollars before the war sold for ten to twelve dollars in 1919. Everyday life got tougher and tougher as the year wore on.[31]

Yet despite the spike in prices, American consumers continued to consume, which helped businesses and farmers. The spending was likely a salve to soothe national feelings in the midst of the tumult of the Red Summer, as business soared right alongside the Red Scare. In 1918 General Motors reported sales of $270 million; in 1919 that number nearly doubled to $510 million. The number of GM employees jumped from 49,118 in 1918 to 85,980 in 1919. Farm profits also boomed. Before the war, farm income had averaged $6.7 billion, but 1919 saw a 152 percent increase, to $16.9 billion.[32]

But economists knew that this inflationary boom would end, and probably rather quickly. As James Grant observed in *The Forgotten Depression: 1921: The Crash That Cured Itself*, this economic expansion was actually an "inflationary distortion of values." Simply put, "what goes up, must come down." The boom wouldn't and couldn't last. This had some in the Wilson administration mighty worried. Joseph Tumulty, the president's top advisor, cabled Wilson while he was in Paris working on the peace treaty. "Issue of high cost of living most acute. . . . You cannot understand how acute situation is brought about by rising prices of every necessity of life." But Wilson's mind was on his League and the plight of Europe. He did absolutely nothing.[33]

Wilson's Federal Reserve, though, did act. To squeeze out the inflation, the Federal Reserve Bank of New York began raising interest rates in November 1919, a move to slow down lending. By using its discount rate—that is, the rate it charges member banks for the money it lends to them—the Federal Reserve can affect the supply of money in circulation. Throughout the war years, 1914 to 1918, and much of 1919, the Federal Reserve kept the discount rate low, increasing the money supply and expanding credit. So it is safe to say that the boom of 1919 was fueled by easy credit and cheap money. At the end of 1919, with the cost of living rising higher and higher, the Federal Reserve acted to slow it down.

But the hike was so steep—a jump from 4 percent to 4.75 percent in the discount rate—that it shocked the stock market; the Dow lost 2.8 percent. And a few months after its initial rate hike, in January 1920 the Fed raised the rate to 6 percent, bringing on deflation and depression that would last until the summer of 1921. According to economist Gene Smiley, "The most common view is that the Fed's monetary policy was the main determinant of the end of the expansion and inflation and the beginning of the subsequent contraction and severe deflation."[34]

By the spring of 1920, demand began to decrease, inventories were piling up, and companies responded by cutting prices. Car sales plunged. In the summer of 1920, GM sold 52,000 cars per month; by November 1920 that number had fallen to 13,000; and by January 1921, sales would be just 6,150 a month. GM stock fell from $35 a share in early 1920 to $25 by July of 1921. Farmers were hurt, too. In the last half of 1920, the average price for the nation's ten leading crops fell by 57 percent. By May 1921, those same crops were bringing in a third of what they had a year earlier. By November 1921, prices had fallen below their 1913 level. Yet farmers' costs remained the same. They were caught in a vicious squeeze.[35]

Aside from the horrors of the Civil War a half a century before, 1919 had been one of the worst years in American history. For many people it seemed as though the country was falling apart. Perhaps one of President Wilson's Secret Service agents said it best, when he noted bluntly, "This country is in a mess." And, what's worse, it seemed as if all of these awful events were in some way connected, that sinister forces were at work to undermine the country. No wonder so many sought a return to normal times. This was the atmosphere in which the nation would have to begin the process of electing the next president of the United States.

CHAPTER 3

THE FIGHT FOR THE REPUBLICAN PRESIDENTIAL NOMINATION

"America's present need is not heroics, but healing; not nostrums, but normalcy; not revolution, but restoration."

—*Warren Harding*

As 1920 dawned, the American people hoped for a respite from the upheavals of the previous year. But with the economy sinking, the country looked to be on the verge of disaster as the presidential election drew near. This would be anything but a mundane, routine quadrennial event; it was a watershed election in many ways. It was obvious to all but the most oblivious that things were not heading in the right direction. Nothing seemed right, and everything seemed wrong, from the economy to the state of society, from politics to baseball. Massive problems plagued the United States of America. Could it recover?

With American democracy, though, comes the right of the people to change the course of the country. Wilson and the Democrats had won the White House and both houses of Congress in 1912 after decades of Republican rule, but they had lost control of Congress in the midterm elections in 1918, just days before the announcement of the Armistice ending the war. With Wilson's popularity in free fall, Democrats feared the loss of the presidency in 1920 and perhaps of more seats in Congress. Even in these early days before professional polling, it didn't take a political genius to conclude that the Democrats were in big trouble, no matter whom the Republicans nominated for president.

The GOP, the party out of power, would be up to bat first in the nominating process. Republicans across the country recognized the extraordinarily weak position the Democrats were in, but what seems like an easy election is not always the best scenario for party unity. In fact, it can be quite disrupting, as party members casting envious eyes on the White House will do whatever it takes to grab the nomination and fulfill their presidential aspirations. And in the spring of 1920, the Republicans had no clear favorite. Party leaders and political pundits had pegged a few top Republicans as likely nominees—a short list that included General Leonard Wood, Senator Hiram Johnson of California, and Governor Frank Lowden of Illinois.

In the wake of the midterm sweep, the party didn't have a front-runner, but looming larger than life itself was former president Theodore Roosevelt. TR had always lamented his decision not to seek another full term after election in his own right in 1904, when instead he chose a handpicked successor, William Howard Taft, to run in 1908. After finishing second as a third-party candidate in his 1912 comeback, Roosevelt was again getting presidential fever. Although he consistently denied the rumors, it was clear he was planning a run in 1920. Many party leaders knew it, and no one was prepared to stop him. And why should they? "It may transpire that Roosevelt will be the one best bet for the party to make," wrote Harding. "It is rather significant to me that he and W.H.T. [William Howard Taft] are assumed to have a get-together meeting and pledge a renewal of their abiding friendship." Harding was referring to a chance meeting the old foes had had in a hotel restaurant, which only fed the growing speculation that Republicans had patched up their differences and Roosevelt was prepared to run again at the head of a more unified party.[1]

Harding himself had played a role in soothing hurt party feelings. He had assailed Roosevelt pretty hard in 1912, after the party split and the formation of the Progressive "Bull Moose" ticket featuring TR and

California Progressive Republican senator Hiram Johnson. But while serving as Republican National Convention chairman in 1916, he urged reconciliation. That was characteristic of Harding, who was a lifelong harmonizer and peacemaker. At the convention he welcomed those "who [had] got[ten] off the reservation in 1912" back to the party. There was no party purge or punishment, for Harding knew that the only way Republicans could hope to be successful was with a united GOP.[2]

TR, for his part, seems to have held no ill will toward the senator from Ohio for past transgressions, but rather something approaching genuine affection. The two had exchanged letters since 1912 and had even collaborated on an amendment to the Selective Service Act of 1917, the army draft bill, signed by Wilson on May 18, 1917. The draft applied to all men aged twenty-one to thirty. But what Roosevelt wanted was for the army to have the ability to raise some volunteer divisions—the idea being that the old Rough Rider would lead those units with the rank of general. It passed in the original version, but the amendment was struck from the final bill. Despite the defeat, TR wrote to Harding to thank him. "I deeply appreciate your patriotic work," he said.[3]

In the summer of 1918, Harding wrote a note of sympathy after TR lost his youngest son Quentin, who, as an American flyer, was shot down over France. Though the nation mourned with the Roosevelts, he wrote, the grief was "tempered with pride, because Quentin found the metal that was in him and gave the highest manifestation of the Americanism which ever must be the hope of the republic." When Harding became president in 1921, he demonstrated his abiding affection for TR, as well as an act of gratitude for the family's support in 1920, by naming Theodore Roosevelt Jr. to his papa's old post, assistant secretary of the navy.[4]

But Teddy's health became an issue after his sickness-filled, trouble-plagued trip on the famed "River of Doubt" in one of the most impenetrable parts of the Amazon. According to Roosevelt himself, the trip took at least ten years off his life. Lying in a hospital bed during the 1918 midterm elections, TR, though, was still setting his plans for the 1920 campaign, so much so that he was already speaking to close associates about possible running mates. And one of the names Roosevelt dropped was Harding's. He even invited Harding to visit him at his home on Oyster Bay. But on January 6, 1919, fate intervened when Roosevelt died unexpectedly. He was sixty years old. The Republican presidential field was now wide open.

If anyone had a leg up on the competition, it had to be General Leonard Wood, a close Roosevelt associate. "General Wood was a magnificent man with a splendid record," wrote Senator James E. Watson of Indiana.[5] An army veteran of more than thirty years, General Wood began his career as a physician, earning a medical degree from Harvard and serving as an army doctor out on the Great Plains. In the Apache War of the 1880s, Wood earned the Medal of Honor in the last fight to capture Geronimo. In the 1890s, he served as the personal physician for Presidents Grover Cleveland and William McKinley. In 1898, along with his young lieutenant colonel Teddy Roosevelt, Colonel Wood formed the Rough Riders cavalry unit as part of the U.S. invasion of Cuba in the Spanish-American War. (Wood's battlefield promotion to brigadier general in Cuba elevated him to full colonel in command of the entire unit, which went on to distinguish itself at San Juan Hill.) After a command role in the Philippines, a stint as governor of Cuba, and a term of service as army chief of staff, General Wood was highly acclaimed by Republicans in Washington, particularly after being snubbed by Wilson for a command role in the Great War.[6]

Family and friends urged Wood to run, as did Roosevelt's political backers and family members. The Roosevelt family "had a real affection for him, and, moreover, a satisfying degree of confidence in his position on public questions," wrote TR's oldest daughter, Alice Roosevelt Longworth.[7] Wood hired TR's campaign manager, and a poll of Republican congressmen in November 1919 showed him with majority support of that caucus.[8] But not everyone was eager. H. L. Mencken held a mixed view of Wood. "I say he is stupid, but I add at once that he seems to be perfectly honest. In truth, he is the only honest candidate yet heard of—perhaps the only absolutely honest candidate in American history."[9] Others thought that having a military man as president was not the right move at this point. "Times have changed," wrote journalist Edward Lowry, "and for the moment, at least, there is a sound public instinct among us against placing military personages in high civil office." Wood might have some good qualities, but it "was easier to decide that he was a better soldier than he was a politician, for he is no politician at all."[10] Walter Lippmann, writing in the *New Republic*, called him a would-be dictator.[11]

Senator Hiram Johnson also had close Roosevelt connections and would be a strong opponent for Wood. A member of the progressive wing of the party, Johnson served as California's governor from 1911 to 1917 and then began his long tenure in the U.S. Senate, which would not end until his death in 1945. In 1912, with the nomination of President William Howard Taft for a second term, Johnson helped establish the Progressive Party and ran with TR on the party's ticket in the famous "Bull Moose" campaign. Though he hoped for the backing of Roosevelt's friends for a run in 1920, Johnson would lose out to Wood. But Johnson did command strong support among liberal Republicans and had to be respected, especially after what had happened four years before in 1916, when he was snubbed by Charles Evans Hughes in what became known as the "forgotten handshake." The resulting backlash against Hughes helped sink the GOP in California and with it the presidency, which only proved Johnson's potential strength. A fierce foe of the League of Nations, Johnson had conducted his own speaking tour to oppose Woodrow Wilson's promotion of the League and to refute his arguments. He drew large, excited crowds along the way.[12]

For Mencken, it was Johnson who seemed to be the best wager. "My bets at the moment are on Johnson. He is almost the ideal candidate. There is no more likely President in the ring," he wrote. "A very shrewd and far-reaching fellow, with a very accurate understanding of the popular mind. A great lover of the plain people."[13] Johnson had strong liberal tendencies—opposing American intervention in Russia, speaking against violations of civil liberties during the Palmer Raids, and strongly supporting the rights of free political speech. Edward Lowry noted that Johnson was like William Jennings Bryan, deriving his political power directly from the people "without the aid of any intermediaries or organization." He was "a herald with a trumpet. He is militant. He summons to arms. He blows a blast outside the walls of Jericho, and if the walls do not fall he uses a battering ram. Like any knight errant he is always ready to tilt a joust against any one who does not measure up to his ideas of a champion of the public weal," Lowry wrote. "He believes he has the courage, the intelligence, the experience, the qualities of mind and character" and "the general fitness" to serve as president. "His problem is to find out how many of us agree with him."[14]

Governor Frank O. Lowden did not have the star power of Wood or Johnson, but he was just as formidable. The son of a blacksmith, he grew up in poverty in the Midwest but did what successful Americans do—he worked hard and pulled himself up by his own bootstraps, working his way through college—and by 1887 he was a lawyer in Chicago. Two years later, he became a law professor at Northwestern. Lowden achieved financial success on his own and compounded it by marrying an heiress of the Pullman Palace Car Company. His first foray into politics landed him in the U.S. House of Representatives, where he served for five years before successfully running for governor of Illinois in 1916.[15]

As governor, Lowden was fiscally conservative, innovative, and principled. He cut taxes, instituted a budgetary system for the state to keep expenditures down, and supported women's suffrage and the death penalty, vetoing a bill that would have outlawed it. He won praise for his ability to work with the other party: Ohio's Democratic governor, James Cox, remarked that Lowden was "one of the most attractive and ablest men of his time." He won wide acclaim for his handling of the Chicago race riot of 1919. "Governor Lowden was tremendously liked by large bodies of people, particularly farmers, who regarded him as a champion of their cause," wrote Senator Watson. With party leaders holding him in high regard, many thought the nomination would likely be "Lowden or a dark horse." Seeing General Wood as his main rival,

Lowden echoed others' concerns about Wood, describing the contrast between Wood's vision and his own as "the goose step vs. the forward step." Lowden certainly had the funds to go the distance with anyone in the field.[16]

With Wood and Lowden seen as the two front-runners, and Johnson possibly third in popularity, other potential candidates could see their stars rise if—or more likely when—the convention became deadlocked. Among the "dark horses" was one of the nation's leading progressives, Senator Robert M. La Follette of Wisconsin, known as "Fighting Bob." He had been at the forefront of many of the major progressive reforms of the early twentieth century. Governor William Sproul of Pennsylvania; Columbia University's president, Nicholas Murray Butler; Massachusetts governor Calvin Coolidge; mining engineer and former Wilson administration official Herbert Hoover; and the most prominent "dark horse" of all, Senator Warren G. Harding of Ohio, rounded out the list of potential nominees.

It is customary for historians to include Harding's name in the list of "dark horses," and he was one, but he did have some national support very early in the cycle. In fact, his name was first brought up publicly by a Kansas City newspaper editor named E. Mont Reily, who in January 1919 circulated a letter to Republicans across the country pushing a Harding nomination. Harding was young, Reily noted, and was from the all-important state of Ohio. With Democrats possibly nominating Ohio governor James Cox, Republicans shouldn't take any chances. Harding was also a regular Republican who always supported the party, he was a great orator, and he believed in "normal things, normal thinking and normal legislation." According to Reily, the Republican slogan for 1920 should be "Harding and Back to Normal." This was the first use of the now-famous phrase that Harding would later tweak and use as his own.[17]

But did Harding even want the White House? As early as the spring of 1918, Harding and his good friend Frank Scobey began discussing it via correspondence. Harding's name had been mentioned plenty in private circles. "It is very comforting and satisfying to have a good many people think well of me for the big office [presidency] but none of this talk has any strong appeal for me," Harding wrote. "I am inclined to think I should like to stay in the Senate but I am not letting the matter worry me to a sufficient degree to keep me awake at nights." In a November letter, Scobey reminded him, "You have always told me you did not want . . . the presidency—but no man is too big for the job if he can get it."[18]

A couple of months later, Harding wrote a lengthy letter to Scobey on the subject of his possible candidacy and his own reluctance:

> I expect that it is very possible that I would make as good a President as a great many men who are talked of for the position and I would almost be willing to make a bet that I would be a more 'common sensible' President than the man who now occupies the White House. At the same time I have such a sure understanding of my own inefficiency that I should really be ashamed to presume myself fitted to reach out for a place of such responsibility. More than that, I would not think of involving my many good friends in the tremendous tasks of making a Presidential campaign. The sorrow of my political life in the Senate lies in the fact that one who has been honored by his state can never hope to return one one-thousand percent of the political obligations which he has incurred. With this feeling should be very reluctant indeed to broaden the field of my political activities.
>
> There are some people who discuss the availability of my name and I am frank to say I am human enough to rejoice that there are people who think well enough of me to mention me in that competition. More than that, it is a mighty gratifying thing to know that one has friends who are willing to give up their time and their means to back a candidacy, but I should be unhappy every hour from the time I entered the race

until the thing were settled, and I am sure I should never have any more fun or any real enjoyment in life if I should be so politically fortunate to win a nomination and election. I had much rather retain my place in the Senate and enjoy the association of friends and some of the joys of living.

While on vacation in Florida in March, Harding told Scobey that he had resisted calls to give a speech there because "if you make speeches outside your own state you are suspected of being a candidate—and I am not."[19]

Harding also conferred with Senator Watson about the presidential nomination on a number of occasions. Years later, in his memoirs, Watson would say that Harding "did not want it, that he was perfectly happy where he was, that he could write for his newspaper and keep it going, that he could fill the position of senator he thought acceptably to his people, that he could play a little golf and have a good time, and that he did not want to take on the incalculable burden of the presidency." Mrs. Harding was likewise "decidedly opposed to it." Harding also told Watson that he was concerned about his health, that his blood pressure was very high, and that he had a weak heart. Florence was worried that the burdens of the presidency might kill him.[20]

But was Harding serious about not wanting to seek the presidency, or was this just the coyness typical of politicians? Harding's letters throughout 1919 suggest he was more worried about the political situation in Ohio and the deteriorating state of the country than about his own position on the national stage. "I am really more anxious about the tranquility of our country than I am personal or party success," he wrote to Scobey. "I really think we are facing a desperate situation. It looks to me as though we are coming to a crisis in the conflict between the radical labor leaders and the capitalistic system under which we have developed this republic."[21]

As for the political situation in Ohio, Harding worried that Wood's campaign in the state would divide Ohio and destroy the present

Republican organization, possibly even threatening his own chances of reelection to the U.S. Senate. As Harding explained in a letter to Scobey, in order to stop a takeover by the pro-Wood crowd, some Ohio Republicans were "insisting that the only way to save the situation in Ohio is for me to permit the use of my name and they are very insistently urging that my refusal to do so would be little less than a betrayal of them into the hands of the enemy. I think you know me well enough to believe that I had rather go into a fight with my friends and lose than to be guilty of deserting them." So, in November 1919, he decided to leave Washington and go to Ohio for ten days to see what he could do. "I do not think there is the slightest question about our ability to completely capture the State. The only thing disagreeable about it is, that I despise being forced into the position of being a presidential aspirant."[22]

But on December 16, 1919, Warren Harding decided to throw his hat into the presidential ring. Although "reluctant," he told Scobey, "I have decided to take the plunge and play the big game." This was partly due to the split in the state party and the prevalent feeling that a Harding presidential campaign would unify it. The official announcement came in a public letter to the Miami County Republican Committee in Ohio, and that organization was the first to endorse him for president. The letter was published in the *New York Times*. "I venture to announce now no platform, nor to emphasize any obvious policy," he wrote. "Men in Congress make records which speak for them. Moreover, I still believe in representative popular government through political parties, believe in party sponsorship, believe conventions representing all the Republicans of the nation should make platforms, that nominees ought to be chosen as exponents of such platforms, and hold such declarations as inviolable covenants to the people." Citing his Senate duty, Harding said that he would not actively campaign for the nomination. "I cannot agree . . . to any personal activity in promoting a pre-convention campaign, not alone because of my distaste for unseemly seeking, but any neglect of important duties in the ensuing five months in the Senate would rightfully forfeit me the confidence which Ohio Republicans have so cordially expressed."[23]

Harding tapped his old political pal Harry M. Daugherty, who had successfully managed his 1914 run for the U.S. Senate, to run his presidential campaign. Harding and Daugherty had been friends for many years. A successful attorney, Daugherty had served two terms in the Ohio legislature but failed to advance further, losing bids for Ohio attorney general, the U.S. House, governor, and the U.S. Senate. But he had a lot of political connections and was a major player in the state party. Daugherty's first mentor was John Sherman, who served in the Senate through 1897, and he had worked for McKinley's presidential campaigns in 1896 and 1900, helped TR in 1904, and managed Taft's campaign in Ohio. In Harding, Daugherty saw someone who could advance as high as politics could take anyone—once remarking that he "looks like a President" and "talks like a President," an assessment many shared. Party leaders and Harding's political friends were not happy with the choice of Daugherty, who had come under fire on numerous occasions for unethical activity, including bribery and extortion, but had skated free. They urged Harding to rid himself of Daugherty to avoid trouble. It was advice he should have taken but did not.[24]

It is widely believed that Harry Daugherty controlled Warren Harding, blazed his path to the presidency, and set himself up with a cabinet post so that he could get in on the graft and corruption. But that understanding of their relationship is inaccurate. Daugherty didn't control Harding, nor did he make him. As Thomas Bailey has written, Harding "was not the 'creature' of . . . the small-town Harry M. Daugherty; rather the reverse."[25]

The men were close friends, and Harding often praised Daugherty in their correspondence, once writing to Daugherty that he "highly valued" his "keen mind, your capacity, your resourcefulness, your industry, your tenacity, your knowledge of men and your estimate of public opinion. One who has so little capacity as I know myself to possess . . . craves the association and cooperation of men of your knowledge and experience." But Harding's friendships had their limitations. "I never count my personal friendships of any particular value to any other person

than myself," he wrote to Daugherty, "and I never base personal friendships on either political or partisan relationships, even though it is con-
ceivable that personal and political friendships may be safely and
helpfully blended together. I can recall that one of the most valued personal friends that I can boast never agreed with a single political thought
or plan of my own."[26]

And Harding was willing to correct his friend if need be. "The
trouble with you . . . in your political relations with me, is that you
appraise my political sense so far below par that you have no confidence
in me or my judgment," he wrote to Daugherty in 1918. "Pray do not
think because I can and do listen in politeness to much that is said to me,
that I am always being 'strung.' I cannot and will not suspect everyone
of wanting to use me. I must and will believe in professed political friendship until I find myself imposed upon. It is the only way that I know of
to political happiness."[27]

Harding explained his relationship to Daugherty succinctly in a letter
to another correspondent. "Daugherty does not own me in any way and
I am under no particular spell in my relationship to him," he said.[28]

On another occasion, he complained to another friend that Daugherty had tried to push him into running for president to save his own
skin in Ohio. "Evidently, from your letter, they have been trying the
same things on you that Daugherty tried on me," he wrote to fellow
newspaper owner and state party secretary Charles E. Hard. "In a
veiled way, he intimated that I was inviting an opposition candidate in
1920 for my place in the Senate. I do not excessively value my popularity or my standing in the party, but I must refuse to be influenced by
any such a threat."[29]

Harding was his own man, and Daugherty would continue to head
his campaign team because Harding trusted him and wanted him there.
"He is vastly much the smartest politician in the bunch and the only one
with vision and acquaintance to carry on a nation-wide campaign," he
wrote to Scobey. In addition, for Harding, loyalty was one of the most
important virtues. He would not abandon his friends. "I think you know

me well enough to believe that I had rather go into a fight with my friends and lose than to be guilty of deserting them." In another letter he reiterated his position. "If a fellow has to sacrifice those he believes to be his friends in order to win other friends he had better not venture on the undertaking at all. I simply will not do it." This attitude would bring mounds of trouble for his future presidential administration.[30]

The presidential primaries were scheduled for March through June in twenty states. Unlike today, when nominations are won or lost during primary season, in 1920 the primaries had little bearing on who would emerge as the nominee, as only a handful of delegates were actually awarded by that process. Candidates, particularly "dark horses," generally entered certain primaries in order to show the vitality of their campaigns, their ability to attract voters, their organization skills, and their capability for raising money. The aim was to generate momentum that could carry over into the national convention. Hoping to jump out ahead of the pack, Wood and Lowden were running heavily financed campaigns. Lowden had his own deep pockets from which to draw—he would spend more than $400,000—while Wood had a lot of deep-pocketed friends. The Baltimore *Evening Sun* reported on June 3, 1920, that Wood had spent more than $60,000 in Indiana alone and had plans to raise $1 million for his campaign, a massive sum in those days. Rumor put it at $6 million. A Senate investigation would later reveal the number to be closer to $1.5 million. Senator Borah alleged that Wood and his team were attempting to "control the Republican convention by the use of money." The mounting criticism of his heavy-handedness did not help Wood's prospects.[31]

Harding was politically astute enough to see what was really going on, especially with General Wood. "Pray don't be disturbed about the publicity claims of some of the candidates," Harding wrote to Charles Forbes, who was serving as a regional campaign manager out west and who later, as a member of the Harding administration, would become infamous. "They are cheating themselves worse than they are the American public and will awaken to a very great disappointment." Harding knew that despite all the money and his big-name campaign managers, Wood was unlikely to carry the Republican banner. "I do not know what the convention will ultimately do but you can write down one thing, that Wood will never be elected if he is nominated and I doubt very much if he can be nominated under any circumstances."[32]

Harding's campaign would compete in a few primaries, including Indiana and his home state of Ohio, but he was careful to avoid states with "favorite son" candidates, where his participation would likely bring division and discord. Harding was not in favor of the kind of campaign being waged by Wood and Lowden. "I do not want an extravagant money spending campaign. If a nomination must come through such a process as that, I do not want the thing at all," he wrote to Scobey. "I think the very strength of my position lies in the fact that we are not spending money." Daugherty mainly concentrated his efforts on getting delegates in the states without primaries to pledge themselves to Harding for the convention, especially as a second- or third-choice candidate, and—with or without Harding's knowledge—on lining up big-money backers to fund the convention campaign, as well as the fall contest. One convert Daugherty won over to the Harding cause in early 1920 was Jake Hamon, a millionaire oilman from Oklahoma who controlled a bloc of fifty delegates. Harding was still expressing ambivalence about running for president: "The only thing I really worry about is that I am sometimes very much afraid I am going to be nominated and elected. That's an awful thing to contemplate."[33]

When the primaries began and his campaign stumbled early, it suddenly looked like Harding might not have to contemplate that possibility for very long. Wood realized that Harding was a vital threat, and Wood's well-funded campaign took on Harding's head-to-head in his own backyard, Ohio. Harding got strong backing from former president William Howard Taft and won the primary with 123,257 votes to Wood's 108,565, but Wood did manage to win 9 delegates and defeat Daugherty's bid to become an at-large delegate. With a split delegation, Harding's victory in his home state was not as strong as had been hoped. And in the neighboring state of Indiana, where Harding actively campaigned and was thought to be a front-runner, he finished in fourth place with only 30,782 votes. He told Daugherty, "It looks like we are done for." Wood won Indiana with more than 85,000 votes. By June, when the primaries were over, Johnson led in popular votes with 965,651, helped in large part by his win in his home state of California, and Wood had come in second with 710,863 votes. Harding was a distant fifth in popular votes, with just 144,762, but he hadn't competed in every state. Wood led the delegate count with 124, Johnson was second with 112, then Lowden with 72, and Harding with 39. Watson, one of Harding's biggest supporters, wrote that he "had made a very poor showing in the campaign," noting that Harding had not won a single delegate in any state he campaigned in outside of Ohio.[34]

But none of this really mattered, certainly not to Daugherty. What mattered was the convention itself. Daugherty knew, as most seasoned politicos did, that with Wood, Johnson, and Lowden leading the pack, it was likely they would beat on one another in Chicago and deadlock the convention. Then dark-horse candidates could make their move as potential compromise nominees. Daugherty had already been looking at that scenario for months. In a press interview in February 1920, a month before the start of the primaries and some four months before the party's convention, Daugherty had made a bold prediction: "I don't expect Harding to be nominated on the first, second, or third ballot, but I think we can well afford to take chances that about eleven minutes after two o'clock on Friday morning at the convention, when fifteen or twenty men, somewhat weary, are sitting around a table, some one of them will say: 'Who will we nominate?' At that decisive time the friends of Senator Harding can suggest him and can afford to abide by the result."[35]

So, in the end, the primaries mattered little. All Harding had had to do was avoid being embarrassed, especially in Ohio, and he could remain a viable alternative in Chicago. Indiana had certainly been a disaster, but he hadn't irritated anyone important during his primary campaign, so his candidacy was still very much alive.

Before the convention convened, Harding made what would be his most famous oration and provided the slogan for the fall campaign. Speaking in Boston, Harding noted the upheavals of the previous years, but his solution to those problems was not more government. "America's present need is not heroics, but healing; not nostrums, but normalcy; not revolution, but restoration; not agitation, but adjustment; not surgery, but serenity; not the dramatic, but the dispassionate; not experiment, but equipoise; not submergence in internationality, but sustainment in triumphant nationality," he said. "My best judgment of America's needs is to steady down, to get squarely on our feet, to make sure of the right path. Let's get out of the fevered delirium of war, with the hallucination that all the money in the world is to be made in the madness of war and the wildness of its aftermath. Let us stop to consider that tranquility at home is more precious than peace abroad, and that both our good fortune and our eminence are dependent on the normal forward stride of all the American people."[36]

Wilson had used more government to fix problems at home and war to make the world safe for democracy abroad, but to Harding that was the wrong prescription. In language that would be echoed by John F. Kennedy four decades later, Harding had another remedy in mind: "If we can prove a representative popular government under which a citizenship seeks what it may do for the government rather than what the government may do for individuals, we shall do more to make democracy safe for the world than all armed conflict ever recorded. The world needs to be reminded that all human ills are not curable by legislation, and that quantity of statutory enactment and excess of government offer no substitute for quality of citizenship." What America needed most was a return to normalcy.[37]

Americans understood well what Harding meant, and they liked it. But many of the nation's journalists at the time mocked his language, and later historians criticized his choice of words as well. One myth associated with "normalcy" is that Harding actually coined the term himself—or, in the telling of one historian, that the word came out of a mistake. Harding "lives in popular memory as the chief executive who, unable to read correctly his own speeches, mistook *normality* for *normalcy*, and thereby provided the best-known categorization of his presidential agenda," wrote Robert F. Martin. But the truth is that the word had appeared in dictionaries for decades. "I have noticed that word caused considerable newspaper editors to change it to 'normality,'" Harding said a couple of months after the speech. "I have looked for 'normality' in my dictionary, and I do not find it there. 'Normalcy,' however, I did find, and it is a good word."[38]

The Republican National Convention opened on June 8, 1920, in Chicago. A majority of the 984 delegates was needed to secure the presidential nomination. On the fourth day of the convention, Friday, June 11, nominating speeches for candidates began. Front-runners Wood, Lowden, and Johnson received nods, but so did Herbert Hoover, Massachusetts governor Calvin Coolidge, Pennsylvania governor William C. Sproul, Columbia University president Nicholas M. Butler, Senator Miles Poindexter of Washington, Judge Jeter C. Pritchard of North Carolina, and Senator Howard Sutherland of West Virginia. In a campaign tactic suited to his dark-horse candidate, Daugherty tried to get the most bang for his buck, arranging for a specific place in line to put Harding's name into nomination and using a great orator for the nominating speech itself. "We had purposely held the nominating speech for Senator Harding back until toward the end," he later wrote. He used former Ohio governor Frank B. Willis, "a man who could make a speech that would lift the tired delegates out of their seats," to formally nominate Harding. Willis called Harding "Ohio's second McKinley" and said he was a "great, stalwart, modest, patriotic American citizen" who had carried the whole GOP ticket in 1914 to victory, including Willis as governor. With the conclusion of the speech, the delegates erupted in a ten-minute celebration.[39]

But the enthusiastic ovation for Harding did not translate into immediate success when the balloting began. After the fourth nominating ballot on Friday, he was actually slightly below where he had been on the first vote, with just 61 delegates. Wood led with 314 delegates, and

Lowden was second at 289. The numbers had remained virtually unchanged through those four ballots. A deadlock seemed likely, and with no presidential nominee in sight, party leaders had to figure a way out of a possible logjam that could continue for days, splintering party unity in the process. So a few party leaders decided to hold a meeting late Friday night to discuss the situation. They met in one of Chicago's finest hotels.

The Blackstone. Room 404. It is purported to be the most famous—or infamous, depending on one's perspective—hotel room in the history of American politics. Here, it is said, in the midst of cigar smoke and adult beverages, a group of U.S. senators—some would later call it a "cabal" and "a Senatorial Soviet"—met in the wee hours of Saturday morning, June 12, 1920, and chose Warren Harding as the Republican nominee for president of the United States.[40] Their choice came despite the fact that Harding's name was not flying around Chicago, at least not on Friday night or early Saturday. The Saturday morning headline in the *Los Angeles Times* told of the gridlock: "Republican Nomination Hangs in the Balance." In the article, Harding was not mentioned. "Nobody is talking Harding," wrote one reporter.[41]

It became clear in the discussion at the Blackstone that neither Wood nor Lowden could win the nomination. At least one prominent senator had already declared that he would not support either one. Johnson was also seen as unacceptable, especially after he spurned offers of the vice presidency. It was obvious that the party leaders were running out of viable candidates. In the early morning hours, discussion centered on Harding. He was "no world beater," said one, "but we think he is the best of the bunch." And he was. Harding was a good, loyal Republican. He was acceptable to all factions of the party and, if any might be hostile, he was a natural peacemaker and harmonizer. Late that night, Harding was summoned to the room and asked if there was anything in his background that could hurt him in the upcoming election. Obviously, there were a number of issues that might come up, such as his past dalliances and the much-repeated rumor from back home that he had Negro blood coursing through his veins. But after considering everything for about ten minutes alone, Harding emerged to say that there was nothing that would disqualify him from the presidency.[42]

The next day, June 12, voting resumed. But Harding's name did not immediately zoom to the top of the heap. He more than doubled his total to 133 delegates, but that took four more votes to accomplish. It was progress, but only slow progress. On the ninth ballot, though, he began to gain rapidly, grabbing 345 delegates. On the tenth, he captured a majority: 645 delegates. Then, on a motion by the chair, the vote was made unanimous. Senator Warren G. Harding of Ohio was the Republican Party's presidential nominee.

The "smoke-filled room" explanation for Harding's nomination is a myth—peddled by the press and politicos of both parties who disliked him, such as Alice Roosevelt Longworth, who wrote, "Daugherty's prophecy that the nomination would be decided by a group of tired men in a smoke-filled room was painfully accurate."[43] David F. Houston, who held two cabinet posts under Wilson, wrote, "Harding will not be a leader. He cannot be. He has never stood for any great cause. He knows very little, has no vision, very little sense of direction, and no independence. He was not nominated to lead. He was selected because he was colorless and pliable." If elected, Harding would be a "tool" of Senate leaders like Lodge, Houston believed, and "the Senate will be supreme." "What a trial it will be to have to witness Mr. Harding's efforts to think and his efforts to say what he thinks."[44]

But the press drove the myth more than anyone else. Harry Carr of the *Los Angeles Times*, in an article under a sub-headline that read, "Predicts Hotel-Room Nominee," reported on the night of June 11, "Tonight the big inside stuff is coming off. Somewhere in a hotel room a few old bucks with wilted collars are picking out a President of the United States."[45] The *Chicago Daily Tribune*'s reporter wrote that early on Saturday morning the senators had decided "to start the Harding drive," for "they had gone as far as they could" in trying to nominate Lowden.[46] The headline in the Philadelphia *Public Ledger* on June 11 was "Deadlock Part of Senate Plan for Dark Horse." The sub-head was equally damaging: "'Congress Hotel Group' First Takes Up Plans for Eliminating Wood and Lowden, Favors Sproul or Harding."[47] A headline in the Baltimore *Evening Sun* opined, "Nomination of Harding Due to Senator's Desire to Control Government."[48] According to the *Sun* reporter, "The point of view of the Senators who nominated Harding is that the balance of power of this Government should be, not in the White House, but in the Senate." As editor Oswald Garrison Villard would note in his memoirs, "We felt that . . . [what] we were witnessing was the spectacle of the old Republican bosses again in complete control of a subservient party and defying all aspirations for reform and progress."[49]

Harding biographer Robert K. Murray has written, "No myth has been more pervasive in American history than this one."[50] As presidential scholar Thomas Bailey has also noted, "Legend to the contrary, he was not the clear choice of the Senate bosses at Chicago in 1920; they did not control the convention; and he was not nominated in a smoke-filled hotel room but in an open assembly." A high-level meeting, or meetings, did take place in the Blackstone Hotel, and Harding's name emerged as a potential nominee after some discussion. That much is true, and in an era before the primacy of the presidential primary, all presidential nominees were chosen, at least to some degree, by party bosses.[51]

In the nineteenth century, especially the latter part of that century, that's the way nearly every single nominee was chosen. There were many "smoke-filled rooms" involving both parties in those days, deals were cut, and promises were made. Stories of such wheeling and dealing were legendary. Even Lincoln, who had instructed his campaign managers to "make no contracts which bind me," found that promises had been made to gain enough support for him to be awarded the nomination at the 1860 Republican convention. After discovering the deals, Lincoln angrily said his managers had "gambled me all around, bought and sold me a hundred times."[52] Benjamin Harrison, after his retirement in 1889, told Teddy Roosevelt that when he had won the presidency, he "found out that the party managers had taken it all to themselves. I could not even name my own Cabinet. They had sold out every place to pay election expenses." It was because of these backroom deals that the idea of primaries was hatched, but it took decades before the primary system became the main avenue to nominate candidates for president.[53]

To those who participated in the meeting, it was simply party business. According to one of Harding's early backers, Senator James Watson of Indiana, there was nothing underhanded about it. "I wish to state without reservation that all the talk that has for years been indulged in about the legerdemain and hocus-pocus employed to nominate Harding is, to use an ordinary street expression, 'pure bunk.' The apparently indelible impression that there was something not quite normal and above-board about it grew largely out of a statement made by Daugherty," Watson said, referring to the bold prediction back in February. "There was nothing insidious, or subterranean, or un-American, or unfair, or unethical about the transaction. It was simply a voluntary gathering of men, all greatly interested in the success of the party, all bent on preventing a split at the Convention, for the purpose of discussing the best way out of the muddle." Party leaders did not want "a prolonged and deadly struggle over the nomination."[54]

Daugherty wasn't directing events; he wasn't even present at the meeting. "Daugherty did not attend this conference and was not even invited to do so," wrote Watson. This was simply how the game was played. And Daugherty understood it well. "All Presidents are made by organization," he would later write. "Our system of party government makes this inevitable." Daugherty had hired an army of two thousand staffers and worked to make "personal contact" with nearly every delegate, refusing to concern himself with the leadership. "We paid no attention to these meetings, but sought out and gripped the hands of the delegates who were to vote. Every man pledged to Harding was busy urging that the deadlock be broken and the Senator be nominated."[55]

Daugherty took the right tack. A meeting in a hotel room was of very little value, since no one would win the nomination without the support of a majority of the 984 delegates. As Murray concluded, after the meeting ended, "No orders ever went to convention delegates as a result of it, nor did it signal the implementation of a senatorial plan to nominate Harding. Of the sixteen senators at the convention, thirteen continued to vote for candidates other than Harding on the first four ballots on Saturday morning," which was the day after the meeting. By Saturday afternoon, "only three of the thirteen switched to the Ohioan, leaving ten still voting for other candidates." In addition, "a few of these senators" opposed to Harding, "such as Henry Cabot Lodge, used the Saturday recess to attempt to create a stop-Harding movement." The truth of the matter is simple politics: "From the time of the Lowden-Wood deadlock, Harding became the most available candidate." As Watson would later write, "The delegates did it themselves!"[56]

Republican-leaning newspapers praised the nomination. The *Los Angeles Times* editorialized that in nominating Harding, the GOP had "made a capital choice. Senator Harding is a good American, a good Republican and a good citizen—and a good winner. At no time in his public career has he been false to the traditions, the ideals, the principles or the candidates of the Republican Party. He is experienced in statecraft, and all his public acts are guided by reason, not by caprice. He is a constructive statesman of the McKinley type. He believes in building up, not in tearing down; and he has never wavered in his adherence to American institutions," the editors wrote. "He holds deep convictions on the important problems facing the American people and he expresses them in forcible and epigrammatic utterance." Harry Carr, a reporter who covered the convention for the paper, said, "Harding is not a transcendent genius; but he is an amiable, gentle-mannered Middle-Westerner with a large fund of sound common sense. He is a good deal on the order of McKinley, and will be a fine sedative for a nation suffering from nerves and from a severe overdose of college professor."[57]

The Philadelphia *Public Ledger* called Harding "a man free from cults and isms, who could be expected to give the nation an administration of public affairs based on sound principles of business judgment," as well as someone who will do what "the business interests of the country—the smallest merchant as well as the greatest banker—desire at Washington, more of practical common sense in the settlement of public questions and less of cast and horse play." According to the paper, Harding "has always won the respect and the confidence of those who know him best," by which it meant his fellow senators, regardless of party. The paper carried statements from Democratic senators on the Republican nominee. Senator Gilbert Hitchcock, Democrat of Nebraska: "Senator Harding is a colleague of mine and a personal friend, and a man of the highest character. I think he fits the Republican platform very well." Senator William H. King, Democrat of Utah: "Senator Harding is a capable and upright American. I am inclined to think that he is the strongest man the Republicans could have named. They decided upon Harding. They wanted the party to go to the country this year as the party of conservatism."[58]

But not everyone in the press was full of praise. Some took the opportunity to savage Harding. H. L. Mencken was especially critical. Referring to Harding as a "numskull," he called the Republican nominee "simply a third-rate political wheel-horse, with the face of a moving picture actor, the intelligence of a respectable agricultural implement dealer, and the imagination of a lodge joiner," in a column in late July. Intellectually, he wrote, Harding "seems to be merely a benign blank—a decent, harmless, laborious, hollow-headed mediocrity" who neither has "the slightest dignity of conviction" nor "cares a hoot for any discernable principle." In another column he mockingly wrote, "Gamaliel has the very rare virtue (in American politics) of being relatively honest—of being almost as honest, in fact, as the average porch-climber, detective or seller of Mexican oil stock."[59]

Charles Thompson, who was the Washington correspondent for the *New York Times* and no friend to Harding, wrote, "[Harding] never attracted me in the least" and "rubbed me the wrong way every time I saw his standardized smile and heard his comfortable good-fellow voice." Thompson spread untruths about the nomination campaign. "Harding was the man whom the delegates least wanted. Nobody was for him, not even his own State of Ohio," he wrote. "Having nominated him without enthusiasm, the Convention adjourned without enthusiasm." Thompson's editor at the *Times*, Charles R. Miller, described Harding as "an undistinguished and indistinguishable unit in the ruck of Republican Senators." He claimed, "We must go back to Franklin Pierce if we would seek a President who measures down to his political stature," and he called Harding "the fine and perfect flower of the cowardice and imbecility of the Senatorial cabal that charged itself with the management of the Republican Convention."[60]

Bad press notwithstanding, Harding was the man at the top of the ticket, and the focus would soon turn to the fall campaign. But could Warren Harding, an Ohio senator who had not been on anyone's radar as a presidential nominee, actually pull off a presidential win? Who was Warren Harding, anyway? The voting public didn't really know. And who would run with him on the presidential ticket? That would be a question for the Republican National Convention.

CHAPTER 4

THE ELECTION OF 1920

"Let them (the people) know it all, and then let them decide. Don't let's cheat 'em; let's make the record full and fair. We mustn't cheat 'em."

—Warren Harding

With the GOP convention a wrap, much of the country was asking the question: Just who was Warren G. Harding, the Republican nominee for president of the United States? He was largely unknown to most of the American public—then just as he is now.

"Some are born great. . . . Some achieve greatness. . . . And some have greatness thrust upon them," wrote Shakespeare in *Twelfth Night*. But in the presidential sweepstakes, there was another saying, a play on Shakespeare's words that seemed to be as true as any law of nature: "Some are born great, some achieve greatness, and some are born in Ohio." From William Henry Harrison, elected the ninth president in 1840, to William Howard Taft, the twenty-seventh in 1908, a period of sixty-eight years, seven U.S. presidents had been born in Ohio. Harding would be the eighth. And according to his many detractors, it was simply his Ohio birth that paved his way to the White House, not greatness in any shape, form, or fashion.

Unjust criticism aside, Warren Harding was Ohio through and through. He has come to symbolize his hometown, but he wasn't actually born in Marion. He arrived in the world at a time of great turmoil on

November 2, 1865, just months after the end of the calamitous War between the States, in Blooming Grove, Ohio, and would be the oldest of eight children. He attended Ohio Central College, moved to Marion as a young man, and bought a newspaper, the *Marion Star*, which became a publishing and financial success. He was soon a pillar of Marion society.

Harding was born a Seventh Day Adventist, but he later became a Baptist. He was a Mason of high degree and joined the Elk Lodge, the Rotary Club, and the local Chamber of Commerce. He was "the Prominent Citizen" in Marion, wrote journalist William Allen White.[1] To another reporter, Charles Thompson of the *New York Times*, he was "deservedly the pride of the community. He was in the forefront of the city's progress; he was always looking ahead and planning for it." He was the "instigator of practically every public improvement," working to get paved streets, electric lights, and a system of parks for the city.[2]

At the age of twenty-five he married Florence Kling DeWolfe. She was the daughter of Marion's wealthiest man, Amos Kling. But after a falling out between father and daughter, a young Florence had found herself pregnant, then abandoned by her common-law husband, Pete DeWolfe. She managed to survive, though penniless and virtually homeless, providing for herself with the help of friends in Marion and by giving piano lessons. Soon she began keeping company with the young bachelor who was editor of the town's newspaper—and who had savaged Amos Kling in its pages, accusing him of shady financial dealings with the city government. Kling hated his daughter's new beau and peddled rumors that Harding had black blood in his veins. He shamelessly referred to Harding as a "n*gger." But her father's enmity did not dissuade the headstrong Florence, who wed Harding in July 1891.[3]

Despite his rocky relationship with his prominent father-in-law, Harding was always interested in politics. He got his first real taste of national politics in 1884 by utilizing his rail pass, one of the perks of owning a newspaper, and attending the Republican National Convention. Four years later, he attended as a delegate. In 1892 he lost his first

race in a campaign for Marion County auditor—one of only two electoral losses in a career that spanned a quarter of a century. His first
political success came seven years later, when he won the first of two
terms in the Ohio state senate, eventually becoming Republican floor
leader in 1902. In 1903 he won election as the state's lieutenant governor
but served only one two-year term. He lost a bid for governor in 1910,
but in 1914 he won a seat in the U.S. Senate, where he would serve until
his nomination and election as president in 1920.

Harding was unlike most other politicians. Ambition, the vice that
turns so many ordinary men into ravenous political wolves, "did not stir
him greatly," wrote *New York Evening Mail* editor Henry L. Stoddard.
Even though Harding was "always a popular figure" back home in
Marion and "was the best known man in town," everyone "called him
Warren." And no matter how high he climbed, he always "remained
Warren."[4] And that's the way Harding wanted it, even as president.
Harding loved to play golf, often played with members of Congress, and
"insisted on being treated without respect for his office," wrote Edmund
Starling, head of his Secret Service detail. "Forget that I am President of
the United States," Harding would say. "I'm Warren Harding, playing
with some friends, and I'm going to beat hell out of them."[5] His humility
was such that as president he refused to allow the U.S. Shipping Board
to name a merchant ship after him.[6]

Charles Evans Hughes, who served as Harding's secretary of state,
called him a "most kindly man."[7] Senator James E. Watson of Indiana
admired him for "his lovable nature" and wrote that he "was as intensely
human in his sentiments and emotions and sympathies as any man I ever
knew."[8] Columbia University president Nicholas Murray Butler said he
was "one of the kindest men who ever lived."[9] Journalist Edward G.
Lowry also made note of Harding's kind nature. He wrote that he possessed a "kindliness and kindness that fairly radiate from him. He positively gives out even to the least sensitive a sense of brotherhood and
innate goodwill toward his fellow man," he wrote. These traits are the
"strongest [impression] Mr. Harding makes upon every one."[10]

Even his political enemies and those who harbored disdain for him could not ignore Harding's thoughtfulness. The ambitious Democrat William McAdoo, Woodrow Wilson's son-in-law and treasury secretary, who had no love for Harding or his administration, which he thought was full of "disgraceful incompetency," believed Harding "was a likeable person. His manner was pleasant and ingratiating; and he was a 'good fellow.'"[11] Oswald Garrison Villard, a founder of the NAACP, grandson of abolitionist William Lloyd Garrison, and a dyed-in-the-wool liberal who thought Harding "corrupt," had to admit that he "had a heart."[12] William Allen White, editor of the famed Kansas *Emporia Gazette* and a leader in the Progressive movement, had almost nothing good to say about Harding in all of his voluminous writings, but he conceded that he had a "loveable personality."[13]

Perhaps no man captured the goodness of Warren Harding better than Charles Thompson, the Washington reporter for the *New York Times*. Thompson, who had a "positive distaste" for a "simple sort of chap" with nothing "stirring in his brain," complained about Harding's "perpetual smile" and "his meaningless geniality," which he said "came to grate on me more and more." But Thompson nonetheless conceded that Harding was "one of the kindest hearted of men. Never was there a man fuller of good feeling." Harding spent hundreds of dollars every Christmas on gifts for the poor in Marion, Thompson related in his memoirs. Harding's father had told the reporter that his son had given the poor "more than any other man in this town." Harding's "generosities were so numerous," wrote Thompson, "and so constant that in Marion you never heard the same story from any two men; they always had their own stories, all different." Harding exhibited "kindness to everybody, a desire to do gracious little things to make life pleasanter."[14]

Two days after he was elected president in 1920, Harding responded to an article in the *Literary Digest* appealing to the American people to help the 3.5 million children who were victims of the Great War in Europe. Harding sent a personal check for $2,500 ($32,000 in 2020 dollars) and wrote a gracious note in favor of the magazine's "splendid appeal." His letter was published in the November 13, 1920, issue. "Because such a movement for relief reveals the true heart of America," he wrote, "because it bespeaks an American desire to play a great people's part in relieving and restoring God's own children, I want to commend and support your noble undertaking." The American people should "share our good fortunes in acts of sympathy and human fellowship. I wish you a success which will reveal anew the unselfishness of our great people."[15]

Harding's generosity was also evidenced in his management of the *Marion Star*, where he was known to hire down-on-their-luck reporters and "never fired anybody," nor did he cut any employee's pay in the thirty-five years he owned the newspaper. And if a story emerged that would "cast ignominy or reproach on some innocent woman or child," Harding would not print it.[16] *Star* employees called him "W. G.," and Harding, as Sheryl Smart Hall, the author of *Warren G. Harding and the Marion Daily Star: How Newspapering Shaped a President*, says, "made a point of telling them . . . that they worked 'with' him, not 'for' him." He also offered to let his employees buy stock in a quarter of the company. "This unheard-of move," notes Hall, "spoke volumes to his employees about his high regard for them and gave them a personal, vested interest in the success of the *Star*."[17] And in his final will, he left generous monetary bequests to his former employees.[18]

Harding also had a great love for animals and loathed those who mistreated them—attitudes often on display in the pages of his newspaper. In February 1885, he wrote about a man who did not treat his horses with proper care. "The man who will drive a team of horses for miles and then hitch them unblanketed to a post to shiver for hours in the cold, is less fit and less likely to get to heaven than the poor dumb brutes are." On another occasion he wrote about the mistreatment of mules, not the most popular animal at the time, but he did not refrain from calling out the abuse and naming names. "If the report we have is true regarding the brutal manner in which J. H. Foster, the drayman, treated his mules this morning, the S.P.C.A. greatly neglects its duty if he is not arrested. It's seldom a mule gets sympathy, but there is a limit to all things." Harding's favorite pets were his dogs, which he often took to work with him. In fact, he loved them so much that when one of them died, he published an obituary in the *Star*. His dog during his time as president, Laddie Boy, was the first White House pet celebrity.[19]

Edmund Starling, the head of the White House Secret Service detail, described Harding as "a handsome man, friendly and cordial, with sympathetic and gentle eyes." In his memoirs, Starling related a story about Harding's kindheartedness toward others, including the lowliest of creatures. Early in the Harding administration, the president's private secretary, George B. Christian, told Starling about the new president. "He loathes prizefighting . . . and hunting. He is sensitive to the infliction of pain on anybody or anything." Christian drove home his point with a story about Harding. "One day I was sitting with him on his front porch when I noticed some ants crawling along the balcony rail. I folded my newspaper and swatted them. He protested. 'Why do you kill those harmless insects?' he asked. 'Have they ever injured you?'" This was Starling's "first insight into the character of a man who could not bear to believe that there was evil in any man or selfishness behind any plea for help."[20]

This kind and gracious nature, which even his enemies acknowledged, went with Warren Harding to the White House. But who would be going to Washington with him? The convention had another important task—to choose Harding's running mate. Whom could they nominate to run alongside Harding? Who could help him beat the party in power, the Democrats?

It has been a custom throughout American presidential history to use the second place on the party's ticket for balance between competing party interests. It may be geographical balance, as it often was in antebellum days, or ideological balance. To balance the 1920 ticket philosophically, Harding offered the vice presidency to the progressive and very popular Hiram Johnson, who declined it. Johnson had already issued a statement in early June, before the convention, that "under no circumstances" would he accept the vice presidency. Harold Ickes, a delegate and progressive Republican from Chicago, wrote that Johnson turned down the offer because "he had only contempt" for the nominee. Harding likely knew this, so his offer was probably not serious, but simply a courtesy. He wouldn't repeat Hughes's 1916 mistake by appearing to snub Johnson. After Johnson refused, Harding told party bosses that he would be content with whomever the convention chose.[21]

Party leaders had it in mind to nominate a more progressive Republican to balance out the ticket ideologically, but according to newspaperman William Allen White, who was a delegate from Kansas, when Senator Medill McCormick of Illinois took the podium and tried to nominate Senator Irvine L. Lenroot of Wisconsin, "the convention revolted" and there were thunderous cries for "Coolidge!" The Oregon delegation began the stampede for Coolidge, and Judge Wallace McCamant rose to nominate the Massachusetts governor. "Enthusiastic acclaim swept the Convention like a wave that ran high over all the other candidates and their adherents," wrote Senator Watson. The convention was in no mood for progressivism. The delegates overwhelmingly wanted a conservative vice president in the mold of Warren Harding.[22]

Coolidge, who as a Massachusetts "favorite son" candidate had only a brief presidential campaign, had made a name for himself the previous fall with his response to the Boston police strike. "No doubt it was the police strike of Boston that brought me into national prominence," Coolidge wrote. "That furnished the occasion and I took advantage of the opportunity." Putting down the strike, he wrote, "increased my political power many fold." The "Yankee Puritan," as William Allen White called Coolidge, had a very impressive resume filled with government service, although none on the national stage. He had served as mayor of Northampton, Massachusetts, in both houses of the state legislature, as president of the state senate, and as lieutenant governor, and he was elected governor in November 1918 by a close margin. Then, in November 1919, after the strike, he won a "decisive" victory, which catapulted him nationally and brought forth his presidential candidacy.[23]

He was known as "Silent Cal" for his quiet demeanor, and stories of Coolidge and his peculiar personality were legendary. Edward Lowry called him "the oddest and most singular apparition this vocal and articulate settlement has ever known: a politician who does not, who will not, who seemingly cannot talk. A well of silence. A center of stillness." The *Washington Post* once quoted Alice Roosevelt Longworth as saying Cal Coolidge "looks as though he's been weaned on a pickle." Perhaps the most oft-told anecdote about Coolidge is the tale of a young woman sitting next to him at a dinner party. She leaned over and said, "I made a bet with a friend that I could get you to say more than three words tonight." Without missing a beat, Coolidge replied, "You lose."[24]

Journalist Edward Lowry wanted to know the great men of Washington, to find out who they really were, what motivated them, what made them tick. But Coolidge was a complete enigma. "I have been eager to pluck out the heart of Mr. Coolidge's mystery," Lowry wrote, "to discover what sort of man he is, to establish a basis for appraisal. And all in vain, for he has revealed nothing, disclosed nothing." But those who served with him knew his good qualities. According to Herbert Hoover, Coolidge "was well equipped by education, experience, and moral courage" for higher office. "He was the incarnation of New England horse sense and was endowed with certain Puritan rigidities that served the nation well. He possessed New England thrift to the ultimate degree, and his tight hold on government expenditures and his constant reduction of public debt were its fine expression." Coolidge was "a real conservative" and "a man of complete intellectual honesty."[25]

A real conservative he was, and a perfect choice to serve as Warren Harding's running mate. The Philadelphia *Public Ledger* said the Harding-Coolidge ticket was "a clean, unmistakable, acceptable Republican ticket. They will give the country a Republican administration. They will not attempt to play Providence to a resentful, jealous, decidedly unready world." While it may be commonplace for parties to seek geographical and ideological balance for their national tickets, that was not the case for the Republicans in 1920. Harding and Coolidge saw the world in exactly the same terms and believed, as the Jeffersonians had, that the least amount of government would be the best for society. Their personalities, though, were polar opposites. Harding is widely known as a man who enjoyed a good time, liked to drink, smoke, and play poker, and had enjoyed the company of a lady friend or two. Calvin Coolidge wouldn't have been caught dead doing any of those things. He was the quintessential Puritan in that regard. Some might even say he was a prude. But he was a rock-solid conservative who treated the people's money with the greatest respect. In fact, Coolidge was so tightfisted with public funds that as president he refused to spend money to fix the leaky White House roof.[26]

Not everyone in the party favored the 1920 ticket. Some were lukewarm, others downright hostile. The antagonism was directed at Coolidge as well as at Harding. Oswald Garrison Villard, who attended the 1920 GOP convention as a journalist for *The Nation* magazine, wrote that it was "from first to last one of the dreariest and most discouraging party gatherings ever held." Villard talked with some newspapermen from Massachusetts after the nomination of Coolidge for vice president, and he reported that many in that delegation "laughed heartily, thinking it a great joke." Robert L. O'Brien of the *Boston Herald* told Villard that Coolidge was the "worst man I ever knew in politics."[27]

The fiercest fire, though, was directed at the top of the ticket. The progressive Harold Ickes was particularly harsh, writing unforgiving invective against Harding in his autobiography and helping fuel the damage to his reputation. One of the few who fiercely opposed the nomination of Harding, Ickes, with few supporters, yelled "No!" on the motion to make it unanimous. Harding had "the backing of the Old Guard. He was a typical small-bone Ohio politician . . . distinctly lacking in character and in essential integrity." This was evident in the "stomach-turning" and "miserable machinations that went on in that Chicago convention." Ickes even went so far as to solicit two of TR's sons—Theodore Jr. and Archie—to "denounce" Harding and "declare that no true Rooseveltian would support him, either in the convention or thereafter." Both refused. So the "ineffable Harding" was "nominated with his Ohio gang hanging onto his shirt tails . . . those turbulent, grasping, selfish men who were thinking little of their country but much of the spoils," Ickes wrote. "From the moment of Harding's nomination I knew that I would not support him. I was outraged and disgusted." Disliking all things conservative, Ickes also took after Coolidge. "The political medicine man from Northampton, Massachusetts, did not appeal to me any more than did the Ali Baba from Ohio, although I must say that Coolidge was never capable of the skullduggery of Harding."[28]

Although she would later come around to some degree, Alice Roosevelt Longworth had "an active distaste" for Harding, "one of the dark horses, whose name had been hardly mentioned in the beginning." She would later claim to have had a conversation with George Harvey, one of the participants at the late-night Blackstone Hotel meeting, who said Harding was chosen because he "could be counted on to 'go along.' In other words, he could be controlled."[29] *New York Times* reporter Charles Thompson had said much the same thing, believing that with Harding the bosses could "control the Presidency." Harding would give "them ease," and they could "shuffle him and deal him like a deck of cards."[30]

William Allen White, who was perhaps one of the most important members of the Republican Party, was a "Roosevelt man" like Ickes and greatly disliked Harding, favoring Hoover instead. White said at a meeting of the Kansas delegation, "If you nominate Harding, you will disgrace the Republican Party. You will bring shame to your country." In July, though, he wrote to Harding, "I have no doubt that you will be able to unite the Republican party"—something that, for White, would be possible only if Harding caved to Progressive demands. That did not happen. But White supported Harding in the fall anyway, only to savage his reputation in later years.[31]

Harding had his work cut out for him in mending party fences, but that was one of the strengths of his candidacy. He reached out to Republicans of various philosophical leanings and worked toward party unity. He exchanged letters with former president William Howard Taft, asking for his counsel: "I do not pretend to know about everything which is interesting to all the varied elements in our American life and I welcome ideas and suggestions and am aiming to be instrumental in restoring a party government where counsel and advice shall abide." In August, the previous Republican nominee, Charles Evans Hughes, visited Harding at his home in Marion and "issued a statement supporting his candidacy." Hughes agreed to campaign for Harding with speeches in Ohio and Indiana. In September, Harding wrote to Henry Cabot Lodge, noting the "important work of uniting the country on a thoroughly American program." Throughout the fall campaign, Harding's voluminous correspondents included the Speaker of the House, governors, and other Republican Party officeholders.[32]

Harding's first official act as the nominee was an acceptance speech. He confided in Lodge that he wanted to hit the "high spots," emphasizing major themes including "the restoration of constitutional government through party, our foreign relations, industrial peace, and the great problem of taxation . . . and economies in government." Always friendly to members of the press, even though some of them were not very friendly to him in the pages of their periodicals, Harding had *Evening Mail* editor Henry L. Stoddard at his home in Marion as he worked on his speech. It was "a confession of faith," he told Stoddard. "Let them [the people] know it all, and then let them decide. Don't let's cheat 'em; let's make the record full and fair," he said. "We mustn't cheat 'em." Harding emphasized this to Stoddard because he had been given advice, which he didn't take, not to say too much. "Frankness was a strong Harding trait," Stoddard later wrote. "And he always meant what he said."[33]

In a very lengthy address that ran nearly seven thousand words long, Harding did not engage in attacks on the opposite party but instead emphasized what he believed and what he wanted to do for the country. He included no less than seventeen "I believe" statements, such as, "I believe the Federal department should be made more business-like and send back to productive effort thousands of Federal employees, who are either duplicating work or not essential at all," "I believe in the protective tariff policy and know we will be calling for its saving Americanism again," "I believe the tax burdens imposed for the war emergency must be revised to the needs of peace, and in the interest of equity in distribution of the burden," "I believe in established standards for immigration, which are concerned with the future citizenship of the republic, not with mere manpower in industry," and "I believe that every man who dons the garb of American citizenship and walks in the light of American opportunity, must become American in heart and soul." Stoddard wrote of him, "He stood for no particular issue. He was a party man, ready to do whatever everybody thought best," but there could be little doubt where Warren Harding stood on the issues.[34]

Now it was the Democrats' turn. President Wilson, despite his growing unpopularity, was not yet ready to concede defeat in 1920, as bad as things looked for his party. Stung by the second vote against his beloved League of Nations that March, Wilson was determined to make the presidential election a referendum on its ratification. But more than that, he wanted to be the Democratic Party's nominee for an unprecedented third term, despite his physical condition. White House usher Ike Hoover said Wilson "was in a receptive mood for the nomination"; in fact he was "anxious and expectant." But, according to the Washington correspondent for *The Protectionist*, a publication of the Home Market Club in Boston, in May of 1920 no reporter in the capital had a clue as to the president's real condition, and much of the country remained in the dark as to exactly what was wrong with their leader. "It is not expected that he will be a candidate for re-election," the reporter wrote, "but he is taking a disconcertedly long time to say he will not." The reason was simple: Like Daugherty, Wilson was privately hoping for a brokered convention, in which stressed Democrats would turn to him. He had no intention of surrendering to the Republicans, and he certainly had no intention of surrendering his leadership of the Democratic Party to anyone other than himself.[35]

The Democrats met in San Francisco at the end of June, but no call came for the beleaguered man in the White House. His party shunned him in favor of a different candidate, someone who could take on Harding without the weaknesses and the baggage carried by Wilson. The top three candidates were Ohio governor James M. Cox, who had also served in the U.S. House; William G. McAdoo, Wilson's treasury secretary and son-in-law, who was known as the "Crown Prince" and badly wanted to succeed his father-in-law in the White House; and the attorney general, A. Mitchell Palmer, fresh off the raids that had brought the chaos and violence across the country under control.

Given his closeness to the president, a McAdoo presidency would essentially be a third Wilson term, and he never shied away from boasting about the previous eight years. "As a matter of fact, the administration of Woodrow Wilson was responsible for more genuine constructive legislation in its eight years of existence than all the Republican administrations of the past fifty years," he wrote. Labeled "the most arrogant person in Washington" by Herbert Hoover, McAdoo led for the first eleven ballots, besting Palmer, with Cox in third place. On the twelfth ballot, Cox moved into the lead and stayed there until he had secured the necessary two-thirds vote to win the nomination, on the forty-fourth ballot. Woodrow Wilson received all of two votes. Cox's nomination was influenced by the thought that Ohio would be crucial if Democrats had any hope of keeping the White House. To further bolster his chances, Cox picked a running mate who had a very familiar political name. Franklin Delano Roosevelt, then thirty-eight years old and serving in his cousin's old job as assistant secretary of the navy, readily joined the ticket.[36]

The opposing nominees for the White House made for a unique presidential campaign. Not only were both men statewide elected leaders from the same state, both were also newspaper owners—Harding had his *Marion Star*, and Cox owned two newspapers in Ohio. This was a first in American presidential history. Harding ran the more traditional campaign, modeled largely on McKinley's 1896 "front porch" strategy. He wouldn't barnstorm the country making speeches and glad-handing; the people would be brought to him, for the most part. Later in the campaign he did briefly hit the trail and give speeches as far away as Oklahoma. It was not that Harding believed himself above the common people—far from it. To one reporter who enthusiastically backed him, he wrote, "You must not seem excessive in your enthusiasm, because that would tend to make me out a very different person from that which I really am. You know me well enough to understand that we are just plain folks, like so many of the American people, though we do have earnest convictions and high aspirations for our common country."[37]

Harding also had some star power in his corner, as many leading actors and entertainers backed his candidacy. Singer Al Jolson, one of the most famous at the time, campaigned for Harding and also wrote a campaign jingle—"Harding, You're the Man for Us." Other famous Americans supporting Harding, more than seventy in all, came to see the candidate in Marion. They included Eddie Foy, Ethel Barrymore, Pearl White, and Anita Stewart, the top stars of their day. Even the Chicago Cubs came to play a local team in Marion in support of Harding.[38]

Cox, on the other hand, traveled widely. Being the clear underdogs in the race, the Democrats understood that to beat the Republicans they would need to reach as many voters as they could and convince them that they had their best interests in mind. A passive campaign would not cut it in 1920. Cox and Roosevelt hit the campaign trail hard, taking to the stump across the country. The campaign was billed as "the most strenuous ever undertaken by a nominee for the Presidency." It even outdid William Jennings Bryan's whirlwind speaking tour in 1896. Cox worked the Midwest, Pennsylvania, and Connecticut in August, then headed out west. From there he headed south to Kentucky, Tennessee, Maryland, then up to New England and Ohio. He gave twenty-six speeches in one day alone. In all he visited thirty states, skipping only the Deep South, which he was guaranteed to win no matter what, and Maine and Vermont. He traveled twenty-two thousand miles, gave nearly four hundred speeches, and spoke to an estimated two million people. Roosevelt, who had not yet been afflicted with polio, traveled eighteen thousand miles, giving ten speeches a day.[39]

As Wilson desired, the League of Nations would be a central issue in the campaign. For Cox, it was a thorny one. Whether he truly supported the League or not made little difference. The political problem he faced was that he had to embrace it and maintain close ties with Wilson, no matter how unpopular he might be. Throwing the sitting president under the bus would make a difficult political situation much worse. So, soon after the nomination came his way, Cox and Roosevelt visited Wilson in the White House to reassure him they would remain firm on the League. Cox was permitted to replace the Democratic Party's national chairman, Homer Cummings, who had been instrumental in Wilson's victories and had paid off the party's debts after the 1916 campaign.[40]

Harding has been accused by historians of muddling the League issue in the campaign by not taking a definitive stand on it, and to some degree that's true. But, at least politically, he had a bit of a problem. His party was divided on the issue, as there were pro-League Republicans, some that supported the League with reservations, and a few who would not support it under any circumstances, and he had to work to keep those divergent groups on board with his campaign. Yet he was always clear about one thing: he did not support the League as proposed by Wilson. The *New-York Tribune* reported in August after a Harding foreign policy speech in Iowa, "League Flatly Repudiated by Harding." He did, however, support some kind of international organization, or what he called an "association," for solving world disputes, although he was never clear about what exactly that would be. In September Harding wrote to Hiram Johnson, one of the League's fiercest critics, about the issue. "We are all going to be heartily agreed about clinging everlasting to American independence, and hold ourselves adamant against the surrender which was contemplated in the negotiations of the President. I do not pretend to specifically point out exactly what I propose to do and think it practical to do, because the big task of the present is to make it reasonably possible for our party to unite in opposition to the surrender which threatened in the course pursued by the President." Harding would later sign onto the World Court proposal.[41]

On the League issue, President Wilson, monitoring the campaign from the White House, was convinced that Democrats would win. "The President expressed a very strong conviction of its favorable outcome," wrote David Houston, then serving as secretary of the treasury. "He said that he was confident that Cox would be elected and that the League would be the issue with which the people would mainly concern themselves, and that on it they would go with Cox." Former Speaker of the House Champ Clark of Missouri was also supremely confident. "Harding and Coolidge will be just as easy to beat as any men they could put up," he said. However, not everyone was so sure. Secretary Houston thought it would be "tragic to have a man of Mr. Wilson's intellect and high standards succeeded by a man of Mr. Harding's mediocre mind and ordinary standards of thinking and action," but, he said, "I did not share the President's confidence."[42] As late as Election Day, November 2, Wilson remained positive, as he had throughout the campaign. After a cabinet member expressed apprehension about the possible outcome, Wilson interrupted him. "You need not worry. The American people will not turn Cox down and elect Harding. A great moral issue is involved. The people can and will see it."[43]

The only really ugly issue that came up during the fall campaign was the old smear that Harding had "Negro blood in his veins." The accusation that Harding had black ancestry came from William E. Chancellor, a college professor and supporter of Wilson. According to one presidential scholar, Chancellor did not like the "more tolerant racial views of Harding and the Republicans, so he invented a scandal that played on cultural fears of race-mixing." This came about soon after Harding gave a speech in Oklahoma stating that he supported full rights for all Americans. But, in fact, the scandal went back to Harding's early days in grade school, when other children made fun of him for the rumor. Florence Harding's father, who hated his son-in-law, had helped spread it. It came up in every campaign Harding ever ran but never gained any real traction, certainly not outside the South. For his part, the kind and gracious Harding refused to attack Wilson personally, as some of his campaign aides desired. "I guess you have nominated the wrong candidate, if this is the plan for I will never go to the White House over the broken body of Woodrow Wilson," he told them.[44]

As the campaign pushed into its final month, an incident in New York City reminded everyone that things were still amiss. At one minute past noon on September 16, a horse-drawn carriage filled with dynamite exploded in New York City's financial district in Manhattan. Thirty people were killed instantly, and another eight died of their wounds within days. The target: the offices of J. P. Morgan at 23 Wall Street. It was the largest act of terrorism in U.S. history up to that time. The crime was never solved, although authorities believed that it was likely the handiwork of the anarchist groups that had carried out the bombings in 1919.

Was anything safe in the country? Where would anyone go to get a respite from all the chaos enveloping the nation? Even the up-and-coming sport of professional baseball proved to be no refuge from pressing national problems. Those who sought escape from the current mood of uncertainty with an afternoon at the diamond were shocked to learn that the 1919 World Series had been fixed, as several players from the Chicago White Sox had been bought off by crooked gamblers and greedy moneymen. The "Black Sox" scandal rocked much of the country and became a media sensation in 1920, as baseball's commissioner, Kennesaw Mountain Landis, banned eight White Sox players for life. Nothing seemed safe.

In the end, neither the personal attacks on Harding, nor the barn-storming of the Cox-Roosevelt ticket, nor the confidence of Wilson made any difference. With the country in a state of upheaval, Warren Harding won by the largest margin in the history of presidential elections up to that time, and on his birthday no less, taking 60 percent of the popular vote: 16,143,407 ballots to 9,141,750 for Cox. The Electoral College was just as lopsided, with Harding winning 404 to 127. Cox won just 11 states, and the only one outside of the old Confederacy was Kentucky.[45] Harding even managed to swipe Tennessee, the first southern state to go Republican since Reconstruction, causing the *Memphis Commercial Appeal* to call it "an avalanche"—the heaviest vote ever recorded in the state. The entire state of Tennessee was "caught in the GOP Cyclone."[46] The solidly Democratic city of Boston went Republican for only the second time in its history. Republicans won New York by a million votes, something that had never happened before, and knocked Al Smith out of the governor's chair. The Republicans in the House of Representatives increased their majority, carrying 303 seats to the Democrats' 131. The Senate would be solidly Republican as well, after a 10-seat gain gave the GOP a margin of 22 seats. Wilson's top aide, Joe Tumulty, summed up the Democrats' point of view: it "wasn't a landslide, it was an earthquake."[47]

For some, Harding's victory could be laid at the feet of the intense dislike of Woodrow Wilson and what had transpired in the country over the previous few years. "Harding was not Woodrow Wilson," noted Professor Lewis L. Gould, "and in 1920 that was all that mattered to the American electorate."[48] As the Los Angeles Times noted the day after the rout, "Eight years of Democratic incompetency and waste are drawing rapidly to a close."[49] Charles Thompson of the New York Times believed that the people "did not vote for Harding; nor did they vote against Cox. In 1920 they did not vote for anybody; they voted against somebody; and the somebody they voted against was not a candidate; it was Wilson." Thompson believed Cox was actually defeated in November 1918, two years before, "when Wilson appealed to voters to show their opinion of him by electing a Democratic Congress, and they showed it by electing a Republican one." This resembled the British system "of calling for a vote of confidence in the Government at a parliamentary election."[50]

For journalist William Allen White and a host of others, the 1920 campaign was a study in contrasts. "Harding was the complete antithesis of Wilson, and the currents of that day were anti-Wilson," he wrote. Harding's "return to normalcy" was a rejection of progressive ideals. The people in 1920 were "tired of [progressive] issues, sick at heart of ideals and weary of being noble," wrote White.[51] Even the fiercely anti-Harding H. L. Mencken recognized it, writing, "[Americans] are weary of hearing highfalutin and meaningless words; they sicken of an idealism that is oblique, confusing, dishonest and ferocious."[52] Progressivism had brought trouble, and the people pushed back. "The reasons for the Republican victory are not far to seek. Almost every class and condition of men and women in the country had some particular thing to be discontented about," wrote the editors of the Baltimore *Evening Journal*. And they struck back hard by electing Warren Harding.[53]

Yet, in truth, there was another explanation for the Republican landslide: the people liked Warren Harding and what he stood for. As White noted, the election "was made upon two fundamental issues—the hate of Woodrow Wilson . . . and the return to 'normalcy.'" The nomination of a progressive Republican might have resulted in a victory but would certainly not have been a landslide with such long presidential coattails. But, whatever the reason, one thing was certain. As Mencken rightfully observed, with the election of Harding as president, "Liberalism was laid in a coffin." And that is what the people wanted.[54]

CHAPTER 5

THE HARDING ADMINISTRATION

*"When elected, I will immediately summon the best
minds in America because it is the only lawful and appropriate course that a President should take."*

—Warren Harding

On Friday, March 4, 1921, Warren Gamaliel Harding, the humble
newspaper editor from Marion, Ohio, had a date with history. But to
him it was like any one of the thousands of days that had preceded it in
his more than fifty-five years of life. After a meeting the previous day
with President Wilson and a night at the Willard Hotel, Harding rose
early on the day he would become the president of the United States, ate
breakfast, read the newspapers, and prepared to head over to the White
House to meet with Wilson for the trip together to the Capitol, which
would be in an automobile, a first in presidential history. Just after one
o'clock, he would stand on the East Portico of the U.S. Capitol, where
he had toiled the previous six years as a United States senator, and take
the oath of office as the twenty-ninth president of the United States.

When Harding woke, the early morning was bitterly cold, with an
icy wind and temperatures just below freezing, hovering around thirty
degrees. By 10:00 a.m., the air had warmed a bit to forty degrees, making
it at least somewhat more tolerable for the throngs of citizens who had
come to Washington to see the inauguration of a new chief executive.
Every hotel was filled to capacity, and many were forced to find

accommodations elsewhere. Harding spent most of the ride to the Capitol tipping his hat to those lining the streets cheering him as he passed by. Making his way into the Capitol building, Harding bade farewell to President Wilson, who was so weak that he had to be lifted into the car for the ride over. He was still so feeble from his stroke that he would be unable to attend the ceremony. Harding was very gracious to his predecessor, despite the nasty comments Wilson had made during the campaign. "Goodbye, Mr. President," Harding told him. "I know you are glad to be relieved of your burden and worries. I want to tell you how much I have appreciated the courtesy you extended to me."

At 1:18 p.m., Warren G. Harding took the oath of office with his left hand on a Bible once owned by George Washington, open at Micah 6:8: "He has shown you, O man, what is good. And what does the Lord require of you but to do justly, to love mercy, and to walk humbly with your God?" After repeating the constitutional oath, administered by Chief Justice Edward D. White, Harding leaned over and kissed the Bible. He then pulled his speech from his coat pocket and began his address to the crowd. His speech was electronically amplified, a first for a presidential inauguration, and broadcast across the country and around the world by radio.[1]

In his inaugural address, President Harding focused on the multitude of major problems facing the country after the upheavals of the previous two years—coming out of what he called the "great storm" in Europe and the "wreckage of war" that had been inflicted on the United States. It was nothing like what had befallen Europe, with its "devastated lands" and "devastated cities." America's problems were mainly economic, centered "in the delirium of expenditure, in expanded currency and credits, in unbalanced industry, in unspeakable waste, and disturbed relationships." Harding vowed to "reduce the abnormal expenditures" and "strike at war taxation," which Wilson had not lowered after the end of hostilities. The new president spoke in favor of "administrative efficiency, for lightened tax burdens, for sound commercial practices, for adequate credit facilities, for sympathetic concern for all agricultural problems," and he recognized "the immediate task of putting our public house in order. We need a rigid and yet sane economy, combined with fiscal justice, and it must be attended by individual prudence and thrift, which are so essential to this trying hour and reassuring for our future," he said.[2]

The nation's new vice president, Calvin Coolidge, had a very positive opinion of the man ushering in this new era of republican simplicity. "It was a clear but crisp spring day," he wrote in his autobiography. "The inaugural address was able and well received. President Harding had an impressive delivery, which never failed to interest and hold his audience," Coolidge said, and "his charm and effectiveness never failed."[3] Many in the press were equally positive. The *Los Angeles Times* praised the inauguration and the new president. "Consciously and serenely, without arrogance or parade, the Republican party . . . resumed control of the United States government," and President Harding, "with the eye of an optimist . . . has begun as the American people would have him begin, in humility rather than in pride," the editors wrote. "There was no note of self-glorification in the inaugural address." With the close of the era of Wilson, "eight years of Democratic extravagance and misrule have come to an end and . . . . Republican restoration has taken place . . . under such sterling leadership" as Harding's.[4]

The *Chicago Daily Tribune* said, "Mr. Harding seems as near to being a representative of American character and product of American life as any man who has ever entered the White House." The paper reported that the night before the inauguration, Harding had said, "I am going to my work with the confidence that all will be well" for the country. "That was not spoken lightly. It was a great assertion of the spirit and vigor of the American people. It expressed sincerely our confidence in our ability to meet all problems and go forward steadily in the path of a benignant destiny," the editors wrote. "Mr. Harding will make mistakes, being human, as his predecessors have before him. He will succeed in the degree that he represents and draws his inspiration from the simple and virile instincts of the American people and makes himself an intelligent instrument of the spirit of American nationalism. It was a mighty manifestation of that spirit which carried him to victory on the shoulders of the greatest majority in our political history."[5]

But not everyone was brimming with confidence. Critics found fault with the new president's choice of words in his address. Wilson had told his cabinet at their last meeting that "there will be one very difficult thing for me ... to stand, and that is Mr. Harding's English."[6] One of Harding's most persistent critics, as we have seen, was the Baltimore *Evening Sun* writer H. L. Mencken. He attended the "simple ceremony" and wrote, in a report published later that evening, that the new president's address "began with a sentence in bad English and ended with a noble phrase from Holy Writ." This new "Warren Gamaliel," Mencken opined, "differed vastly from the simple rustic who was lifted out of oblivion" in Chicago in 1920. He was "infinitely better dressed," but also "more solid, more deliberate in movement, more conscious of the glare upon him."[7] Three days later, in a column entitled "Gamalielese," Mencken charged that Harding "writes the worst English that I have ever encountered. It reminds me of a string of wet sponges."[8] Wilson's son-in-law, "Crown Prince" William McAdoo, wrote that Harding's speeches "leave the impression of an army of pompous phrases moving over the landscape in search of an idea."[9] The poet E. E. Cummings declared that Harding was "the only man, woman or child who wrote a simple declarative sentence with seven grammatical errors."[10]

Harding also had his defenders. As Robert Murray has written, "Surprisingly, few contemporaries agreed with Mencken's or Wilson's views. Reporters covering the administration often marveled at Harding's vocabulary and while they quibbled from time to time with his syntax, they thought his choice of words was superb."[11] The *New York Times* opined, "Mr. Harding's official style is excellent. It carries where finer writing would not go. Mr. Harding is not writing for the super-fine weighers of verbs and adjectives, but for the men and women who see in his expressions their own ideas, and are truly happy to meet them. It is a good style, let the pundits rage about it as they will."[12]

But now that he was president of the United States, Harding had little time to worry about his critics, for he had troubles aplenty. On

Inauguration Day, the *Chicago Daily Tribune* made note of the plethora of problems. "Few of his predecessors have confronted more momentous problems on the threshold of the presidency than Mr. Harding," the editors wrote. "The greatest war in history, resulting in the greatest destruction of life and wealth in history, has been followed by a peace hardly less demoralizing." The economy was in terrible shape, they declared, pointing to the "depression, unemployment, industrial adjustment, [and] the struggle with the persistent high cost of living." But President Harding, they said, "looks upon this situation from the American point of view and will test action by his conception of American interests rather than by some dubious formula of universal welfare."[13] As Robert Murray has noted, "From Wilson he received a disintegrating presidency, a confused and rebellious Congress, a foreign policy in chaos, a domestic economy in shambles, a society sundered with hatreds and turmoil."[14] It would not be an easy administration.

With the crumbling national economy and millions out of work, and in keeping with his view of republican simplicity, Harding saw no need for an inaugural celebration. Although he was known to love a good party, the new president cancelled the inaugural ball and the extravagant festivities that have come to signify a new incoming administration. Even the liberal magazine *The Nation* praised Harding for abandoning "elaborate plans" for his inauguration. "Jeffersonian simplicity, so much sneered at, is the true ideal for an American President," the editors wrote.[15]

Harding also threw open the White House for visitors. It had been shut down by Wilson during the war and his long illness. After the inauguration and the modest parade that Harding reluctantly agreed to, which included only those troops who were actually in Washington, thousands of visitors were allowed to walk around the White House grounds at the invitation of the new president. In fact, after the inauguration, when the maid in the residence began closing the curtains so that no one could see inside the mansion, the new First Lady, Florence Harding, stopped her. "Let 'em look in if they want," she said. "It's their White House!"[16]

This simple act made an impression on many, including journalist Edward G. Lowry. The "social-political atmosphere of Washington had been one of bleak and chill austerity suffused and envenomed by hatred of a sick chief magistrate that seemed to poison and blight every ordinary human relationship and finally brought to a virtual stoppage every routine function of the Government," he wrote. A "general condition of stagnation and aridity . . . had come to affect everybody here. The White House was isolated. It had no relation with the Capitol or the local resident and official community. Its great iron gates were closed and chained and locked. Policemen guarded its approaches." Harding changed all that on his first day. Opening the White House to the public, Lowry wrote, was a "new manifestation of peace on earth good-will to men." Mr. Harding, he continued, "has undeniably made a good start. He made an immensely favorable first impression. He got started on the right foot. He quickly won for himself a great body of local favorable public opinion."[17]

Though he would be derided as a lazy and inactive president, Harding went to work immediately to set up his administration and focus on the nation's business. He had always been a hard worker as a newspaper editor and in his various political offices, and he would be a hard-working president. Harding rose early every day and was at his desk by 8:00 a.m. He held appointments from 8:00 a.m. until 10:00 a.m., at which time he attended cabinet meetings every Tuesday and Friday. He demanded that his cabinet secretaries come to the meetings prepared to discuss the major issues of the day. Owing to his good-natured personality, at noon he always took time to shake hands with visitors to the White House. After a work-filled afternoon, Harding did not break for a relaxing evening in the residence. His typical day of work usually did not end before midnight, and there was never any time built into his schedule to take a nap, as other presidents have been known to do. William H. Crawford, a reporter who spent a week observing Harding in the White House, wrote that the president breached "the eight-hour law twice every day, his usual day lasting about seventeen hours." A typical workweek for President Harding was eighty-four hours, Crawford noted. White House workers confirmed these observations, according to Louis Ludlow, who wrote, "Mr. Harding put in more hours of toil per day, on the average, and more hours in the aggregate, than any other President within their recollection."[18]

Openness and availability would be hallmarks of Harding's presidency. "President Harding's keen desire to please and his accessibility to all sorts of visitors made his days especially arduous. Visiting the Executive Office, I usually found his Secretary's room filled with persons seeking an audience," wrote his secretary of state, Charles Evans Hughes, to whom Harding once confided that the presidency was "the damnedest job!" Hughes would note the striking contrast between the Harding and later Coolidge administrations. "There was a marked change when Mr. Coolidge became President. As he was taciturn and non-committal, visitors got little advantage from a personal interview."[19] Harding, noted Edward Lowry, was "a genial, kindly, generous, good-hearted big fellow who loves his fellow man, who loves simple things, who is without austerity or bitterness, who is not cantankerous, who is easy to get along with," traits that he showed "in his daily relations with his visitors."[20]

This ease of access applied to the press as well. Harding had "perhaps the best relationship with the press of any president before or since," noted historians Ronald and Allis Radosh. Harding held press conferences twice a week, "the first president to hold news conferences on a regular basis."[21] Being a newspaperman himself, the first and only president with such a distinction, Harding had a natural affection for reporters, and he treated them fairly. Wilson, noted Lowry, had "stood behind his desk, his visitors filed in and stood in a thickened crescent before him." Questions were "answered crisply, politely, and in the fewest possible words. A pleasant time was not had by all." But Harding was different. "He met the incoming throng at the door and shook hands with every one of them. For most of them he had an individual word of greeting. Apparently it was the most natural thing in the world for him to do. He made it a very simple, unaffected action."[22]

When it came to selecting his cabinet, Harding wanted what he called "the best minds" to serve in his administration. During the campaign, he had written to the governor of Washington State that his appointments were "going to receive most earnest and serious attention at the proper time. The one particular ambition in my work is to see that the country gets one of the strongest Cabinets that can be brought together." Harding had said repeatedly that he wanted to "immediately summon the best minds in America . . . because it represents the American spirit and because it is the only lawful and appropriate course that a President should take."[23] In this course of action, Harding was simply following the model set up by the founding fathers. The whole reason for a cabinet, or, as the Constitution words it, "executive departments," is so that the president can get the very best advice on various policy matters. A president was never expected to know everything, so the founders wisely allowed Congress the authority to create departments covering necessary functions, and the president, with the "advice and consent" of the Senate, the authority to choose officers who have the necessary knowledge to run those departments.

Choosing the "best minds" would not be so easy to accomplish. "I am beginning to realize what a job I have taken over," Harding wrote to Malcolm Jennings in December 1920. "The man who has a Cabinet to create has one tremendous task. I find I am called upon to be rather impersonal about it and put aside some of my very intimate views of men and give some consideration to the public estimate of available timber." But he was determined to pick his own secretaries and not allow the Senate to control him. While his many critics accuse Harding of being nothing more than a tool of the "Senate cabal" that "engineered" his nomination so as to control him in the White House, Harding showed a remarkable degree of independence in his cabinet picks. As Charles Dawes wrote to him, "I fully appreciate that you are not making up your cabinet along the lines of least resistance—that, when your cabinet is announced, it will be your own cabinet."[24]

As he was selecting his cabinet during the interim between his election and inauguration, Harding was getting a strong push even from the press, particularly the *New-York Tribune*, which was harping on him to select his one-time presidential foe Leonard Wood for a spot. "My own judgment is, that the Cabinet will be big enough and strong enough to appeal to the confidence of the country," he wrote a friend. "I could not, under any circumstances, hope to appeal to public confidence by permitting any one newspaper to dictate to me what my choice must be."[25] Soon he spoke to the press and outlined the three considerations that would govern his picks: "First, there is the man's qualification for public service. That is the most important consideration of all. Second, there is the attitude of the public concerning the man under consideration. Third, there is the political consideration. As to that—well. This is going to be a Republican Cabinet!"[26]

And soon after taking the presidential oath and concluding his inaugural speech, Harding demonstrated another flash of independence when he walked into the Senate chamber and onto the floor without invitation—which was his solemn right as a former senator—to personally submit his cabinet selections to the Senate and ask that they be voted on and approved at once. And they were. It was something no other president had ever done.[27]

Harding's cabinet picks represented different aspects of the nation he now led. "The Cabinet list was a cross-section of upwardly mobile America: a car manufacturer, two bankers, a hotel director, the editor of a farm journal, an international lawyer, a rancher, and an engineer," wrote Paul Johnson. "It included only two professional politicians."[28] And that's the way Harding wanted it. The cynic H. L. Mencken was a bit more critical, describing the cabinet as "three highly intelligent men of self-interest, six jackasses and one common crook."[29]

In a move that was unprecedented at the time, Harding wanted to include Vice President Coolidge in all cabinet meetings and discussions. This practice was actually started during the presidential transition period. Coolidge and his wife traveled to Marion after the election to stay with the Hardings after Christmas. "They received us in the most gracious manner. It was no secret to us why their friends had so much affection for them," Coolidge wrote in his autobiography. "We discussed at length the plans for his administration. The members of his Cabinet were considered and he renewed the invitation to me, already publicly expressed, to sit with them." They also discussed policies "for restoring the prosperity of the country," which would include "reducing taxes and revising the tariff." It was obvious to Coolidge that Harding "was sincerely devoted to the public welfare and desirous of improving the condition of the people."[30]

Although today the vice presidency is a much-valued office, one with vast influence over policy and involving hands-on work with the president, this was not always the case. From its inception in the days of Washington and Adams, the vice presidency was a miserable place to be, considered by many of its unfortunate occupants to be a "career-killing" position with no real power to do much of anything, except perhaps in the never-discussed role of waiting for the president to die, since the vice president is but one heartbeat away from power. Senator James Watson once noted that the vice presidency "is usually regarded as the 'final resting place' of a politician."[31] Daniel Webster had a similar viewpoint but a much deadlier rhetorical aim. When asked about taking the job, he is said to have remarked, "I do not propose to be buried until I am dead."[32]

The office was considered so undesirable that party leaders generally had to beg someone to take it. Thomas R. Marshall, vice president for Woodrow Wilson, once used a parable to describe the job's obscurity. "There once were two brothers. One ran away to sea, the other was elected vice president. Neither one of them was heard of again." The job, said Marshall, is like "a man in a cataleptic fit; he cannot speak; he cannot move; he suffers no pain; he is perfectly conscious of all that goes on, but has no part in it." John Nance Garner, who would go on to serve as vice president during the first two terms of FDR, was a bit more colorful in his description, once remarking that the office was "not worth a bucket of warm piss." It was generally thought that the role of the vice president was to be neither seen nor heard.[33]

Worse still, the founders actually considered the vice presidency a legislative office, not an executive one, with its main function being president of the Senate. The nation's second vice president, Thomas Jefferson, who once called the role a "splendid misery," acknowledged the original intentions of the framers with respect to the vice presidency. "I consider my office as constitutionally confined to legislative functions," he wrote to Elbridge Gerry in 1797, "and I could not take any part whatever in executive consultations, even were it proposed." The office was seen that way for nearly 150 years, with the vice president presiding over the Senate, then going home when Congress was not in session. There would be no official home in the nation's capital for the nation's second officer until 1974. The vice president either lived in a hotel or rented a residence during the session.[34]

When Calvin Coolidge was offered the second spot on the Harding ticket, Grace Coolidge, who understood the potential pitfalls, quickly asked her husband, "You aren't going to take it, are you?" To which the governor replied, "I suppose I'll have to." When the official nomination came in July 1920, Vice President Thomas Marshall sent Coolidge a witty telegram: "Please accept my sincerest sympathy." The new Republican vice-presidential nominee wrote his father an almost apologetic letter. "I am sure Senator Harding is a good man, and an old friend of mine. I hope you will not mind," he wrote. John Coolidge replied that he was "surprised and pleased to hear of your nomination" and hoped that his son would not be "greatly disappointed." But Coolidge wrote in his *Autobiography* that he "was pleased to accept [the nomination], and it was especially agreeable to be associated with Senator Harding, whom I knew well and liked."[35]

And Coolidge would fare better than his predecessors, as Warren Harding began the first steps in what would be a transformation of the vice presidency into its modern form. Having served as a lieutenant governor, Harding understood how those serving secondary offices can be pushed aside. Soon after their respective nominations, Harding and Coolidge met in Washington for a brief conference before the start of the fall campaign. In a statement to the press, Harding announced his intentions for his vice president. "I think that the Vice President should be more than a mere substitute in waiting," he said. "In establishing coordination between the executive office and the Senate the Vice President ought to play a big part, and I have been telling Governor Coolidge how much I wish him to be not only a participant in the campaign but a helpful part of a Republican administration. The country needs the counsel and the becoming participation in government of such men as Governor Coolidge." Coolidge was a fellow fiscal conservative with vast experience in government, and Harding very much desired the benefit of his opinions.[36] "Silent Cal" attended cabinet meetings at Harding's request—something that, as John Dean has written, "resulted in a nearly seamless transition of power following Harding's death."[37]

To help achieve "normalcy" and to calm turbulent economic waters, Harding made some very wise choices when setting up his administration, carefully selecting heads of departments during the transition period so they would be ready to hit the ground running on the day of the inauguration. One of the appointments most crucial for the recovery of the economy was secretary of the treasury. He would preside over seventy thousand employees and have duties that covered the currency, customs and excises, public buildings, the Coast Guard, collecting taxes, settling foreign debts, and enforcing the Volstead Act, the new Prohibition law. To take care of such vast responsibilities, Harding chose Andrew Mellon, of the famed and fabulously wealthy Mellon family. Mellon was a man of great achievement; though he had never held political office, he was very popular with conservative Republicans in Congress. His father, Thomas Mellon, who had died in 1908, had made his fortune in banking, finance, and industry. Secretary Mellon inherited his deeply held conservative beliefs from his banker father, who had written in his autobiography, "Ignorance of economic principles blinds our governing class to the evils of extravagance and undue public burdens, increasing the cost of living to rich and poor alike." Those words, which Andrew Mellon the younger took to heart, formed the basis of his economic philosophy, which lined up perfectly with that of both Harding and the Republican Congress.[38]

Andrew Mellon became the head of the Mellon empire upon the death of his father and eventually branched out to other ventures, including the financing of the Alcoa aluminum company. At the time of his appointment to the Harding cabinet, Mellon ran at least sixty companies and was one of the richest men in America, with a net worth hovering between $300 and $400 million—which today would make him a billionaire.[39] Mellon was at least a hundred times richer than his nearest cabinet competitor, Herbert Hoover, and supposedly the "runner-up to John D. in the Open Money-Getting Championship," as Edward Lowry wrote.[40] His appointment, explained Professor Lewis L. Gould, "reassured the financial community of the president's conservatism and fiscal soundness."[41] Mellon "understood business better than any Treasury secretary since Hamilton," according to scholars Larry Schweikart and Michael Allen. There was little doubt that Mellon would run the Treasury Department like he ran the family enterprise, with sound business practices.[42]

One of the "best minds" to serve in the Harding cabinet, or any cabinet in U.S. history, for that matter, was Herbert Hoover, who would lead the Commerce Department. Hoover was himself mentioned as a presidential candidate in 1920, and he had won a few delegates at the national convention. Originally from Iowa and orphaned as a young boy, Hoover stayed with his grandmother for a short time before moving to Oregon to live with one of his uncles, a physician. With his uncle's help, Hoover was able to attend the newly opened Stanford University in California, where he studied geology. A brilliant mining engineer, Hoover worked around the globe and developed techniques used to extract important metals such as silver, lead, and zinc. He also invested in gold mines.[43] He was "a creative artist in mining," wrote Edward Lowry. "He developed a new department in his profession. He made good mines out of bad ones; successful ones out of unsuccessful ones; solvent mining concerns out of bankrupt mining concerns. He made money and a reputation in the process." By the age of thirty-seven Herbert Hoover was retired and a multimillionaire, worth around $4 million.[44]

During the early years of World War I, before U.S. entry, Hoover led relief efforts that kept Belgium and other parts of the continent from starving. He even met with German officials and persuaded them to allow food shipments for famished refugees. This made Herbert Hoover an international hero. As head of the Food Administration for Wilson, Hoover, under the conviction that "food will win the war," organized efforts to conserve food—to supply the troops abroad, but also to make sure the people at home had adequate resources. He promoted "Meatless Mondays" and "Wheatless Wednesdays." His efforts to combat waste increased the food supply by 15 percent and allowed him to ship twenty-three metric tons of food overseas. After the war, he once again led relief efforts in Europe that won him international accolades.[45]

In private, though, Hoover was shy, sensitive, modest, not very articulate, and talked very little. Harding had to work to persuade him to join his administration and even offered him his choice of departments to administer: Commerce or Interior. Once he agreed and settled on Commerce, the president had to persuade the conservative Senate to approve him. The trouble stemmed from some of the nominee's progressive views that did not sit well with conservative senators Henry Cabot Lodge and Boies Penrose—particularly Hoover's support for the ratification of the Treaty of Versailles, which he had backed "in order to save what was left of the European structure," and his opinion that joining the League would cause "no harm" to the country. The choice of Hoover also didn't sit well with Mellon, who considered him "too much of an engineer." Conservatives desperately wanted Mellon at the Treasury but were, like Mellon, lukewarm, to put it mildly, about Hoover.[46]

Harding quickly grew tired of the pushback he was getting from the Senate. "I do not want the administration to quarrel with the Senate or any considerable faction in the Republican Party," he wrote to Daugherty in February 1921, a month before his inauguration. But, in regards to

Hoover, he wrote, "I do hold him in very high esteem and think his appointment would appeal to the cordial approval of the country. The more I consider him the more do I come to think well of him. Of course, I have no quarrel with those who do not think as I do, but inasmuch as I have the responsibility to assume I think my judgment must be trusted in the matter."[47] Finally, he sent Lodge and Penrose a terse note: "Mellon and Hoover or no Mellon."[48] The sniping stopped immediately, and Hoover was approved without further delay on March 4 with the rest of Harding's cabinet. As Andrew Sinclair has written, "Nothing shows Harding's determination to be independent more than his appointment of Hoover."[49] And nothing better disproves the lie that Harding was being controlled by a "Senate cabal" than his support for Hoover.

Although not an official cabinet pick, Charles Dawes, who was considered for treasury secretary, would have a major role in the administration's economic policy in a new executive branch agency. Until the administration of Warren Harding, the U.S. government did not operate under a budget, nor did the president have much to do with appropriations other than approving or rejecting spending bills. The various executive departments made their own requests to Congress for funding independently of one another, so there was no consolidated mechanism for keeping track of the nation's spending because no unified budget existed. In fact, there was no easy way for anyone to know exactly how much the government was spending annually. To address this problem, the Bureau of the Budget was created by the Budget and Accounting Act of 1921, which President Harding readily signed in June 1921. Fifty years later the Bureau of the Budget would become the Office of Management and Budget, or OMB. With the establishment of this new agency, the president would be responsible for crafting a consolidated budget and sending it to Congress for approval.

The president would appoint a director to oversee the new agency, and Harding chose Dawes for the post, writing that it was "probably the most important appointment I am to be called upon to make. In view of the many duties imposed I do not suppose there will be so important an office in the administration." He wrote to Dawes on June 9, the day before he signed the bill, "Nothing would please me more than to call a man of your outstanding prominence and eminent qualifications to such a service."[50] The great-great-grandson of revolutionary alarm rider William Dawes, Charles Dawes had served in the army during World War I, rising from major to brigadier general, but most of his time had been spent in engineering and logistics, not combat. Before the war he had been a lawyer in Lincoln, Nebraska, run unsuccessfully for Congress, then gotten into banking, building the Central Trust Bank in Chicago. He had also served as comptroller of the currency in William McKinley's Treasury Department from 1898 to 1901. Harding had confidence that Dawes, with his banking experience, had the ability to get a handle on the skyrocketing spending that had come with the war and to craft plans to balance the budget. It would be essential to cut spending and begin producing budget surpluses so that the national debt, at $26 billion and climbing, could be reduced, and Dawes would be instrumental in helping Harding get America's fiscal house in order. For President Harding, that was priority number one.[51]

CHAPTER 6

REBUILDING A DEPRESSED ECONOMY

"We need a rigid and yet sane economy, combined with fiscal justice, and it must be attended by individual prudence and thrift, which are so essential to this trying hour and reassuring for our future."

—*Warren Harding*

When Warren Harding settled into the presidential chair, a host of national problems were staring him directly in the face. But his most immediate pressing concern was the state of the economy. Resolving the difficulties in America's overseas relationships or restoring domestic tranquility would matter little if unemployment and inflation continued to climb and the GDP continued to shrink—as it had been doing for a year. In fact, as 1921 dawned, the nation was a year into a full-fledged depression, "one of the most severe this country has ever experienced," as Harding's treasury secretary, Andrew Mellon, wrote.[1] According the National Bureau of Economic Research, the slump lasted a year and a half, beginning in January 1920 and ending in July 1921.[2]

During that period of eighteen months, the conditions for many average Americans were downright miserable, and the overall economy was on the verge of a major collapse. The nation's output fell 23.9 percent in nominal terms, production declined 31.6 percent, stock prices dropped 46.6 percent, and corporate profits saw a 92 percent decrease. These numbers translated into a difficult job market. Unemployment shot up from 4 percent to nearly 12 percent in just a year, meaning nearly five million Americans were without jobs, according to one study. Another tabulated the unemployed at six million, making the unemployment rate 19 percent. The three million members of the American Expeditionary Forces (AEF) returning home from the war helped contribute to the unemployment crisis. Food prices fell by two-thirds from the summer of 1920 to the summer of 1921, devastating the nation's farmers. In all, the gross national product (GNP), a measure of the wealth generated in the nation in a year, fell 17 percent, and twenty thousand businesses failed, including a Kansas City haberdashery owned by Edward Jacobson and Harry S. Truman, the future president. U.S. Steel, one of the nation's largest companies, did not close but had to cut wages three times in one year.[3]

As Harding said in his inaugural address, much of this had come about because of Wilson's war, which had cost the United States $50 billion, well more than half of the nation's GNP. American debt, which had been just $1.2 billion in 1916, stood at nearly $26 billion in 1919—the bulk of it from Liberty Bonds sold to pay for the war. Worse still, the Allied powers were on the hook for more than $10 billion in American loans that were unlikely to ever be repaid (save for Finland, they never were). Annual spending, just $700 million and change in 1916, stood at $18.5 billion in 1919, a 26-fold increase. In fact, before 1912, total federal spending had never been much higher than $700 million in any year. With the rapid demobilization of the AEF, the spending for 1920 was reduced considerably, but it still stood at more than $6 billion, nearly ten times what it had been in 1916. American cities may not have been devastated, and American casualties may not have reached the horrific levels they did for the warring European powers, but the economic damage was very real for the average American.[4]

Harding and his team set out to achieve four economic objectives they believed would end the depression quickly and get the economy back on track: cut spending, slash income tax rates, protect the American economy from floods of cheap goods and cheap labor from Europe, and get the government out of the way of the private sector. The result was the swift end of the depression and one of the greatest economic booms the nation has ever seen. And although Harding is often labeled "feeble," he was at times very bold in his actions. He was audacious enough to veto popular spending bills that he believed were fiscally irresponsible.

Harding was determined to stop the progressive tide, which had begun in earnest with Theodore Roosevelt in 1901 and reached its zenith under Woodrow Wilson—a twenty-year expansion of government power. When Harding told the people during the campaign that the country did not need "heroics," "nostrums," and "revolution," but "healing," "normalcy," and "restoration," he was offering a recipe for sound conservatism. With Harding in the White House, the people could no longer expect Washington to act as a lifeboat to rescue them from the nation's problems.

This was not simply campaign conservatism; it was what Harding truly believed. In his inaugural address, he spoke out against the new tendency to look to government for answers. The nation must understand that "no statute enacted by man can repeal the inexorable laws of nature. Our most dangerous tendency is to expect too much of government, and at the same time do for it too little," he said. "No altered system will work a miracle. Any wild experiment will only add to the confusion. Our best assurance lies in efficient administration of our proven system." He pledged to work "for the omission of unnecessary interference of Government with business, for an end to Government's experiment in business, and for more efficient business in Government administration." This spelled the end of progressivism, which had targeted business for regulation and increased taxation, including the "excess profits tax" imposed during the war.[5]

In the days before the Great War, Americans by and large had almost no relationship with the federal government—a fact the progressives sought to change. Unlike today, when our government is involved in so many aspects of our lives and knows so much about us, the only occasions when most citizens came into contact with any aspect of the federal government was the mailman or if they had a family member in the military service, as small as it was in those days. Progressives wanted the government more involved in the lives of American citizens, especially in their economic livelihood. Although the progressives differed in many ways from their populist kin, they did agree on many issues: regulation of railroads and industry, a graduated income tax, expansion of the currency—all measures designed to make the government more responsive to the needs of the people. And many old populist ideas became law under progressive governance, especially under Wilson, whom one scholar has called the nation's "most visionary President."[6]

The idea of a national income tax had always excited those who wanted to expand the size and scope of the federal government. But there was a major impediment to such a tax in the U.S. Constitution, which prohibited direct taxation not apportioned among the population. During the Civil War, the federal government did impose a wartime income tax on all incomes over $600, with progressive rates for higher incomes, but it was only a temporary war measure, allowed to expire in 1872. In 1894, Congress attempted the first peacetime income tax with the Wilson-Gorman Tariff Act, a revenue bill that lowered tariff rates and imposed a small tax on individual incomes and corporate revenue to make up the difference from the loss of customs duties. However, a lawsuit brought on behalf of bank stockholders reached the U.S. Supreme Court, which struck down the new levy in 1895 as an unconstitutional direct tax in *Pollock v. Farmers' Loan & Trust Co.*[7]

To get around this legal barrier enacted by the founders, the nation's progressives drew up a new constitutional amendment, the Sixteenth, that would allow for an income tax. In 1909, under President William Howard Taft, who favored an income tax on corporations, Congress passed the new amendment, and in February 1913, just days before the inauguration of Woodrow Wilson, the Sixteenth Amendment was officially ratified and made part of the Constitution, the first change since Reconstruction. Progressives were now free to enact a permanent tax on incomes.

Many warned about the potential dangers of such a tax. "When men once get the habit of helping themselves to the property of others, they are not easily cured of it," wrote the editors of the *New York Times*, who called the amendment "unnecessary."[8] Warnings notwithstanding, in a major political triumph for the new Wilson administration, the nation's first permanent income tax became law on October 3, 1913, when President Wilson signed the Underwood-Simmons Act. Like its 1894 predecessor, the 1913 income tax was sold to the American people as a mechanism to bring about a more equitable distribution of the nation's wealth. The 1913 income tax law would affect only the most affluent, less than 4 percent of all Americans, and the tax rate was rather paltry. Progressives in Congress had wanted a rate of 68 percent on all income over $1 million, but their amendment was defeated. There was a 1 percent tax on all net incomes. But each individual was granted a $3,000 exemption (roughly $75,000 in 2020 dollars), with an additional $1,000 for married couples ($4,000 would equal $100,000 in 2020), thereby exempting more than 96 percent of the citizenry. It was a progressive tax: the tax rate increased as one's income increased. But the highest tax rate was just 7 percent, and it was only for those fortunate enough to earn half a million dollars per year or more ($12 million in 2020 dollars). All corporations, insurance companies, and joint stock companies paid a 1 percent tax. In the first year the tax was in effect, the Bureau of Revenue received 368,000 tax returns and took in $28 million in revenue, far below congressional expectations—but it was a start for the progressives.[9]

The second big achievement for the Wilson administration, and arguably the most far-reaching, was the establishment of the Federal Reserve System, which Arthur Link called the "crowning achievement" of Wilson's first term. Almost three months after signing the income tax law, Wilson signed the Federal Reserve Act, which established the central banking system that is still in existence today. The original plan came about during a 1910 meeting on Jekyll Island, Georgia, of a group of bankers including J. P. Morgan, John D. Rockefeller Jr., and Senator Nelson Aldrich, whose daughter had married Rockefeller Jr. in 1901. The system, which required all U.S. banks to become members, consisted of a network of twelve regional banks, a new paper currency called Federal Reserve notes, and a Federal Reserve Board consisting of a chairman appointed by the president, the secretary of the treasury, the comptroller of the currency, and the president of the New York Federal Reserve Bank to govern it all. The board meets in secret, its records are not public, its decisions are final, and it is not subject to the dictates of Congress or the president. Today its powers are vast and its influence over the American economy is enormous. Under this new law, the Federal Reserve Board, rather than Congress, would determine how much currency would be in circulation at any given time—mainly by adjusting the discount rate.

Wilson also pushed through other new laws on the progressive wish list. The Clayton Antitrust Act of 1914 was the first such law since the original Sherman Antitrust Act of 1890, and it provided stiffer penalties for business monopolies, cartels, and trusts if they engaged in price discrimination or set up "interlocking directorates." The Federal Trade Commission Act of 1914 also enacted tough new regulations to counter what were deemed unfair business practices. The commission could issue "cease and desist" orders to any business found to be engaging in violations of the law. These two new laws gave Washington more power over business than it had ever had.

When war came for the United States in 1917, progressivism did not stop, as some historians claim, but marched forward with increased speed. Not only was the very act of intervention in the war in Europe the implementation of a progressive ideal—"to make the world safe for democracy"—but in war conditions, the progressive ideas of government control over the economy were implemented with very little opposition. At least some of the inspiration for FDR's New Deal in the 1930s came from Wilson's wartime progressivism.

The Wilson administration created more than five thousand agencies and boards, including Hoover's Food Administration and the all-important War Industries Board, which oversaw much of the American economy. The Committee on Public Information, headed by George

Creel, a former newspaperman, controlled the flow of information the public received and was, in reality, nothing more than a propaganda agency. To assist with the war effort, the nation's radio service was nationalized, as was the entire national railroad network in 1917; it remained under government control until 1920. To help pay for Wilson's war, the Federal Reserve increased the money supply by 1,000 percent, which caused prices to rise by 50 percent during the war years.[10] The dismantling of this massive governmental monstrosity—which Robert Higgs called Wilson's "wartime socialism"—helped create the post-war depression.[11]

On taking office, President Harding immediately began to reverse the course Wilson had taken, looking to cut taxes, reduce spending and regulations, reform the tariff, assist farmers, and reconsider the Allied loan situation (European powers owed billions of dollars in both private and public loans). Since the problems the nation faced were simply too great to wait, Harding used his constitutional authority to call Congress into special session in April to begin the great task that lay ahead. He had discussed this with congressional leaders—including Speaker of the House Frederick H. Gillett and Senator Lodge, both from Massachusetts—the day after his inauguration, inviting them to the Oval Office for a sit-down meeting. The discussion centered on the special session and legislative priorities, and the top two policy items were tax reform and an emergency tariff bill.[12]

On March 22, 1921, less than three weeks after his inauguration (until the ratification of the Twentieth Amendment, presidents took office in March), President Harding officially issued a proclamation calling Congress into special session on April 12 to tackle "national problems far too pressing to be long neglected." The government should not be discouraged, he wrote in his special message to Congress, but rather "we must be the more firmly resolved to undertake our work with high hope, and invite every factor in our citizenship to join in the effort to find our normal, onward way again." The president said that the administration and Congress together had to address the most "pressing problem at home," which was to "restrict our national expenditures within the limits of our national income" and "lift the burdens of war taxation from the shoulders of the American people." Only then could the government begin to reduce the "staggering load of war debt" with "orderly funding and gradual liquidation." Congress also had to consider tariff reform, revising the laws "to protect American trade and industry," he wrote.[13]

In the intervening period, Harding held his first cabinet meeting on March 8, his fourth full day in office. Unlike Wilson, Harding very much wanted the opinions of all of his cabinet secretaries on every subject, so he convened cabinet meetings twice a week, every Tuesday and Friday at ten in the morning. The meetings were closed to everyone except the president, vice president, and cabinet members, and no record was kept of their discussions. Harding wanted a free and open atmosphere so that members could discuss serious issues without fear of leaks or exposure of unpopular positions.[14]

Harding's openness and transparency extended to all of his cabinet officers. As Hughes would write, "Important matters of administration would be fully discussed at cabinet meetings. The president usually opened these meetings with a brief word and called on each of us in turn for whatever statement we cared to make. Vice President Coolidge attended the meetings and spoke last."[15] Harding's cabinet consisted of "strong men, idealists of the practical sort, to whom the President turned, sometimes pitifully, for information and guidance. He knew them . . . and could trust them," noted journalist William Allen White.[16] Returning the country to "normalcy" would be a "colossal task," wrote reporter Henry L. Stoddard, "as difficult as directing it on a war basis." Harding understood his own limitations and sought the best available men to assist him in running the administration. "The experience he lacked was to be found in those men," according to Stoddard. In Harding's cabinet choices, the major ones anyway, "he ran against the narrow views of his party leaders. They could see no politics in the choice of such men, but Harding had a larger conception of the country's need."[17]

With Mellon at the Treasury and Dawes in charge of the budget, there could be little doubt that the administration would have a very pro-business attitude. Harding had said the "business of America is the business of everybody in America. . . . This is essentially a business country. . . . We must get back to methods of business." Coolidge would later famously remark, in a pithier variation on Harding, that the "business of America is business." If business didn't flourish, then the country wouldn't either. And one way to help business would be to refrain from enforcing the progressive regulatory laws passed from 1901 to 1914, particularly the Clayton Antitrust Act, which the Supreme Court weakened in 1922.[18]

And the American business community stood ready to expand and grow as soon as news of Harding's election was realized. Newspaper headlines between the election and the inauguration displayed the attitude of much of the country. The *Wall Street Journal* said, "Wall Street Sees Better Times after Election." The day after the election the *Los Angeles Times* announced: "Eight Years of Democratic Incompetency and Waste Are Drawing Rapidly to a Close." "Harding's Advent Means New Prosperity." "Inauguration 'Let's Go!' Signal to Business." On March 5, 1921, the editors predicted "good times ahead," writing, "The inauguration yesterday of President Harding and the advent of an era of Republicanism after years of business harassment and uncertainty under the Democratic regime were hailed" by the nation's business leaders. I. H. Rice, the president of the Merchants and Manufacturers Association, told the press, "Good times are now ahead of us. Prosperity is at our door. We are headed toward pre-war conditions. . . . Business men are well pleased with President Harding's selections for his Cabinet and by the caliber of men he has chosen we know that he means business."[19]

To get the economy moving again, the first order of business for Harding would be to slash the crippling wartime taxes that had hit both individuals and businesses hard. The new income tax had soared during wartime. The progressives in 1913 had sought confiscatory taxation of the wealthy and were beaten back then, but war had achieved it for them with tax increases, or "war revenue" acts, as they were billed, in 1917 and again in 1919, a year after the war had ended. The 1917 act tripled corporate taxes while raising income, excise, and postal rates. In 1919, the top rate, which had been capped at 7 percent on the wealthiest Americans in 1913, topped out at 77 percent on incomes over $1 million. The lowest income-earners paid nothing in 1913 but by 1919 paid 4 percent in taxes, and they were still paying it in 1921. And the fact that it was up to individual taxpayers to figure their own taxes, then mail in their checks to the government, allowed many Americans, especially the wealthy, to evade the income tax. But the Treasury was still receiving billions in revenue in 1918.[20]

Mellon sought a huge drop in the top marginal tax rate, a drastic cut from 77 percent down to 32 percent in one fell swoop. Like Harding, Mellon can be characterized as a "supply-sider." He wanted to reform the tax code and reduce rates on the rich so that they would actually pay more in taxes, not less. Mellon understood the principle that would later be called the Laffer curve—that lower rates would not necessarily mean lower revenue. If taxes on the wealthy, or any class for that matter, were too high, Americans would simply avoid paying them by doing less work and taking fewer chances. This was especially true for the investor class. Why invest money in new ventures if the government was going to swipe a large chunk of it? As Mellon said in his 1924 book on taxation, "The history of taxation shows that taxes which are inherently excessive are not paid. The high rates inevitably put pressure upon the taxpayer to withdraw his capital from productive business." According to Mellon, under the high-tax regime many wealthy Americans were buying tax-exempt securities, such as municipal bonds. Lowering tax rates would encourage the rich to move their investments out of tax-free securities and into taxable investments like stocks. The economy would gain in productivity, employment would increase, and more revenue would pour into the Treasury. Mellon was not alone in his thinking. Not only did Harding approve, but so did the chairman of the House Ways and Means Committee, Joe Fordney.[21]

But Congress as a whole was not buying it, and tax-cut legislation was stalled in the House and Senate for months. By the fall, though, the

Revenue Act of 1921, a bill to reduce tax rates, was ready for passage, and Harding signed it just before Thanksgiving. It did not give Mellon everything he wanted, but it did make some significant changes. It repealed the wartime excess profits tax on business and lowered the top rate to 32 percent, but it raised the corporate rate from 10 to 12.5 percent and provided for a capital gains tax of 12.5 percent. It was a start, and Mellon would be successful in pushing additional tax reform throughout the decade.[22]

As both Republicans and Democrats have learned in recent years, massive tax cuts without corresponding cuts in spending cause massive budget deficits and more debt. But the Harding plan called for massive reductions in appropriations.[23] "There is no more important duty confronting public officials everywhere than the enforcement of the utmost measure of economy with good administration," Harding wrote in a private letter.[24] Spending in 1919, the year after the end of the war, had been a staggering $18.5 billion, far higher than the $700 million it had been in 1916. With the demobilization of the AEF, spending naturally fell considerably, but by 1921, when Harding took over, it was still at nearly $6 billion, with most of the reductions having come via the Republican Congress, not the Wilson White House.[25] Harding wrote that it was "gratifying to be able to say . . . that probably no other government in the world has during a similar period so drastically reduced expenditures as has the Government of the United States during the last two years on the insistence of the Republican Congress."[26] But there was still much to be done. As Woodrow Wilson's treasury secretary, David F. Houston, said in 1920, "We have demobilized many groups but we have not demobilized those whose gaze is concentrated on the Treasury." They would be demobilized under Harding, Mellon, and Dawes, however.[27]

Within a week of taking office, Mellon began explaining to Congress and to the public how things worked: that the government does not make money but has to take it from the American people. In a note to many of the nation's big bankers, Mellon reminded them that "the situation calls for the utmost economy. The Nation cannot afford extravagance. The people generally must become more interested in saving the Government's money than in spending it." In other words, the government programs were over. Within a month he wrote to the House Ways and Means Committee chairman, "The Nation cannot continue to spend at this shocking rate. The burden is unbearable. This is no time for extravagance or for entering upon new fields of expenditure. The Nation cannot afford wasteful or reckless expenditure." Government spending "should not even be permitted to continue at the present rate."[28]

Harding wholeheartedly agreed. The president assured Senator Joseph M. McCormick of Illinois that "the administrative departments are now in full sympathy with the program of rigorous and unremitting economy through which, I believe, we will be able during the next year to cover back into the Treasury so large a sum that the aggregate of taxation may be reduced to $3,500,000,000 a year." That was still far more than federal spending of less than $1 billion per year before the war. As Harding pointed out, "half the present total expenditures of the Government arise from wars of the past," in the form of servicing the national debt, "war risk insurance, vocational training, the maintenance of hospitals," and pensions for veterans. In fact, roughly 20 percent of the budget funded the new Veterans Bureau.[29]

In June 1921, nine days after his appointment of Dawes, Harding spoke to 1,200 top managers in the government to lay out his economic policies, particularly spending cuts. "The present administration . . . is committed to a period of economy in government," he said. "This statement is made not with any thought of criticizing what has gone before. It is made in a new realization of the necessity of driving out the loose, unscientific expenditures of government. There is not a menace in the world today like that of growing public indebtedness and mounting public expenditures. There has seemingly grown up an impression that the public treasuries are inexhaustible things, and with it a conviction that no efficiency and no economy are ever to be thought of in public expense. We want to reverse things."[30]

During his short one-year tenure at the Budget Bureau from July 1921 to June 1922, Dawes reduced spending by nearly $1.8 billion, slashing the budget from $5.1 billion to $3.3 billion, a little more than what Harding had predicted was possible. The savings, however, were not concentrated in military appropriations alone, as nearly $1 billion was in discretionary, nonmilitary spending. Dawes had come out of the private sector, and he didn't change his stripes when he got to Washington; he was such a budget hawk that his agency spent only half of its approved operating budget. The federal budget surplus in 1922 was $736 billion, up from $509 million the previous year. Dawes's successor, Herbert Lord, cut spending even further, helping generate surpluses every year of the 1920s and enabling a third of the national debt to be retired.[31] According to economics professor John A. Moore, the "Harding-Coolidge era represents the only time during the twentieth century when the federal government reduced its nonmilitary expenditures in absolute terms."[32]

Harding was pleased with the results Dawes was achieving. In the fall of 1921, he told the press it was "plain that we are working our way out of a welter of waste and prodigal spending at a most impressive rate." He did his part as president to keep unnecessary spending under control—with both courage and conviction, particularly with respect to a proposal to provide a financial bonus to those soldiers who had served in World War I, in what one modern-day scholar called Harding's "most forceful presidential act."[33]

In the summer of 1921, Congress began crafting a plan for a soldiers' bonus. The bill would provide a paid twenty-five-year insurance policy equal to $1.00 for every day of domestic service and $1.25 for every day of overseas service. Veterans would receive certificates that matured in 1945, but they could also borrow up to one-fourth of the certificate's value. This was to adequately compensate veterans for the low pay they had received during the war. Harding, sensitive to excessive spending and the shaky economy, appealed directly to the Senate, imploring them not to pass the bill. In a special message to Congress on July 12, the president wrote, "Our Government must undertake no obligations which it does not intend to meet. No Government fiat will pay our bills. The exchanges of the world testify today to that erroneous theory. We may rely on the sacrifices of patriotism in war, but today we face markets, and the effects of supply and demand, and the inexorable laws of credits in time of peace." Furthermore, a "modest offering to the millions of service men is a poor palliative to more millions who may be out of employment."[34]

The proposal for the bonus, or "adjusted compensation," as the American Legion called it, also met the resistance of Secretary Mellon, who called it "class legislation" and pointed out that the government was already spending $500 million per year on disabled vets and that estimates were the new compensation package might run to $5 billion, ten times the current level of spending. Mellon was not a hard-hearted man, though. He thought further compensation for disabled vets a fair proposal—but not for those who had not sustained any injury in combat or otherwise. He wrote to Charles Hamlin of the Federal Reserve, "It would be the greatest relief to the Treasury and the country as a whole if the bonus question could be disposed of, once and for all."[35]

President Harding was not necessarily opposed to paying a bonus to soldiers; he just did not believe the time was appropriate, given the economic situation. He wrote to several members of Congress of his opposition. The president said he was "well persuaded in [his] own mind that Congress is determined upon such enactment," and understood that "there is a widespread public sentiment, whether artificially promoted or otherwise, in behalf of a compensation to the service men," but nevertheless, he was "equally persuaded that it is futile to undertake such legislation without including taxation provisions to meet the obligations imposed." Simply put, Congress needed to find a way to pay for the bonus, not run up more debt.[36]

Harding made the same general points to the chairman of the House Ways and Means Committee, Joe Fordney—that additional revenue would be needed to meet the new obligation. One proposal was a general sales tax, which, Harding explained to Fordney, would "distribute the cost of rewarding the ex-service men in such a manner that it will be borne by all the people whom they served, and does not commit the Government to class imposition of taxes or the resumption of the burdens recently repealed." The president had "spoken approvingly" of the proposed soldier bonus, but he thought that it should be enacted at a time when the nation could afford it "without such injury to the country as will nullify the benefits to the ex-service men themselves which this expression of gratitude is designed to bestow." Harding simply wanted a postponement of the bonus to allow the nation to get its fiscal house in order—to "await the day when we may safely undertake to pay it once in full, so that the award may be turned to real advantage."[37]

Congress acquiesced to this pressure, but only for a short time. In September of the following year, 1922, as midterm congressional elections neared, the Fordney-McCumber Adjusted Compensation Act passed both houses of Congress. On September 19, President Harding, unmoved by the usual pressures of election season, vetoed the bill. In his veto message to Congress, the president wrote that the bill "fails, first of all, to provide the revenue from which the bestowal is to be paid. Moreover, it establishes the very dangerous precedent of creating a Treasury covenant to pay which puts a burden variously estimated between four and five billions upon the American people, not to discharge an obligation which the Government always must pay but to bestow a bonus which the soldiers themselves while serving in the World War did not expect." Harding vetoed the popular bill mere weeks before the midterm congressional elections—something that, it cannot be overemphasized, most modern presidents would not have dared to do.[38]

Congress, not willing to be outmaneuvered, decided to counter Harding's move. The House overrode the veto on September 20 by a vote of 258–15 after only a few minutes of debate. The original Senate vote passing the bill had been 47–22, a tally that did not include a number of members who had been absent. When the Senate received the veto, 16 senators who had not voted on the original bill were present. Senator

Porter J. McCumber of North Dakota, one of the bill's authors, criticized the veto as one man overruling the will of Congress, but the Senate fell four votes short of overriding the veto, 44–28.[39]

Harding, writing to Dawes, said he believed that the veto had "met a very considerable amount of favor, but I am very sure to be very much complained against for many months to come by a very considerable number of ex-service men. However, I can stand that without annoyance in view of the fact that I have the satisfaction of knowing I did the wise and best thing."[40] The business community, desiring smaller government, agreed with the president and supported the veto, and a number of major newspapers, including the *New York Times*, also approved.[41] The *Chicago Daily Tribune*, always very supportive of the president, disagreed with Harding's veto of the bonus bill but gave him credit "for using his judgment and acting upon his convictions."[42] Even Harding's persistent critic H. L. Mencken praised the veto. "It was his manifest duty as President to oppose this bold and shameless effort to loot the public treasury for the benefit of professional heroes of the war, three-fourths of whom never heard a shot fired in anger," he wrote.[43] A similar bill was eventually passed into law in 1924, when Congress overrode a Coolidge veto.

But while current spending was being slashed, the national debt, blown up by the war, still stood at $26 billion, and annual interest payments were running at $1 billion. Harding was most upset by how much taxpayer money had been wasted by the War Department. "The habit of vast expenditures without proper consideration for results is the inevitable fruit of war," he wrote to Senator McCormick. Massive sums had been spent on weapons and ammunition that never went into action, while the Shipping Board, created to build and procure transport ships, spent $3.5 billion, yet only one ship built by the board ever carried U.S. troops to Europe, and it was a cargo vessel that ferried only fifty soldiers. All of these "extravagances," as Harding called them, had helped run up the massive debt, which now had to be serviced.[44]

The most immediate problem was that $7.5 billion of the debt was in the form of short-term loans, which were due to be paid in May 1923, with the interest rate at 7 percent. First Mellon persuaded the Federal Reserve to cut interest rates to 5 percent, believing the Fed's hiking of interest rates beginning in 1919 had created "the present unfavorable conditions." His next move was to refinance these short-term loans at the lower rate, saving taxpayers $200 million in interest payments. This brought the United States back from the brink of an economic cliff. By the third year of the Harding administration, the national debt had fallen to $22.3 billion, helped by Dawes's large annual budget surpluses.[45]

To pay off their debts, foreign governments were flooding the American market with cheap goods, hoping to gain a favorable balance of trade and fill their coffers. But returning to high, protective tariffs would guard the gate of the American market. It had long been Republican orthodoxy that trade protectionism promotes overall economic growth, protects workers and their jobs, and strengthens the industrial base, essential to national greatness. This line of thinking ran from Alexander Hamilton to Henry Clay (before the Republican Party was even founded) to Abraham Lincoln to Theodore Roosevelt and finally to Warren Harding, and he had no plans to deviate from it. "I believe in the protective tariff policy and know we will be calling for its saving Americanism again," he said in his speech accepting the Republican presidential nomination.[46] In his inaugural address, he told the American people that it "has been proved again and again that we cannot, while throwing our markets open to the world, maintain American standards of living and opportunity, and hold our industrial eminence in such unequal competition. There is a luring fallacy in the theory of banished barriers of trade, but preserved American standards require our higher production costs to be reflected in our tariffs on imports. Today, as never before, when peoples are seeking trade restoration and expansion, we must adjust our tariffs to the new order."[47]

The progressive Woodrow Wilson had sought lower tariffs when he became president. More than a quarter of a century of Republican protectionism was ended with the Revenue Act of 1913, which lowered tariffs across the board and instituted the income tax in order to make up for any lost revenue. In 1918, Wilson made global free trade part of his Fourteen Points. Point Three read: "The removal, so far as possible, of all economic barriers and the establishment of an equality of trade conditions among all the nations consenting to the peace and associating themselves for its maintenance." Americans soundly rejected that line of thinking in the election of 1920.

Harding, in calling Congress into special session within three weeks of entering the White House, asked for an emergency tariff bill. "I believe in the protection of American industry, and it is our purpose to prosper America first," he wrote to Congress. "The privileges of the American market to the foreign producer are offered too cheaply today, and the effect on much of our own productivity is the destruction of our self-reliance which is the foundation of the independence and good fortune of our people. Moreover, imports should pay their fair share of our cost of government. One who values American prosperity and maintained American standards of wage and living can have no sympathy with the proposal that easy entry and the flood of imports will cheapen our cost of living. It is more likely to destroy our capacity to buy."[48]

But it was the nation's farmers who needed the tariff bill the most, Harding believed. For secretary of agriculture, Harding had chosen Henry C. Wallace, a Midwest farmer who edited a journal called *Wallace's Farmer*. Farming was in the Wallace blood. His son, Henry A. Wallace, would serve as agriculture secretary during Franklin Roosevelt's first two terms and then as vice president during his third, and he would run for president in 1948 as the nominee of the resurrected Progressive Party. Considered an expert on agricultural issues, the senior Wallace had been an advisor to Harding during the campaign, and Harding soon asked him to join the administration. "If the verdict of Tuesday is what we are expecting it to be," Harding wrote to Wallace just before Election Day 1920, "I shall very much want your assistance in making good the promises which we have made to the American people." To Congress, Harding emphasized the importance of the new tariff by saying, "American agriculture is menaced." Farmers needed protection from the flood of imports coming from Europe. "It would be better to err in protecting our basic food industry than paralyze our farm activities in the world struggle for restored exchanges," he wrote. Congress complied in May with a bill to establish tariff duties on agricultural imports and erect barriers to European dumping.[49]

By 1922, the country was booming. In his annual treasury report for 1923, Mellon wrote that "labor has been in strong demand, and in most localities fully employed," "the volume of production has been the greatest in our history," and "the traffic handled by the railroads has surpassed all records." The stock market, at 71.95 at the end of 1920, sat at 98.77 by January 1923 and 121.25 by January 1925. The nation's GDP in 1920 was $91.5 billion, and it fell to $69.6 billion in the depression year of 1921. By 1922 it was at $74.1 billion, and in 1923 it was at $85.1 billion. The economy had clearly expanded greatly. As Mellon's work showed, Harding had made an excellent choice for treasury secretary. In a December 1922 speech, Congressman Simeon D. Fess of Ohio praised Mellon as the "greatest Secretary of the Treasury since Alexander Hamilton."[50]

The results of the Harding program are impressive, and some scholars have recognized that fact. "Warren Harding's administration deserves immense credit for executing a swift, clearly articulated, and well-executed response to the crisis at hand," writes economics professor John A. Moore. Harding "inherited a postwar recession. As a result of his administration's prompt action private-sector confidence was restored and the economy bottomed out in July 1921, just four months after the president assumed office. Although Harding is frequently viewed as a weak president, his words and policies regarding the nation's economy suggest otherwise."[51]

Conservative and libertarian-minded economists have long understood Harding's role in solving the "forgotten depression" and reviving the American economy. "Harding's inchoate understanding of what was happening to the economy and why grandiose interventionist plans would only delay recovery is an extreme rarity among twentieth-century

American presidents," writes Thomas Woods. "That he has been the subject of ceaseless ridicule at the hands of historians, to the point that anyone speaking a word in his favor would be dismissed out of hand, speaks volumes about our historians' capabilities outside of their own discipline."[52] Despite his shortcomings, Harding "understood the fundamentals of boom, bust, and recovery better than any 20th-century president." In fact, as Woods wrote in 2009, this "despised figure was . . . a better economist than most of the geniuses who presume to instruct us now."[53]

According to economist James Grant, Harding not only presided "over a macroeconomic miracle cure" for a depression but also "overhauled the creaky machinery of federal budget-making." Instead of fighting over the legacy of Reagan, or of FDR, "who inherited a depression that he didn't actually fix," a "forward-thinking politician might lay claim to the Harding legacy instead."[54] Economist John A. Moore agrees: "Largely undone by the New Deal and then forgotten, Harding's policies merit renewed attention because they guided the country out of recession and into prosperity in a remarkably short period. Curiously, modern advocates for a smaller government and reduced taxes look to the recent Reagan administration as an example. Harding's administration was actually the first to successfully apply these general principles."[55] And for historian Jim Powell, "America's greatest depression fighter was Warren Gamaliel Harding. . . . Hopefully, greater awareness of Harding's success might help give policymakers more confidence that the best thing they can do for an economy is to get out of the way."[56]

These efforts by Harding and his administration quickly paid big dividends. The roaring twenties were set in motion by the end of 1921. As Coolidge wrote in his 1929 memoirs, during 1920 the "country was already feeling acutely the results of deflation. Business was depressed. For months following the Armistice we had persisted in a course of much extravagance and reckless buying. Wages had been paid that were not earned. The whole country, from the national government down, had been living on borrowed money." Coolidge contended that the solution was "to work and save. Our productive capacity is sufficient to maintain us all in a state of prosperity if we give sufficient attention to thrift and industry." And with Harding, he wrote, "the country had adopted that cause, which has brought an era of great plenty." Coolidge would continue the program that Harding had put in place for his nearly six years in the White House, producing the greatest boom in American history.[57]

CHAPTER 7

PUTTING AMERICA FIRST

"I think it's an inspiration to patriotic devotion to safe-guard America first, to stabilize America first, to prosper America first, to think of America first, to exalt America first, to live for and revere America first."

—*Warren Harding*

With the awful events of 1919 and the economic depression of 1920–21, Americans turned inward, wanting to concentrate on the problems plaguing their own nation rather than those of Europe, and they liked the man from Marion and his pledge to "return to normalcy," which was as much about putting America and Americans first as anything else. As a Republican, and like many conservatives within the GOP, Harding passionately believed that the first priority of government was at home, not in some faraway land. The prevailing idea of a great many national Republican politicians at the time was to put the country above any personal or partisan causes. Wilsonian Democrats had shown themselves to be the party of social meddling, foreign crusades, and global markets, and that had given the Republicans a huge advantage in the 1920 election. As Robert Murray has written, no other phrase, "with the exception of 'return to normalcy,' was as descriptive of or as appealing to the Harding administration" as "America First."[1]

For Warren Harding, "America First" was not, as his many detractors claim, some catchy slogan conjured up by his handlers to help propel him to the White House in 1920; it was a deeply held principle that he expressed throughout his career, including at the 1916 Republican convention four years before. At that time, as the European war raged into its third year and President Wilson was gearing up to run for a second term, the Republicans had met in their national convention in Chicago to pick a candidate who could retake the White House, which they had held for forty-four out of the previous fifty-six years. Republicans had controlled the presidency for such a lengthy period that it had almost come to be seen as the party's birthright. The "Grand Old Party" had had a lock on the White House and much of Congress nearly continuously since the election of Lincoln in 1860.

As the 1916 Republican convention gaveled in on June 7, the assembled delegates first had to choose a convention chairman. And the overwhelming choice was Senator Harding. In his lengthy address to the convention upon his selection as chairman, Harding spelled out the long-held principles of the Republican Party, summed up in the slogan "America First." Ironically, Wilson would run his campaign under that banner, along with his memorable slogan of "He Kept Us Out of War." But the true believers in "America First" were Republicans. "We believe in American markets for American products," Harding told the delegation, "American wages for American workmen, American opportunity for American genius and industry, and American defense for American soil."[2] Senator Chauncey Depew of New York pronounced Harding's address "a very acceptable keynote speech. His fine appearance, his fairness, justice and good temper as presiding officer captured the convention. There was a universal sentiment that if Hughes declined the party could do no better than to nominate Senator Harding."[3]

But, despite the appeal of such lofty patriotic rhetoric, the Republican Party, badly split between its conservative and progressive wings, lost to the Democrats in a close vote, 277 for Woodrow Wilson in the Electoral College and 254 for Charles Evans Hughes. A plurality of Americans believed Wilson would keep them out of the carnage across the Atlantic. Yet, little more than a month after his second inauguration, Wilson led America into the Great War. Senator Harding voted for the war resolution in April 1917, believing it to be his patriotic duty, and he remained a supporter of the war.

For those scholars who contend that Harding had no foreign policy experience when he entered the White House (aside from perhaps the one speech at the 1916 Republican convention), his life, both in and out of politics, tells a different tale. He had traveled widely before he emerged onto the national scene, probably more than most of his presidential predecessors. He had been to Europe three times before winning his Senate seat in 1914, and had also been to Egypt, the Caribbean, Hawaii, and Panama. In the Senate, not only did he serve on the Foreign Relations Committee with Lodge, but he also chaired the Senate's Committee on Naval Affairs, Pacific Islands, and Territories and the Committee on the Philippine Islands—and in that important capacity he opposed President Wilson's plan for Filipino independence. This experience did not make him an expert, but he was by no means ignorant of the problems in American foreign policy either.[4]

Harding named a "best mind" to handle U.S. foreign affairs—Charles Evans Hughes of New York, who had been the 1916 presidential nominee. Hughes was a graduate of Brown University and Columbia Law School, practiced law, and had taught a course on constitutional law at Cornell in the 1890s. In 1906 he had won the New York governorship, beating publisher William Randolph Hearst, and he had served on the U.S. Supreme Court as an associate justice for six years, from 1910 until 1916, when he resigned his seat on the Court in order to accept the Republican presidential nomination. Hughes nearly won the White House, coming within a handful of votes of besting Woodrow Wilson and changing the course of American history. On Election Night, as more and more states fell into the Republican column and almost every political prognosticator believed Wilson was going down to defeat, Hughes went to bed thinking he was the nation's president-elect. When late returns in California came in and tipped the election to Wilson, a reporter phoned the Hughes residence. When the butler answered and informed the man that "the President is sleeping," the reporter shot back,

"When he wakes up, tell him he isn't the President anymore."[5] His "forgotten handshake" with California governor Hiram Johnson—when Hughes visited California and even stayed at the same hotel as Johnson but didn't arrange a meeting or get his endorsement—likely cost him the state of California and the grand prize.

Despite his near miss, Hughes had great qualities to serve as secretary of state, according to Edward Lowry, including "sobriety, steadfastness, trustworthiness, honesty, industry, intelligence, capacity, application, and the will to succeed." As Lowry wrote, "He has been as successful in private life as in politics," with "character, an educated, trained mind, shrewdness, and common sense." Hughes would serve as secretary of state for the combined term of Harding and Coolidge before retiring in 1925. In 1930 he went back on the Supreme Court, this time as chief justice upon the death of William Howard Taft, owing his appointment to Herbert Hoover.[6]

Like Harding's other cabinet picks, Hughes would be given free rein, in his case, to run the State Department and the foreign policy of the United States. When Harding announced his choice to the press on February 21, 1921, he responded to a question from a reporter by deferring to Hughes. "You must ask Mr. Hughes about that," he said. "That is going to be another policy of the next Administration. From the beginning the Secretary of State will speak for the State Department." He then turned and walked away, leaving the press to question Hughes alone. This was certainly a radical departure from administrations past—something that Hughes acknowledged in his autobiography. "President Harding was a most kindly man; always eager to please his old friends and to make new ones. He found it difficult to say no. To me, he was a most agreeable Chief, always accessible, anxious fully to understand each problem as it arose" and "good enough to leave me the organization of the State Department," he noted. "I realized that I must take a full measure of responsibility when I felt definite action should be taken. I did not go to him with a statement of difficulties and ask him what should be done." Soon after taking over the reins at State, Hughes began cleaning house by ousting every employee he deemed "incompetent." But despite the long leash Harding had given Hughes, the two met often and talked on the phone regularly.[7]

Although some scholars characterize Hughes as an exception to the isolationism pervading the Harding administration, "America First" was the theme of Hughes's acceptance speech for the Republican presidential nomination in 1916, an address entitled "America First and America Efficient." He spoke of "paramount national needs," a "dominant sense of national unity," and making sure the Republican Party was an "organ of the effective expression of dominant Americanism." Hughes would be a perfect fit for the Harding administration, working to implement three major components of an "America First" policy—in foreign affairs, international trade, and immigration.[8]

One of the first major foreign policy issues facing the president was the League of Nations. Even though the Senate had twice rejected Wilson's proposal, the issue had been a major one in the recent presidential election, and even though the voters had seemingly rejected the idea, Harding wanted to solidify his opposition to it and his dedication to "America First." In his inaugural address, he said, "The recorded progress of our Republic, materially and spiritually, in itself proves the wisdom of the inherited policy of noninvolvement in Old World affairs. Confident of our ability to work out our own destiny, and jealously guarding our right to do so, we seek no part in directing the destinies of the Old World. We do not mean to be entangled. We will accept no responsibility except as our own conscience and judgment, in each instance, may determine." Like Washington and Jefferson, Harding sought to keep America out of entangling and permanent alliances.[9]

But the League proposal, in and of itself, was not really the problem; the rules governing the League were—namely the objectionable articles in the charter that seemed to suggest American troops could be called into combat without the approval of Congress, which effectively took the decision-making power out of the hands of the people's representatives and handed it to foreign bureaucrats with virtually no oversight. In his inaugural address, President Harding spoke of his dislike of such agreements, saying, "America can be a party to no permanent military alliance. It can enter into no political commitments, nor assume any economic obligations which will subject our decisions to any other than our own authority." There would be no U.S. membership in the League of Nations under President Harding.[10]

But that did not mean the issue of an international organization was dead. Scholars have accused Harding of waffling on the issue during the 1920 election, but he remained committed to keeping the United States out of the League, at least on the basis of Wilson's proposal, and joining some alternate association of nations, such as the World Court. During the campaign, Harding had said quite clearly, "I am for co-operation among nations. America must take her part in the world's affairs. But we hold there is no need of an American surrender of sovereignty to play a righteous nation's part."[11]

To get a clearer view of Harding's views, in mid-September 1920 the president of Cornell University, Dr. Jacob Gould Schurman, wrote asking for his opinions on foreign affairs and specifically what international associations he might favor. Schurman wanted to read Harding's reply at a conference of college and university presidents on international affairs.[12]

In his response, Harding reiterated his opposition to Wilson's League without the Lodge Reservations, and he noted that his Democratic opponent was in favor of it. He said, "I am opposed to an offensive and defensive alliance of powers seeking to dominate the rest of the world." But Harding also said what he was for, not simply what he was against. "I heartily favor an association of nations inspired by ideals of justice and fair dealing, rather than of power and self-interest," he wrote. "The Hague tribunal gives us the foundation of such an organization. Under the conditions now prevailing in the world, with the world fully realizing the awfulness of modern war, it is wholly possible to perfect The Hague tribunal so that its determinations shall be effective and accepted without surrender of national rights." Harding sought to "improve, to save and build upon whatever is good rather than to abandon the good there is and repudiate the world's aspirations for peace." Any international association, though, must respect national sovereignty, for neither he nor his party would "surrender the supreme inheritance of national freedom and self-determination."[13]

A little more than a month after his election, President-elect Harding wrote to Senator Henry Cabot Lodge on the issue. While Harding firmly believed that the country did not want the League, he wrote, "I am equally convinced that the country does wish us to do some proper and helpful thing to bring nations more closely together for counsel and advice. I can not at this moment see why anyone should shy seriously at an honest effort to find common ground from which we may proceed hopefully in seeking to carry out such an enterprise." But Harding did make a promise to Lodge, which he asked him to convey to the members of the Senate Foreign Relations Committee: that he would not "adopt any program without first thoroughly going over the matter with them." Unlike Wilson, Harding was always very deferential to Congress.[14]

Secretary of State Charles Evans Hughes was also on board with the plan. "We favor and always have favored, an international court of justice for the determination according to judicial standards of justiciable international disputes," he said in a speech in Boston in October 1922. Hughes, along with the president, wanted to make sure that the U.S. government could participate "in the election of judges of the International Court . . . so that this Government may give its formal support to that court as an independent tribunal of international justice." A few months later, on February 2, 1923, President Harding sent a special message to the Senate urging American membership in the World Court, officially known as the Permanent Court of International Justice at The Hague. "The whole story of civilization has been the story of the efforts to substitute the domination of justice under law for armed might," Harding wrote in a private letter. "I may say frankly that it is inconceivable to me that the American people, who have so long been devoted to this ideal, should refuse their adherence now to such a program as is represented by this tribunal." But no one should suggest "that our country surrender any of its control over its own fundamental rights and destinies." This was not like Wilson's League proposal. It was simply a proposition to ensure that "the rule of law may be substituted for the rule of force."[15]

Although it might seem a stretch to call such thinking "America First," it is important to consider the context of Harding's ideas. America, and the world, had just witnessed the most horrific war in human history up to that time, a conflict that many believed might be repeated in the not-too-distant future, perhaps with results that would be much worse, especially given the apparent failure of Versailles and the League. World War I was, in many respects, the first industrialized "total war," with newer and more powerful weapons than had ever been used before. Future technological advancements would only make war worse, not better. This was an experience that many in America and in Europe, especially France, did not want to see repeated, so it's easy to see why there were those who sought any available avenue to keep the peace among the nations of the world. There needed to be some mechanism, they thought, by which rogue nations could be disciplined, short of war. Harding, like many Republicans, simply wanted to make sure America would not be forced into action that it did not consent to participate in. Perhaps a World Court would be the right approach. The House voted in favor of joining the World Court in 1925, two years after Harding's death. The Senate followed suit in 1926 but with several reservations, which could not be worked out. In the end, President Coolidge dropped the idea.

One potential snag was that, officially at least, a state of war continued to exist between the United States and Germany because of the U.S. Senate's failure to ratify the Treaty of Versailles, while some fifteen thousand American troops still occupied the Rhineland. Harding had mentioned the "technical state of war" in his special message to Congress in April 1921 on the subject of "urgent national problems." Congress soon passed the Knox-Porter Resolution, declaring the state of war that existed between the United States and Germany and the Austro-Hungarian Empire at an end. Harding signed it on July 2, 1921. In January 1923, Harding ordered the withdrawal of U.S. troops from the Rhineland.[16]

The issue of the new Soviet Union was also a thorny one. When the Bolsheviks took power in Moscow in 1917, creating a communist state, Woodrow Wilson did not recognize the new regime. That was a policy that Harding would keep. In fact, the U.S. government did not recognize the Soviet government until FDR in the 1930s. But the United States still had to deal with Russia. Although Hughes served as secretary of state, and thereby was the head of U.S. foreign affairs, Commerce Secretary Hoover had experience dealing with Russia, so his office handled many issues there through the Bureau of Foreign and Domestic Commerce. Hoover wanted the Soviets to drop communism because otherwise there could be "no real return to production in Russia, and therefore Russia will have no considerable commodities to export and consequently, no great ability to obtain imports." Efforts to establish trade seemed to be futile.[17]

The biggest problem with regard to the Soviet Union was not trade but famine. Droughts in parts of Russia, along with the realities of war and communism, might cause the deaths of millions of people if something were not done. Acting under the American Relief Administration, Hoover organized a massive operation. Within two years, there were 200 Americans in Russia operating 18,000 separate food stations. Medicine and clothing were also provided. In all, the U.S. government spent $28 million in Russian relief aid, and another $58 million came from private sources. Nearly 550,000 tons of food were shipped to Russia and distributed to those in need. This may have helped strengthen the Soviet government in the long run—but men as charitable as Harding and Hoover were not going to stand by while millions starved in a famine.[18]

Closer to home, American relations with Latin America had been in a state of decay for nearly twenty years, beginning a downward slide when Theodore Roosevelt, operating under the new Roosevelt Corollary to the Monroe Doctrine, decided that the United States had the right to intervene anywhere in the Western Hemisphere when necessary. Over a period of two decades, the United States had intervened militarily in Mexico and other Latin American nations on a number of occasions and for a wide variety of reasons, from debt collection and national finance to war and hemispheric security issues. Harding's immediate predecessor, Woodrow Wilson, had continued the policy, intervening in Mexico in 1914 to depose the Huerta regime in a 2-day operation that cost 17 Americans and as many as 175 Mexicans their lives, then again in 1916 with an intervention to capture Pancho Villa that lasted three years. The situation eventually became so untenable that U.S.-Mexico diplomatic relations were severed. Wilson also occupied Cuba during World War I to keep it from falling into German hands, and he sent troops to Haiti in 1915 because of debt issues and to the Dominican Republic in 1916 because of internal instability. Many of these occupations lasted for years and gained for the United States no goodwill in the Latin American region.

Unlike his internationalist predecessor, President Harding was a non-interventionist who did not believe it to be the mission of the United States to interfere with the internal affairs of other nations. True, he had supported World War I as a United States senator, voting to declare war on Germany, but he wasn't on board with Wilson's objective of making the world safe for democracy or, worse, imposing democracy on other nations. According to Harding, it was "none of our business what type of government any nation on this earth may choose to have." As he wrote to Theodore Roosevelt, Harding believed that the United States had to "establish the fact that democracy can well defend itself," but he had "not thought it helpful to magnify the American purpose to force democracy upon the world."[19]

In keeping with that spirit, he ordered no interventions or occupations in Latin America or anywhere else. Harding's election, and his ideals, pleased Mexico greatly. Mexican president Alvaro Obregon believed that the troubles plaguing the United States and Mexico were at an end. He had called Woodrow Wilson the "most terrible enemy" of Mexico but hailed Harding's inauguration as "a day of deliverance." Harding wrote Obregon a note of introduction during the transition period, citing his desire "for the most cordial and helpful relations between our two republics." The two leaders exchanged a number of letters during Harding's tenure. In July 1921, Harding wrote a long formal letter in which he expressed his belief that the relationship between the two countries "has not been fundamentally impaired" and that the only question remaining to be answered was "the manner in which we may re-establish and renew the outward form of its expression." The new relationship paid dividends. In August 1923, a few weeks after Harding's death, diplomatic relations between the United States and Mexico were restored.[20]

Instead of resorting to force and pressure, Harding sought to repair America's relations with its neighbors to the south with kinder words and less threatening action. He did leave troops in Nicaragua and Haiti, but he withdrew them from Cuba in 1922, and he took the first steps to bring troops home from the Dominican Republic and allow for free elections there. In fact, the proposal was known as the Harding plan. By September 1924, a year after Harding's death, the Dominican Republic was returned to native rule. Using diplomacy rather than guns, Harding's administration settled a border dispute between Peru and Chile and another dispute between Costa Rica and Panama, and Harding himself was asked by the president-elect of Panama to help facilitate diplomatic relations between Panama and Colombia.[21]

The situation between Panama and Colombia was dicey, because Panama had once been part of Colombia, and the Colombians had never forgiven the United States for its meddling nearly twenty years before with the construction of the Panama Canal. For many years, the United States had wanted to build an interoceanic canal through the Isthmus of Panama to facilitate commerce and naval power. A French company had tried and failed, going bankrupt in the process. The United States took over the operation and began negotiations with Colombia. In early 1903, the United States, then led by Theodore Roosevelt, entered into a treaty with Colombia that gave the United States the authority to build a canal through the isthmus. The treaty stipulated that in exchange for rights to the canal zone, a strip of land 10 miles wide, the United States would make an initial payment of $10 million to Colombia followed by $250,000 annually for the duration of a 100-year lease. The U.S. Senate ratified the treaty, but the Colombian Senate rejected it, holding out for a better deal—which angered President Roosevelt.

The failed French company, hoping to sell its discarded equipment to the United States, organized a revolution in Panama, where there was already a well-established separatist movement. The extent of U.S. involvement is unknown, but it is clear that America was sympathetic to the revolution. Interestingly enough, the USS *Nashville* did make a judicious arrival at Colon, a Panamanian port on the Atlantic side, just as the revolution was breaking out, which prevented Colombia from being able to land troops to put down the revolt. The revolution was successful, and two weeks after it broke out the United States recognized the new nation of Panama and signed the Hay-Bunau-Varilla Treaty in November 1903. The United States paid the French company $40 million for its equipment, gained control of the canal zone, and paid Panama $10 million plus annual payments of $250,000, essentially the same deal that Colombia had rejected.

Construction of the canal began in 1904 and lasted until 1914. Yet the manner in which the deal had been brokered did not reflect a lot of credit on the United States. During the Wilson administration, Secretary of State William Jennings Bryan negotiated a treaty with Colombia in which the United States expressed sincere regret for anything that had alienated the Colombians and agreed to pay them $25 million in what can only be described as conscience money. The treaty languished for years during the Wilson administration, but under Harding, the Thomson-Urrutia Treaty was signed in April 1921.[22]

Without question, Harding's greatest achievement in foreign policy was the Washington Disarmament Conference, or the Washington Naval Conference, as it is sometimes known. This was the first arms control conference in U.S. history. After such a horrific war in Europe, an alternative idea to the League proposal was international disarmament. In that pre-modern, pre–Air Force era, the most feared weapons belonged to the world's navies—particularly battleships, devastatingly effective sea weapons akin to modern-day aircraft carriers. A naval arms race between Britain and Germany was one cause of World War I. The rivalry had begun in 1897 when Germany, under Kaiser Wilhelm II, passed the Naval Law to increase the size of its navy. To Britain, this aggressive move appeared as a vital threat. British policy required the Royal Navy to maintain at least twice the naval vessels as the next two powers combined, so Germany's effort to build up its naval fleet forced Britain to increase its already gargantuan navy in order to maintain its supremacy. Both nations began a furious building program involving battleships, with Germany also constructing large numbers of submarines, or U-boats. And the very existence of such vast military might was an incentive to use it. Therefore, post-war thinking was that limiting those weapons might just prevent future wars on such a massive scale.

The idea for an international disarmament conference actually originated with Senator William Borah of Idaho, who introduced a Senate resolution in December 1920. In May 1921, during Harding's special session, it passed the Senate 74–0 and the House 332–4. In his inaugural address, Harding spoke of the disarmament conference, saying that the United States was "ready to associate ourselves with the nations of the world, great and small, for conference, for counsel; to seek the expressed views of world opinion; to recommend a way to approximate disarmament and relieve the crushing burdens of military and naval establishments." The nation was also "ready to encourage, eager to initiate, anxious to participate in any seemly program likely to lessen the probability of war." He also brought up disarmament in his special message to Congress in April, in relation to cutting national defense spending. But, as he told Congress, there was no need to "entirely discard our agencies for defense until there is removed the need to defend. We are ready to cooperate with other nations to approximate disarmament, but merest prudence forbids that we disarm alone." Things moved quickly from there. In August, he sent out invitations to eight nations for the conference, set for November 1921.[23]

Support for the disarmament conference was widespread. Many newspapers, members of Congress, and peace organizations that believed in some form of limitations backed the idea.[24] There was also support from a most unlikely source. "I have high hopes of this Washington Conference," said Winston Churchill, who had served as First Lord of the Admiralty during part of World War I. "It has been called together by President Harding in a spirit of the utmost sincerity and good will."[25] Harding had always supported a large navy, but he believed the conference was the right move. He wanted to see the "peace of the world, the proximate end of the frightful waste of competing armaments, and the establishment of peace on earth, good-will toward men."[26] His feelings were on full display in May 1921, when he traveled to Hoboken, New Jersey, and there on the docks watched as 5,212 wooden caskets containing the remains of American servicemen from France arrived for burial. In his brief remarks, Harding tearfully promised, "I find a hundred thousand sorrows touching my heart, and there is a ringing in my ears, like an admonition eternal, an insistent call, 'It must not be again! It must not be again!'"[27]

The day before the conference was to open, Harding attended a solemn ceremony at Arlington National Cemetery to dedicate the Tomb of the Unknown Soldier, containing the remains of an AEF member who had died in France. The next day, Harding opened the conference with a short speech. The purpose of the conference, said the president, was "a coming together from all parts of the earth to apply the better attributes of mankind to minimize the faults in our international relationships." It was not the call of the United States alone, he said, but "the spoken word of a war-wearied world, struggling for restoration, hungering and thirsting for better relationship; of humanity crying for relief and craving assurances of lasting peace." The nations of the world "demand liberty and justice. There cannot be one without the other," he said. "Inherent rights are of God, and the tragedies of the world originate in their attempted denial." And that denial is made possible by machines of war. The peoples of the world "who pay in peace and die in war wish their statesmen to turn the expenditures for destruction into means of construction, aimed at a higher state for those who live and follow after." That was the purpose of the conference, "a service to mankind."[28]

Harding then turned the proceedings over to Hughes and his team. In choosing the American delegation, the president had not repeated the mistakes made by his predecessor at Versailles. When President Wilson traveled to Paris to negotiate, he insulted many by not including a single member of the U.S. Senate, then led by the GOP. Nor did he take along any major Republicans, including only a token member of the opposition party who was a minor official. Secretary of State Hughes would obviously lead the delegation, and included would be not only Commerce Secretary Herbert Hoover, Senate Foreign Relations Chair Henry Cabot Lodge, former secretary of state Elihu Root, all Republicans, but also Oscar W. Underwood, leader of the Senate Democrats.[29]

In a well-received address to the conference, Hughes astonished the delegates by announcing that the United States would cut 30 capital ships, including 15 still under construction, totaling nearly 850,000 tons, and would end further naval construction for 10 years. This was an extremely important proposal because Japan was very skeptical of the conference and America's true aims in calling it. Tokyo had already announced that it "could not consent even to consider a program of disarmament on account of the naval building program of the United States." Before the war, the United States built two capital ships per year. In 1916, in preparation for the possibility of war, the Naval Appropriations Act approved funds for 10 capital ships, 6 cruisers, and 140 smaller ships within a three-year period. In 1920, the American navy had asked for the construction of 88 naval ships, which caused both Britain and Japan to increase their shipbuilding programs. So there can be little doubt that this proposal by Hughes helped break any potential logjams and ensured that the conference went forward. Had Washington exhibited an obstinate attitude about reduction of its own fleet, there would have been little motivation for any other nation to accede to reduction demands. Hughes went on to propose that the British cut 19 ships and Japan 17. In total, 66 ships would be scraped, altogether more than 1.8 million tons. One British reporter noted that Hughes had destroyed in mere minutes more ships "than all the admirals of the world have sunk in a cycle of centuries."[30]

The cuts also served another purpose for the spendthrift Harding administration, as they would greatly aid in the reduction of federal spending. At the time, the cost of one battleship was $40 million, so the United States would save hundreds of millions of dollars. This was also part of Harding's reasoning for the conference. He wrote to Senator McCormick that he hoped it would "lighten the burden of both armament and taxation."[31]

In the end, the world's five greatest naval powers—the United States, Britain, Japan, France, and Italy—agreed to reduce their respective fleets considerably. Germany's fleet had been scrapped at Versailles. The conference set a ratio of 5–5–3–1.75–1.75, which meant that the United States and Britain were permitted 500,000 tons for capital ships, Japan 300,000, and France and Italy 175,000 each. The limitations did not affect smaller ships such as destroyers, cruisers, and submarines. The Japanese felt slighted by such a low number, but they were able to negotiate a promise from the United States not to build any more fortifications on Guam, Wake Island, Samoa, or the Aleutians. In the end, the Five-Power Naval Treaty was a major victory for America. As one scholar wrote, Britain "yielded to a modification of her complete command of the seas." This led to "the beginning of American leadership in the world." Britain would now be dependent on America, rather than America being dependent on Britain.[32]

The conference was responsible for other notable achievements—a ban on the use of gas and chemical weapons on the battlefield, which was an important accomplishment given the horrors that had taken place in France during the war, and, even more important, several treaties signed with the objective of easing tensions in the Pacific, mainly over

China and Japan. As Harding had written to the governor of the Hawaii territory before the conference, "The Pacific ought to be the seat of a generous, free, open-minded competition between the aspirations and endeavors of the oldest and newest forms of human society."[33]

American relations with China began in the late eighteenth century, when the two nations first began trading. But by the nineteenth century, the Chinese empire was weak and crumbling, a ripe target for European imperialists. As they had done in their earlier "Scramble for Africa," the major powers of Europe moved into China and carved out spheres of influence, with each nation—mainly Germany, Britain, and France—overseeing a specific area where it exercised complete control. They strictly managed trade, applied their own laws, and set up their own courts within their sphere. Chinese citizens were tried not under Chinese law but under the laws of the nation that controlled that area.

The United States feared being shut out of lucrative trade with such a large nation. This desire to trade with China was a main reason the United States took control of the Philippine Islands, which were known as the "Gateway to China." With these European spheres of influence, the United States would be cut out of a large portion of Chinese trade. In response, the United States introduced what was called an "Open Door" policy in regards to China, proposed by Secretary of State John Hay, who served under McKinley and later Theodore Roosevelt. To initiate this policy shift, Hay issued two diplomatic notes. The first, in the summer of 1899, was a statement directed to all nations who had an interest in China, urging them in their spheres of influence to agree to respect certain Chinese rights and also the principle of fair competition. The United States was not asking for special treatment or favors of any kind, but seeking a policy whereby trade and commerce would be open to all nations without any favoritism or discrimination. Europe essentially ignored Hay's first note.

The very next year, 1900, a Chinese ultra-nationalist group known as the Boxers staged a violent rebellion under the cry, "Kill the foreign devils." They besieged the embassies of various foreign nations in the capital city of Peking (now Beijing). Two hundred whites were murdered, and several hundred diplomats were besieged in their embassies. A multinational rescue force of some eighteen thousand troops, involving all nations with an interest in China, including the United States, was quickly assembled and deployed to save the diplomats. The military force put down the rebellion and freed the diplomats. Not content with military success, European powers slapped huge financial reparations on China, totaling a third of a billion dollars. More troubling, at least as far as the United States was concerned, was the fact that the Europeans did not withdraw their troops from China after the rebellion was put down. The United States feared that China would now be permanently occupied by those powers, who would assert their sovereignty over their respective spheres. In response, on July 3, 1900, Hay issued a second Open Door Note, announcing that the policy of the United States would be to preserve the territorial, administrative, and commercial integrity of China. The European powers did not respond to this second note either.

At the Washington Conference, all nations with an interest in China signed the Nine-Power Treaty, agreeing to observe John Hay's "Open Door" policy. It had taken two decades, but the Open Door was now a reality. While Japan signed the treaty, it was obvious from the recent actions of the Japanese that they considered their burgeoning island nation an emerging power in Asia and wanted to make further inroads into China and other areas of the Pacific realm. The specifics of Hay's second Open Door Note would stand in the way of Japanese ambitions and invite potential conflict. Tensions and disagreements between Japan and the United States dated back to at least 1898 and the Spanish-American War, when the United States took the Philippine Islands and annexed Hawaii, also considered by the Japanese to be in their sphere of influence. Japan had had a number of conflicts with other nations as well.

In 1895 Japan had defeated the Chinese and gained control of what is now the Korea Peninsula, which had been controlled by China. Ten years later, in 1904–1905, the Japanese engaged in a war with Russia. The Russians, then building a trans-Siberian railroad, represented a vital threat in the far eastern region that was very close to Japan and its interests in China. In their shocking defeat of the Russians, the Japanese bombed the Russian fleet at Port Arthur without warning, in what would become a typical military tactic. Although the United States had absolutely nothing to do with the war, President Theodore Roosevelt got involved in the peace process, holding talks at Portsmouth, New Hampshire, in 1905. An agreement was hammered out, but neither nation was happy with what it received from the peace treaty. Roosevelt won the Nobel Peace Prize for his efforts, but Japan was privately fuming over the American interference.

Several executive agreements were also worked out between the United States and Japan under Roosevelt. In 1905, the United States and Japan signed the Taft-Katsura Agreement, a secret deal in which the United States agreed to give Japan a free hand in Korea—in violation of the Open Door policy—and in exchange Japan recognized the predominant American position in the Philippines. In 1908, both nations signed the Root-Takahira Agreement to support the status quo in the Pacific. Not content to let sleeping dogs lie, President Roosevelt sent the Great White Fleet of sixteen battleships on a worldwide tour, including of Tokyo Bay, a clear case of TR attempting to intimidate Japan with a show of naval force.

In 1912, rumors surfaced that a Japanese fishing syndicate with close ties to the Japanese government was attempting to purchase or lease significant portions of land in Baja California from Mexico. The U.S. government feared that this move would give the Japanese a potential site for a submarine base, whereby they could intercept traffic from the Panama Canal. So, a second corollary was added to the Monroe Doctrine, the Lodge Corollary, which simply extended the scope of the Monroe Doctrine to include non-European nations and also private syndicates that had a close relationship to a foreign government. The Japanese move into Baja was thwarted.

Adding insult to injury, a few years later Japan felt slighted by the Treaty of Versailles. The Japanese had had their eyes on Germany's colonial possessions, but that conflicted with Wilson's principle of self-determination for all peoples. Clearly, the tensions that would eventually culminate at Pearl Harbor in 1941 began decades before. In an attempt to help alleviate the building pressure, the major powers at the Washington Conference signed the Four-Power Treaty. The United States, Britain, France, and Japan agreed to preserve the status quo in the Pacific, pledging not to seek new territorial gains and agreeing not to change or alter territorial boundaries in the Far East. Japan was not happy about this agreement either, with one diplomat remarking, "We have discarded whiskey and accepted water." Yet the agreement would hold until the 1931 Japanese invasion of Manchuria—which the United States, at the time embroiled in the Great Depression, could do nothing about.[34]

Harding was pleased with the results of the conference, noting that it "recorded a great accomplishment in putting a definite end to costly naval competition and in the prohibitions regarding certain inhumane methods of warfare," as well as achieving "guarantees . . . for future peace" in the Pacific.[35] At the time, public opinion on the conference was generally positive. Even many of Harding's harshest critics praised him for its success. Alice Roosevelt Longworth applauded the conference as a "success" with "definite results achieved."[36] Oswald Garrison Villard said it "shall never be forgotten." Harding, he wrote, "was superb."[37] Even Kansas newspaperman William Allen White, who was no fan of Harding's, praised it. "President Harding did one important thing," he wrote. "He called the Disarmament Conference," and "the Republicans . . . pointed with pride to what Harding had done."[38] Edmund Starling, Harding's lead Secret Service agent, noted that the conference "ended in success. It was quite different from the Peace signing at Versailles. This meeting radiated good feelings and renewed confidence."[39] Not everyone was thrilled, particularly with the ship reductions, causing the comedian Will Rogers to joke, "The United States never lost a war or won a conference."[40]

Scholars have generally approved of Harding's conference as well. The agreements at the conference "unquestionably reduced tension in the Pacific and postponed war for a number of years in that area," wrote Maxim Ethan Armbruster. For Thomas Bailey, a scholar of U.S. diplomatic history, the "disarmament part proved illusory," but the "general air clearing was praiseworthy, and may have averted war in the Pacific for a decade." The conference was the only such U.S. international meeting of the 1920s and '30s "to achieve really significant results." And for his efforts, Harding was twice nominated for the Nobel Peace Prize, in 1922 and 1923.[41]

In regard to Europe, the major issue concerning the United States was debt. Not only did the United States owe a lot of money as a result of Wilson's war; it was owed a lot of cash as well. The allied nations of Europe borrowed $10 billion from the United States to finance their war. The money had been used to buy war materials from U.S. industries, so it was not a total loss to the United States if the loans went into default. It was a case of the American government's loaning money to foreign nations to buy American goods. In total, there were more than twenty debtor nations, but the three greatest debtors were Great Britain with $4.3 billion, France with $3 billion, and Italy with $1.6 billion. Interest amounted to $475 million per year, payable in gold. By 1922, European debtors already owed $1.5 billion in interest alone.[42]

Through the early 1920s, even after the war had been over for several years, Europe was still in a state of disarray. The face of the continent had been changed considerably by the war. There were nine new nations, while the Austro-Hungarian Empire, the German monarchy, and the Ottoman Empire were all gone. European economies were in depression; there was massive infrastructure damage, especially in France; and unstable currencies not backed by gold abounded. Russia had fallen to communism. Germany faced massive popular upheaval, sickness and starvation, and huge reparations payments—owed mainly to Britain and France, not the United States. These massive reparations totaled $32 billion, with a 26 percent annual interest rate, and were not scheduled to be completely repaid until 1989. As Mellon wrote, Europe was "in a state of political turmoil and disagreements which prevented any solution of the reparations problem and hindered her economic recovery. Her currencies went from bad to worse, industry dragged along at a slow pace, and in many countries, all incentives to save and accumulate capital virtually disappeared."[43]

It looked unlikely that Europe would ever be able to repay its loans to the United States, especially given the high tariffs imposed on its trade goods entering the U.S. market. Some argued that if American tariffs were lowered, then Europe would make enough money in trade with the United States to eventually pay back the loans. But Harding and the Republican Congress were unwilling to allow Europe to feed off the American market—so as to essentially repay American loans with American dollars. The tariffs would remain in place, and Europe would have to figure out how to repay the United States Treasury some other way. Britain and the nations of the continent sought full debt cancellation, but Mellon opposed it, and so did Congress.

Understanding the need to do something quickly, in 1922 Congress created a debt commission. It would include five members, all appointed by President Harding: the secretary of the treasury, who would chair the commission, the secretary of state, one other cabinet member, one member of the Senate, and one member of the House. The commission also had preconditions: all debts had to be paid in full in twenty-five years, by 1947, at 4.25 percent interest.[44]

The World War Foreign Debts Commission, consisting of Secretary Mellon, Secretary Hoover, Secretary of State Charles Evans Hughes, Senate Finance Committee chairman Reed Smoot, and Ohio congressman Theodore Burton, met in early 1923. Since Britain owed nearly half the total bill, the commission sat down with British representatives—Chancellor of the Exchequer Stanley Baldwin, Governor of the Bank of England Montagu Norman, and British ambassador to the United States Auckland Geddes. Mellon took charge like the banker he was, and they worked out a deal that was eventually ratified by Congress and the British Parliament. Britain would make an immediate cash payment to the United States that would bring down the total to $4.6 billion. The balance would be paid off in sixty-two years, in annual installments, with the first ten years at 3 percent interest and 3.5 percent from 1933 to 1984. France got a similar deal.[45]

Trade policy was another central component to Harding's "America First" agenda. Although tariff policy concerned economic growth and rebuilding a shattered economy, it also had an "America First" component to it. Harding's entire objective in foreign policy was to put America, not foreign nations, first in every aspect of the nation's affairs. As he said on the campaign trail in 1920, "I think it's an inspiration to patriotic devotion to safeguard America first, to stabilize America first, to prosper America first, to think of America first, to exalt America first, to live for and revere America first."[46] To Henry C. Wallace, his secretary of agriculture, he wrote, "I am a good deal more interested in maintaining productivity in our country than I am in adjusting the commercial balances of the world. You must expect that the propagandists of the importers and the international bankers will circulate a great deal of matter which tends to challenge the wisdom of a protective tariff policy. Personally, I am willing to go before the country in favor of protection to our American industry."[47]

Congress had already passed the Emergency Tariff Act in 1921 to help stop European dumping. But Harding and Republicans in Congress wanted a more permanent law. So, the next year, in 1922, Congress passed the Fordney-McCumber Tariff Act, which doubled existing tariff rates, raising them to 38 percent, but allowed two-thirds of foreign imports to enter the U.S. market duty-free. In the negotiations between Congress and the executive branch on the tariff bill, Harding won a major concession by requesting and receiving a provision that would allow him, as president, to unilaterally impose retaliatory tariffs against nations that discriminated against U.S. goods.[48] This new provision, Harding wrote to McCumber, was "extremely essential" "to meet the new conditions" in the world.[49] The resulting manufacturing boom was nothing short of another industrial revolution in the United States, bringing soaring economic growth and increasing wages to America's workers.[50]

Legislation on immigration during Harding's presidency, as on trade, had an "America First" component to it. He wanted to protect American culture from foreign influences, to keep the nation safe from terrorism, and to defend American wages. And despite the beliefs of some contemporary scholars, the desire to stem the tide of immigration was not based on race, or at least not solely on race. Limits on immigration to the United States had begun with the Chinese Exclusion Act of 1882, and the exclusion of the Chinese and Japanese would continue under any new plan, but the new restrictions were aimed mainly, in Thomas Bailey's phrase, at "the war-ravaged hordes of Europe." A flood of new immigrants from Europe would not only take jobs away from native-born Americans but also continue to bring in a dangerous element that had already caused havoc in the country—Bolsheviks and anarchists.[51]

Political violence as a result of immigration was nothing new in the United States, nor would cracking down on it be a fresh step. In the most tragic example, Leon Czolgosz, a crazed anarchist with Polish immigrant parents, had assassinated President William McKinley in September 1901 at the World's Fair in Buffalo, New York, shooting him in the abdomen. The new president, Theodore Roosevelt, went after those responsible, writing in his first annual message to Congress three months later: "I earnestly recommend to the congress that in the exercise of its wise discretion it should take into consideration the coming to this country of anarchists or persons professing principles hostile to all government. . . . They and those like them should be kept out of this country; and if found here they should be promptly deported to the country whence they came." A little more than a year later, Roosevelt signed the Immigration Act of 1903, which specifically excluded anarchists, most of whom came from Russia and eastern Europe, and helped slow the tide of anarchist violence.[52]

After the rash of Bolshevik violence in 1919, many Americans, including many members of Congress, were ready for a new immigration crackdown. Although organized labor supported immigration restrictions in order to protect jobs and wages, groups such as the

American Legion and the American Protective League wanted restrictions because of the foreign ideologies—whether socialism or bolshevism—that some immigrants brought with them. Even large corporations were on board. During a special session called by Harding in the spring of 1921, Congress debated and passed an immigration bill within hours. The House passed it by voice vote, while the Senate approved it by a tally of 78 to 1. Harding signed it into law in May.[53] He wrote that the law was "calculated both to limit the inflow of population during a period of depression and to hasten the day when we may effect true Americanization of all newcomers to our shores."[54]

The bill's sponsor in the House, Committee on Immigration chair Albert Johnson of Washington State, wanted to exclude all immigrants, but the final bill, the Per Centum Act, called for a quota of 3 percent, meaning that just 3 percent of the number of each country's nationals already living in the United States, as measured by the 1910 census, would be allowed in as immigrants. From July 1, 1920, until June 30, 1921, 805,228 immigrants had come into the country, and nearly twice that number had been expected over the following year, but the new law restricted it to a little more than 309,000. The following year, the numbers were only a bit over 350,000, with most new immigrants coming from northern and western Europe. These restrictions helped limit the number of radicals entering the country, ameliorated the employment situation, and improved workers' wages throughout the decade.[55]

Harding's foreign policy triumphs were quite impressive. The idea that the United States retreated into isolationism during the 1920s is incorrect—particularly with regard to Europe. According to historian A. J. P. Taylor, "American policy was never more active and never more effective in regard to Europe than in the nineteen-twenties. Reparations were settled; stable finances were restored; Europe was pacified; all mainly due to the United States." In addition, Harding improved relations with Latin America, especially Mexico, greatly relieved victims of a famine in Russia, concluded peace treaties with Germany and Austria, slashed foreign dumping into the American market, restricted immigration to protect jobs and wages, and called a successful disarmament conference, which the 1924 GOP platform called "the greatest peace document ever drawn." And all of this Warren Harding accomplished in less than three years in office.[56]

CHAPTER 8

HARDING, NATIONAL HEALER

*"The one thing we must assiduously avoid is the develop-
ment of group and class organizations in this country.
The demagogues who would array class against class
and group against group have fortunately found little to
reward their efforts."*

—Warren Harding

On June 16, 1918, a rail-thin, balding sixty-two-year-old man stood on
a platform at a public rally in Canton, Ohio, to speak out against the
Great War raging in Europe, a conflict the United States had been
involved in for more than a year, with no end in sight. The aging speaker
was no obscure activist; he was Eugene Victor Debs, a longtime labor
leader and the nation's foremost socialist, who had been a candidate for
president on the Socialist Party ticket in 1900, 1904, 1908, and
1912—garnering a few more votes each time, as both his movement and
his personal popularity grew, much to the chagrin of the U.S. government. Debs—described as having "burning eyes"—was a dynamic
speaker, had opposed the war from the start, and now took aim at the
powers that had forced it on the people.[1]

Debs had been an activist his whole life, mostly on behalf of railroad
workers. He began working for the railroad at age fourteen and joined
a locomotive union. He eventually moved to the forefront of the labor
movement, in 1893 organizing the American Railway Union (ARU) to
aid unskilled railroad workers. The following year Debs participated in
a massive rail strike that began in Pullman, Illinois, targeted at the

Pullman Palace Car Company. The strike paralyzed two-thirds of the nation's rail traffic and soon turned violent, prompting President Grover Cleveland to send in federal troops. Debs defied a federal court injunction against the strike and was thrown in jail for contempt. His appeal, *In re Debs*, was rejected by the Supreme Court in 1895. It wouldn't be Debs's last trip to the clink. When he got out, he became a socialist and helped build the Socialist Party in America as its father and spiritual leader.[2]

After years in the public eye and four campaigns for the presidency, Debs was a prominent national figure who could legitimately attack U.S. involvement in the war in Europe, particularly the forced conscription of young men to fight in it and the jailing of those who were speaking out against it. In June of 1918, Debs traveled to Canton, Ohio, to visit three socialists who were incarcerated for opposing the war, and then to nearby Nimisilla Park for his public speech. Knowing that there were likely federal agents in the crowd, Debs, speaking extemporaneously as he most often did, jabbed at the spies in his midst and the hypocrisy of the whole affair. It had become "extremely dangerous to exercise the constitutional right of free speech in a country fighting to make democracy safe in the world," he said. "They may put those boys in jail—and some of the rest of us in jail—but they can not put the Socialist movement in jail."[3]

To Debs, the war was nothing more than a crusade for the benefit of Wilson and those in power, while the poor were being cut down like lambs at the slaughter, sacrificed to line the pockets of the affluent. "Wars throughout history have been waged for conquest and plunder," and always at the behest of the nation's rulers, he said. "The master class has always declared the wars; the subject class has always fought the battles. The master class has had all to gain and nothing to lose, while the subject class has had nothing to gain and all to lose—especially their lives." The master class has "always taught and trained you to believe it to be your patriotic duty to go to war and to have yourselves slaughtered at their command." But their "patriotic duty never takes them to the firing line or chucks them into the trenches," he said.[4]

Unsurprisingly, the U.S. attorney for the Northern District of Ohio attended the speech—and he had agents taking down every word the speaker uttered. Within two weeks, Debs was arrested and jailed on ten counts of violating the 1917 Espionage Act, which had been passed soon after Congress declared war on Germany. His arrest under this law officially made Debs a traitor, which, incidentally, was the exact word Woodrow Wilson had used to describe him—a "traitor to his country," the president had said.[5]

The Espionage Act that Debs was prosecuted for violating gave the president broad powers to deal with foreign spies, subversives, and traitors. It also gave Wilson vast powers over trade, and he could even restrict certain incendiary or treasonous materials from the mail. This last power would be administered by the postmaster general. In 1917 that was Albert Sidney Burleson, who believed there existed "a limit" to freedom of speech in such trying times. Material that could be restricted included any publication that "begins to say that this Government got in the war wrong, that it is in it for the wrong purposes, or anything that will impugn the motives of the Government for going into the war. They can not say that this Government is the tool of Wall Street or the munitions-makers. . . . There can be no campaign against conscription and the Draft Law." Postmaster General Burleson stopped distribution of *The Masses*, a radical journal edited by Max Eastman, and any others were warned against making the smallest violations of the Espionage Act. For example, the *New Republic*, which supported the war effort, was threatened with losing its distribution if it continued to run ads for the National Civil Liberties Bureau.[6]

The law forbade anyone to interfere with the military draft, to encourage others to do so, or to consort with the enemy in any way. In 1918, the original act, which had been written in very vague language, was clarified and greatly strengthened with passage of the Sedition Act, which widened the scope of the government's powers over speech. In language nearly identical to that of the 1798 Sedition Act, which had caused an uproar among Jeffersonians, the Sedition Act made it illegal

for anyone to "utter, print, write, or publish any disloyal, profane, scur-
rilous, or abusive language about the form of government of the United
States, or the Constitution of the United States, or the military or naval
forces of the United States" or to "willfully display the flag of any foreign
enemy." Violators faced a possible twenty-year sentence in prison and a
fine of up to $10,000. With these two laws, and the mechanisms used to
enforce them, the land of liberty seemed to be transformed into a police
state, all while waging a war to protect democracy around the world.[7]
As H. L. Mencken wrote at the time, "Between Wilson and his brigades
of informers, spies, volunteer detectives, perjurers and complaisant judges
. . . the liberty of the citizens has pretty well vanished in America."[8] Debs
was sentenced to ten years in prison.

A year after the war's conclusion, with Debs still behind bars in an
Atlanta prison, the U.S. Supreme Court, in *Schenck v. United States*, upheld
the Espionage Act in a case involving two socialists who had been detained
for distributing thousands of flyers urging men not to comply with the draft.
A unanimous Court ruled that the perpetrated act was not protected speech
under the First Amendment. In his written opinion, Justice Oliver Wendell
Holmes held that Congress had a right to restrict such action. Likening it to
a man "falsely shouting fire in a theater and causing a panic," Holmes rea-
soned that the right to free speech was limited and that the government must
be allowed to prevent "substantive evils" in the case of a "clear and present
danger" to the nation. A week later, in *Debs v. United States*, a unanimous
Court also upheld Debs's conviction under the Espionage Act. Later that
year, in *Abrams v. United States*, the Court upheld the Sedition Act, which
was eventually repealed by a Republican Congress in December 1920. But
the Espionage Act remained on the books.

In the meantime, the Justice Department had arrested tens of thousands for opposing Wilson's war, oftentimes for the most innocent of
activities. One man was jailed simply because he explained to someone
why he did not want to buy Liberty Bonds, even though the conversation
took place in the man's own home. A Hollywood movie producer received
a ten-year prison term for making a film about the American Revolution

that focused on atrocities committed by the British. Since the former mother country was a staunch American ally in the war against Germany, such speech was no longer allowable. A state official in Wisconsin was put in jail for two and a half years because he criticized a Red Cross fundraiser. The famous writer Upton Sinclair, author of *The Jungle*, was arrested in California for reading the Bill of Rights in public. Roger Baldwin, a founding member of the ACLU, was jailed for a public reading of the Constitution in New Jersey.[9]

Even while incarcerated in an Atlanta penitentiary, Debs ran his fifth campaign for president on the Socialist Party ticket in 1920 against Harding and Cox. Facing the insurmountable obstacle of a candidate in the slammer, the Debs team came up with a rather ingenious campaign slogan. Rather than run away from his imprisonment, they embraced it. Campaign buttons read: "For President Convict No. 9653." And Debs gained more than 900,000 votes, his best showing ever.

Although Warren Harding did not agree with the beliefs of Eugene Debs—or many of the other dissenters who were denied their rights to free speech—he did not support the government's policy of imprisoning them for such long sentences. The crisis was over, and it was time to move on. As Harding wrote to his friend Malcolm Jennings, he had "heard men in Congress say things worse than the utterances upon which he [Debs] was convicted and the men in Congress, of course, went scot free."[10] Harding wanted to release Debs, but he faced considerable opposition. Wilson had refused to do so, even though his attorney general, A. Mitchell Palmer, had recommended it. The *New York Times* had stated that Debs "is where he belongs. He should stay there." The American Legion opposed freeing him, as did First Lady Florence Harding. But the president also had some firepower in his corner: George Bernard Shaw, H. G. Wells, Clarence Darrow, and Upton Sinclair. And William Allen White, one of Harding's most persistent critics, backed him and even brought some supporters to the White House.[11]

Harding's clemency in the cases of Debs and other political prisoners was not a spur-of-the-moment decision for political reasons, especially given the opposition he faced. He had actually discussed the matter with his campaign manager (and later attorney general) Harry Daugherty before the inauguration and told him to look into the possibility of releasing Debs early. For his part, Daugherty originally opposed the commutation of sentence for Debs. But Harding—in another instance of showing that Daugherty did not control him—persisted. After meeting with Debs and finding him to be "sincere, truthful and honest," Daugherty recommended he be released from prison at the end of the year, but Harding changed the date from December 31 to December 24. "I want him to eat his Christmas dinner with his wife," said the president. Harding's only stipulation was that Debs visit him in the White House as soon as he could. Two days later, Debs was in President Harding's office. "Well, I have heard so damned much about you, Mr. Debs, that I am now very glad to meet you personally," Harding excitedly exclaimed. After the meeting, Debs told reporters that Harding was "a kind gentleman, one whom I believe possesses humane impulses." To his friend Malcolm Jennings, who opposed commuting Debs's sentence, Harding wrote that it "was the right thing to do."[12]

President Harding did not issue a blanket amnesty for all those jailed for violating the Espionage and Sedition Acts, but he did release many of the incarcerated, one at a time, until, according to one scholar, he had "nearly emptied the nation's jails of wartime political prisoners." For doing so, Harding received praise from one of his most persistent critics, Oswald Garrison Villard, who had taken on the cause of political prisoners and had lobbied for their release. Releasing most of them was proof that Harding "had a heart," he wrote in his memoirs. Villard went to the White House to thank Harding "wholeheartedly for his action." In their conversation, it became clear that Harding had a genuine affection for these citizens. Villard recounted that Harding knew a German saloonkeeper in Marion "whom he . . . described with genuine understanding and with real sympathy for the plight many such men found themselves in when the war came." Villard noted, "Woodrow Wilson might have lived forty years near such a man without knowing of his existence or in any degree understanding him." Such was the vast difference between Woodrow Wilson and Warren Harding.[13]

Another major difference was their respective views on race. Although the nation's great Civil War had been over for more than half a century when Harding served as president, the issue of race relations was very much alive in 1921, especially after the horrors of the Red Summer. The federal government had made some strides toward an integrated bureaucracy in Washington over the previous fifty years, with blacks gaining notable jobs in different departments. Theodore Roosevelt had even invited Booker T. Washington to the White House for dinner, setting off the usual knee-jerk reaction in the South. But when Woodrow Wilson came to town, that all changed. Wilson's administration was the apex of segregation in the federal government, as the president ensured that the minimal gains made in the previous decades were reversed. A product of the Reconstruction-era South, Wilson believed in strict segregation and did not approve of racial equality. He even fought the racial equality provisions that other nations sought during the Versailles negotiations. Under his administration, Washington was re-segregated—not only the federal government but much of the city as well. Black officials were removed from offices, and the House of Representatives passed a Wilson-backed law to make interracial marriage a felony in D.C. Booker T. Washington remarked in 1913, the first year of the Wilson presidency, "I have never seen the colored people so discouraged and bitter as they are at the present time."[14] Things were moving backward for black people.

Although whites could never truly know what blacks had to deal with on a daily basis, Warren Harding had at least some understanding of the problem. Throughout his life, he himself had dealt with racial abuse of sorts. It was widely believed, going back to his childhood, that Harding's family line contained "negro blood." Harding was often called "n*gger" by his classmates when he was a child in grade school, and later by his father-in-law, and the issue emerged during his presidential campaign in 1920. His experience made him more sensitive to racial injustice than many others in his day. He was not a man to hold racist views himself or to act toward anyone in a bigoted way. Harding's friend Alfred Cohen, with whom he had served in the Ohio legislature, wrote that Harding was "devoid of racial or religious prejudices. His entire life is a testament to kindness and charity to all."[15]

Harding was not tolerant of real or perceived racial injustices. He called them out in his newspaper. "The colored people are holding a series of meetings at their church in the North End, and doing what good they can," he wrote in one article. "Services are impeded, however, by the very ungentlemanly white attendants who go there for fun and annoy the minister and members a great deal by their racket. A fitting rebuke was given by the minister the other night when he remarked that 'they were welcome only as gentlemen.' If this hint is not accepted the police should teach the rowdies a lesson."[16]

Harding did not shy away from the issue of race relations during his campaign for the presidency, and he hoped it would be addressed in the party's platform. "I can well believe that the Republican National convention will make every becoming declaration on behalf of the negro citizenship, which the conscience of the Party and the conditions of this country combine to suggest," he wrote in a private letter. In his speech accepting the Republican nomination for president, Harding told the nation that he believed "the Federal Government should stamp out lynching and remove that stain from the fair name of America" and that "the Negro citizens of America should be guaranteed the enjoyment of all their rights, that they have earned the full measure of citizenship bestowed, that their sacrifices in blood on the battlefields of the Republic have entitled them to all of freedom and opportunity, all of sympathy and aid that the American spirit of fairness and justice demands." And just days before becoming president, Harding wrote to the secretary of the NAACP, "I think the obligation of our Republican Party is greater today than ever before, after the colored citizenship of this country has made its splendid demonstration of patriotic devotion during the world war."[17]

As president, Harding would not follow Wilson's example of imposing racial segregation in the federal workforce. During the fall campaign and in his first months in the presidency, he met with James Weldon Johnson of the NAACP on several occasions to discuss racial issues, and he followed up by appointing blacks to offices in several federal departments, including as minister to Liberia and to important jobs in the Labor and Interior Departments. By the late summer of 1921, 140 blacks had been appointed to federal positions and nearly a quarter of the post office in Washington was made up of black employees. There was the usual pushback. When Harding sought to appoint a black man to the post of registrar in the Treasury Department, a congressman from Oklahoma objected, citing the fact that "five hundred white women" would be working for him. That was unacceptable to many Americans at the time.[18]

Lynching had long been a problem in the United States, especially after federal troops were removed from the South in 1877. According to an April 1919 report by the NAACP, *Thirty Years of Lynching in the United States, 1889–1918*, 3,224 people had been lynched in the United States, with 2,522 being black Americans. Of the total number, just 219 were lynched in the North, with less than half, 101, being black. Things were so bad that in May 1919 a mixed audience of 2,500 attended a National Conference on Lynching in Manhattan. The keynote speaker was Charles Evans Hughes, who would later serve as Harding's secretary of state. "We are hearing much these days of the drawing together of the nations in cooperation to establish international justice," he said. "I say that duty begins at home. The salvation of democracy must lie in the days of peace after victory."[19]

The history of lynching, as well as the awful racial violence in 1919, should have proven to many that something had to be done about race relations. One of the worst incidents took place in Harding's first hundred days in office, from May 31 to June 1, 1921, in Tulsa, Oklahoma. An allegation that a black man had assaulted a white woman in an elevator caused a two-day race riot that resulted in the destruction of

Greenwood, a prosperous black section of the city that was known as "Black Wall Street," but which the *Tulsa Daily World* derisively referred to as "Little Africa." By the time order was restored with troops and martial law, thirty-five blocks had been torched and a thousand black homes destroyed, and although the official death toll stands at three dozen according to an official state of Oklahoma report, as many as three hundred may have died in what the local papers called a "race war." President Harding expressed "regret and horror" on receiving the news and demanded a complete investigation.[20]

Rather than ignore such tragedies, as Wilson likely would have done, Harding wanted to do something meaningful. A few days after the horror of Tulsa, the president traveled with the First Lady to Pennsylvania to speak to the graduating class at Lincoln University. Known as the "Black Princeton," it was the first historically black college that awarded degrees. "Much is said about the problem of the races. There is nothing that the government can do which is akin to educational work in value. One of the great difficulties of popular government is that citizenship expects the government to do what it ought to do for itself. No government can wave a magic wand. The colored race, to come into its own, must do the great work itself; the government can only offer the opportunity," the president told the assembled graduates. "Nothing is so essential as education; I am glad to commend the work of such institutions as this," he continued. "It is a fine contrast to the unhappy and distressing spectacle we saw the other day in one of the Western states. God grant that in the soberness, the fairness and the justice of the country, we shall never again have a spectacle like it," he said of Tulsa. Harding offered his congratulations to the four hundred graduating students and "shook hands with each one of them." The university proclaimed the day "the high water mark in the history of the institution." The *New-York Tribune* called it a "fine scene."[21]

In sharp contrast to his segregationist predecessor, President Harding also wanted to take some practical action. He called for a federal civil rights law, a federal anti-lynching law, and a commission on race, and he traveled to Birmingham, Alabama, in the heart of the old Confederacy, to give a speech to a segregated audience on providing blacks with equal political rights and equal opportunities in education. That represented the height of political courage at the time.

In his Birmingham speech, the president did not call for outright integration or equality in all things but a policy of fairness for the black man, including political equality and educational opportunities. "Despite the demagogues, the idea of our oneness as Americans has risen superior to every appeal to mere class and group," Harding said. American democracy was a lie if blacks were denied political equality. "I would say let the black man vote when he is fit to vote; prohibit the white man voting when he is unfit to vote," he told his enthusiastic black listeners and the largely silent white section of his audience. "I would insist on equal educational opportunity for both," the president said, and he hoped that the "tradition of a solidly Democratic South and the tradition of a solidly Republican black race might be broken up." In economic matters, he called for "equality proportioned to the honest capabilities and deserts of the individual." But more than just harmony between the two races, Harding called for unity to pervade American politics. "The one thing we must assiduously avoid is the development of group and class organizations in this country. There has been time when we heard too much about the labor vote, the business vote, the Irish vote, the Scandinavian vote, the Italian vote, and so on. But the demagogues who would array class against class and group against group have fortunately found little to reward their efforts," he said, because the "idea of oneness as Americans has risen superior to every appeal to mere class and group." He hoped that that could be so true of race relations that the nation could "lay aside old prejudices and old antagonisms, and in the broad, clear light of nationalism enter upon a constructive policy." With this extraordinary speech, Harding became the first president of the twentieth century to call for civil rights and the first to ever do so in the South.[22]

The denunciations came quickly after the courageous address, and from the exact quarter that one would expect. Southern senators denounced Harding's address, with Senator Pat Harrison of Mississippi calling it "ill conceived," "unfortunate," and a "blow to white civilization." Senator Tom Watson of Georgia said, "We are not going to permit social or political equality of the kind the President advocates because we know it would mean the destruction of the civilization our ancestors handed down to us." Republicans, though, applauded the speech. Senator William M. Calder of New York said he "heartily endorsed the President's views." Oswald Garrison Villard, a founder of the NAACP and grandson of the famous abolitionist William Lloyd Garrison, believed Harding to be sincere in his desire to help blacks, saying the president "clearly favored justice for the Negro which was the more interesting as he was charged with having Negro blood in his veins."[23]

Not content with mere words, Harding soon threw his support behind a federal anti-lynching law authored by Representative Leonidas Dyer that would make lynching a federal crime. In fact, he had already called for such a law in his first message to Congress in April 1921. The Dyer Bill, with the support of the president, passed the House in January 1922, but it was filibustered by the strong bloc of Southern Democrats in the Senate and killed. Harding has been criticized for not doing enough for blacks and pushing harder for equality, but his actions in support of civil rights were remarkable for the time and far greater than any other president's up to that point.

Harding also had affection for other minority groups. The often-neglected American Indians were treated well by the president. He met with them as often as he could, making a long trip west in 1923. During the 1920 presidential campaign, the Society of American Indians sent twenty delegates to Marion to meet with Harding and ask for protection of their "racial rights." Harding told the guests assembled on his front porch that the country "might do well to bestow 'democracy and humanity and idealism' on the continent's native race rather than to 'waste American lives trying to make sure of that bestowal thousands of miles across the sea.'" What Harding wanted for Native Americans was full assimilation, but he was never able to get anything done on the issue in his twenty-nine months in office.[24]

Harding was also very favorable to the Jewish people, one of the most persecuted groups in history. During the fall of 1920, Albert Lasker, a Jew who was one of Harding's close friends, ran the advertising aspect of his campaign and did a masterful job. When Harding became president, he appointed Lasker as head of the U.S. Shipping Board, "the first ever high-profile presidential appointment of a Jew," notes Carl S. Anthony. He also appointed Rabbi Joseph S. Kornfeld as minister to Persia.[25]

Writing to Gustave Hartman, a Jewish Republican in New York running for a judgeship, Harding decried the persecution, violence, and murder against Jews in foreign lands. He said he had raised "protests against the outbursts, amounting practically to emotional insanity, which are most often responsible for the pogroms for massacres of innocent victims . . . even sometimes in our own" country. "We fail lamentably where we do not preach effectively tolerance as well as justice and security and respect for the rights of others as much as liberty," he wrote. "And while these views as to all peoples, irrespective or race or creed or condition [sic], I am especially earnest in my protests against the frequent reversions to barbarity in the treatment of the Jewish citizens of many lands, who have commanded always my admiration by their genius, industry, endurance, patience and persistence, the virtue and devotion of their domestic lives, their broad charity and philanthropy and their obedience to the laws under which they live."[26]

Harding's affection for the Jewish people included a desire to see the creation of a Jewish homeland in the Middle East. As he wrote to the Palestine Foundation Fund, "I am very glad to express my approval and hearty sympathy for the effort . . . in behalf of the restoration of Palestine as a homeland for the Jewish people. I have always viewed with an interest, which I think is quite as much practical as sentimental, the proposal for the rehabilitation of Palestine and the restoration of a real nationality."[27] Words like these demonstrate that Warren Harding had no hate in his heart for any group of people anywhere in the world.

Another group whose members had good reason to be angry was not a racial minority but was important all the same: organized labor. President Harding was without question a solid Republican who was considered a businessman's president and who was on board with the pro-business policies in his party's platform—something that has caused ignorant scholars to launch more unjust attacks against him. Historian Eric Foner, known mostly as a Lincoln scholar, unfairly slammed both Harding and his successor for their anti-labor policies: "Harding and Coolidge are best remembered for the corruption of their years in office (1921–23 and 1923–29, respectively) and for channeling money and favors to big business. They slashed income and corporate taxes and supported employers' campaigns to eliminate unions. Members of their administrations received kickbacks and bribes from lobbyists and businessmen."[28]

But Foner's take is inaccurate, to be charitable. In fact, Harding had sympathy for the workingman. Having come from humble origins himself, and having had to work menial jobs, Harding understood the plight of labor. As owner of the *Marion Star*, he not only treated his workers very well; he allowed them to unionize. He supported unions and the right to collectively bargain, though he did not like strikes or the use of violent tactics. He sought to find alternative solutions to the problem of the often-contentious relationship between management and labor. In his inaugural address, he said, "I had rather submit our industrial controversies to the conference table in advance than to a settlement table after conflict and suffering."[29]

The "conflict and suffering" Harding spoke of concerned the labor disruptions, with perceived Bolshevik origins, that had pervaded the country in 1919. "My most reverent prayer for America is for industrial peace," he said, "with its rewards, widely and generally distributed, amid the inspirations of equal opportunity. No one justly may deny the equality of opportunity which made us what we are. We have mistaken unpreparedness to embrace it to be a challenge of the reality, and due concern for making all citizens fit for participation will give added strength of citizenship and magnify our achievement." He spoke about the Bolshevik influences many believed were behind the upheaval. "If revolution insists upon overturning established order, let other peoples make the tragic experiment. There is no place for it in America. When World War threatened civilization we pledged our resources and our lives to its preservation, and when revolution threatens we unfurl the flag of law and order and renew our consecration. Ours is a constitutional freedom where the popular will is the law supreme and minorities are sacredly protected. Our revisions, reformations, and evolutions reflect a deliberate judgment and an orderly progress, and we mean to cure our ills, but never destroy or permit destruction by force."[30]

Labor strikes and the accompanying violence were nothing new in America. The late nineteenth and early twentieth centuries saw a rash of labor strikes and anarchist violence. The most violent incident in what was a very violent era took place in Chicago in May 1886. A protest led by the Knights of Labor demanding an eight-hour workday turned deadly when an unknown person threw a dynamite bomb into a crowd, killing eleven people, including four police officers. A number of anarchists were rounded up, tried, and convicted, and four were executed for murder. In another horrific incident, on December 30, 1905, former Idaho governor Frank Steunenberg was killed when a bomb strapped to a gate outside his home exploded, killing him instantly. It had been placed there by a member of the Western Federation of Miners union. It was these incidents that caused Americans to associate labor strikes with Marxism, anarchism, socialism, and communism. With the disturbances of 1919, labor was certainly in need of some assistance.

Harding's first move was to fix the ailing economy so that jobs would be created and the unemployment rate would fall. Second, he cut the number of immigrants coming into the country so that jobs would go to Americans and not foreigners and wages would rise with the restriction of labor. Organized labor groups supported that step.

Serious labor trouble began in the spring of 1922 when two signifi-cant strikes hit within months of each other. In April, 400,000 miners in the bituminous coal industry walked off the job. In July, members of the railroad shop workers' union went out on strike. Interestingly, this was something Harding had seen coming three years before, in the fall of 1919, in the midst of the labor strikes and Bolshevik scare. "The coal miners and the railroad forces are clearly maneuvering for a show-down and they are backed by the great organization at which Gompers is the head," he wrote to his friend Frank Scobey. Samuel Gompers was the head of the American Federation of Labor. "I think the situation has to be met and met with exceptional courage," he wrote. "When things get threateningly bad, they have to be corrected, no matter what the cost."[31]

These two walkouts had complex causes, but they were essentially about two age-old labor issues: working hours and wages. Labor had made great strides during the war years, with increased union member-ship and increased wages for workers. Management sought to roll these gains back after the war, particularly when the economy went south in 1920. Coal miners wanted their workday shortened to six hours and their workweek cut to five days; management wanted an eight-hour day and a six-day week. Bituminous coal miners had seen their wages fall from $1,386 per year to $1,013, and the situation had gotten violent, with nineteen strikebreakers and two strikers killed in Illinois in June. A law firm representing an Ohio coal company demanded that the president send in federal troops to protect the property of its client, but Harding refused. "It is pretty well established that the use of federal troops is neither authorized or justified until there is a certification of the state's inability to maintain law and order and put down violence," he wrote in reply. That was not the case in Ohio, at least not yet. Harding, in his calm, kindly way, wanted to use a less aggressive approach. He tried to mediate labor difficulties but ultimately failed in his endeavor.[32]

Harding's anti-union, anti-labor attorney general, though, wanted to get tough with the strikers, particularly the strikers targeting the railroads. Daugherty, the nation's chief law enforcement officer, saw the strikes as potentially harmful to the nation's economic recovery. (Daugherty was pulling out the old playbook, taking a page from the Grover Cleveland years. In 1895, President Cleveland's attorney general, Richard Olney, had gone to federal court and gotten an injunction under the Sherman Antitrust Act against the workers from the Pullman Palace Car Company in order to break a strike and force laborers back to their jobs. That strike, incidentally, also involved the railroads and had been organized by none other than Eugene V. Debs.) Daugherty marched into the courtroom of Judge James H. Wilkerson in Chicago and, according to Robert K. Murray, got "the most sweeping injunction in American labor history." When it was brought up at a cabinet meeting, Hoover and Hughes opposed the injunction and, at least according to Hoover, Harding was persuaded to side with the strikers and told Daugherty to drop at least parts of the injunction. Daugherty, on the other hand, claimed that Harding supported him fully. Harding, in a letter to Charles Dawes in September 1922, wrote that the court action "was pretty drastic, but it was well considered and very much deliberated on before the step was taken. I am glad to know that General Daugherty made so good an impression." Either way, the injunction did end the railway workers' strike and kept the nation's rail lines open and operating.[33]

Although Harding did not have great success in helping organized labor, despite the fact that he said he spent 90 percent of his time during the summer of 1922 on the strikes, his administration did manage some advances. One major achievement was helping the steel industry gain an eight-hour workday. A major steel strike in 1919 shut down half the nation's steel industry, something that could have been disastrous for the country as a whole. After much negotiation, the steel industry finally agreed to end its twelve-hour workdays, with the president writing an encouraging letter to the CEO of U.S. Steel, Elbert H. Gary, commending him for the proposal and offering to "tender any prudent assistance" he might desire. "I do not believe there is anything that could be done that would be of greater assistance in making for an equitable adjustment of our economic situation. Your lead in this matter would have a tremendously helpful effect throughout the country," Harding wrote. Sadly, the final announcement of a new eight-hour workday for steelworkers came on the day he died, August 2, 1923.[34]

Despite failing to help labor as much as he might have desired, Harding did calm national waters on several major issues including labor, at least insofar as the public was concerned. His commutation of Debs's prison sentence and his release of many other labor organizers with the stroke of his pen helped heal the deep wounds caused by the war. And although Harding couldn't get an anti-lynching bill through the Senate, the number of lynchings in the United States fell considerably in 1923 and 1924. Because of his efforts, the country enjoyed relative peace and harmony for the next decade.

CHAPTER 9

THE SCANDALS

*"I have no trouble with my enemies. I can take care of
my enemies all right. But my friends . . . they're the ones
who keep me walking the floor nights!"*

—*Warren Harding*

President Harding had his fair share of political enemies, as every high
official does, but even some of Harding's harshest critics recognized
his better qualities as the economy continued to improve into 1923 and
national tempers calmed. For a political enemy like William Allen White,
a self-professed Roosevelt Republican, to compliment Harding at all was
remarkable, and yet White admitted that "it was evident that the man
tremendously desired to do what he regarded as the right thing"—
though what Harding and White considered "the right thing" could
differ widely. But even doing "the right thing" caused trouble for Warren
Harding, as 1923 turned into a nightmare year for the president.

President Harding was responsible for everyone he appointed to
office. Although he made some very wise choices, some turned out to be
not quite so judicious. "Had Harding appointed a dozen Mellons, he
would have been remembered as a great president," wrote Larry Schweikart and Michael Allen, "but he did not, of course, and many of his
appointees were of less than stellar character." Of this there can be little
doubt. Herbert Hoover noted that, for all his good choices and good
qualities, Harding "had another side which was not good." Hoover was

referring to some Harding appointments that brought shame and disrepute on the president and the country. Hoover was also upset that Harding had weekly poker games with some of these men, which he said "irked me to see . . . in the White House." In 1923, about the time some of the scandals became known to him, Harding stopped those poker games and even quit drinking.[1]

In the end, it was a few of his friends who deceived him. "The President had been betrayed," wrote Agent Edmund Starling. "Harding was ruined by his friends, just as Wilson was ruined by his enemies."[2] Alice Roosevelt Longworth was a bit less charitable, but she wrote in the same vein, saying that the scandals were "the result of electing to the presidency a slack, good-natured man with an unfortunate disposition to surround himself with intimates of questionable character to whom he was unable to say no, friends who saw financial opportunities for personal power ripe for the picking and were unscrupulous in taking advantage of the weakness of character of the President."[3] But Harding was not truly weak. As Starling noted, his problem was that "he trusted everyone," probably too much, and that brought on the trouble, as a few of his friends obviously did not hold him in the same regard he held them. His unscrupulous associates took advantage of his kindness by helping themselves to as much loot as they could get. But there was no way for Harding to know that those he chose for office, many of whom were close friends, would deceive him, which is precisely what happened.[4]

The year 1923 would be a difficult one for President Harding. He would face a number of problems, some political, others private. In the midterm elections the previous fall, the Republicans had lost a number of congressional seats in both houses of Congress. The president's party still held a majority, but the loss felt like a stinging rebuke. The First Lady had battled a serious kidney ailment and been near death at one point, something that weighed heavily on the president's mind, but she eventually pulled through. Harding himself also suffered from a severe bout of the flu in early 1923. But the trouble within his administration—rumors that all was not right with some of his appointees were flying—weighed heaviest of all. As Harding said to William Allen White in 1923, "My God, this is a hell of a job! I have no trouble with my enemies. I can take care of my enemies all right. But my damn friends, my g*d-damn friends, White, they're the ones that keep me walking the floor nights!" This statement has been used by some to argue that Harding obviously knew about the scandals and did nothing about them. But the facts are clear: when he had evidence of wrongdoing, he acted.[5]

To get out of Washington for a while and be amongst the people, Harding scheduled a long summer trip to the West that would take him as far away as Alaska. He was the first president to visit the territory. It was not billed as a campaign swing in preparation for 1924 but as a "Voyage of Understanding." Although he was likely to be a candidate for a second term, Harding did not want to engage in politics but to interact with people as their president. The trip would prove to be far from relaxing, as more news reached Harding about scandals in his administration.

"There was gratitude, there was friendship, there was a comradic warmth about Warren Harding," wrote the journalist Henry L. Stoddard. But the president was beginning to learn that some of his friends were dishonest, and for a man like Warren Harding, that was a very tough pill to swallow. "It seemed the task of gratitude, and the test of loyalty, to stand by them, and he did stand by them. He could see no wrong in their ways or their purposes, could see no reason why the ways of Marion and of Columbus as he knew them could not be the ways of the White House." But they weren't, and he learned that lesson the hard way from three major scandals during his administration—the Veterans Bureau, the Justice Department, and Teapot Dome.[6]

The first scandal that Harding became aware of was at the new Veterans Bureau. One of the inevitable consequences of war is the aftermath, and not just the destruction of infrastructure and wealth but the destruction of lives and bodies, and those bodies—hundreds of thousands of troops wounded in World War I—had to be repaired. To do that, the federal government embarked on a new course. Not even to handle the horrors of the War between the States had Washington created a federal agency for veterans. But after the Great War it did. Woodrow Wilson signed a bill on the day he left office to begin the process of appropriating money for wounded veterans.[7]

Heading the new bureau under Harding was Charles Forbes, who had previously worked in the Wilson administration. Forbes was an immigrant from Scotland. He had come to America when he was a lad just four years of age. His family lived first in New York City and then moved farther and farther west. Like most new arrivals, Forbes came up hard. He served twice in the military as a young man and fought in France during the Great War, where he won the Distinguished Service Medal. Forbes got into the construction business in Seattle, and his work eventually took him to Hawaii, where his firm had a contract to work on the new U.S. Navy base at Pearl Harbor. It was there that he first met Senator and Mrs. Harding. Forbes worked for Harding's presidential campaign on the West Coast, earning himself a job in the new administration, mainly at the insistence of the new First Lady. Harding named Forbes the head of the War Risk Insurance Bureau, which soon became the Veterans Bureau. Some of Harding's closest confidants, including Daugherty, did not want Forbes in the administration, but Florence, whom Harding called "the Duchess," got her way, as she usually did.[8]

Under Forbes's tenure, the bureau employed thirty thousand people and accounted for 20 percent of the entire federal budget. The Veterans Bureau built hospitals for wounded vets, and with his background in construction, Forbes was an ideal candidate for the job. But with so much money flowing, it was difficult for all but the truly honest to resist skimming off the top—which is exactly what Forbes did, taking kickbacks on land purchases and hospital construction. He also sold government medical supplies for far less than their value, pocketing the money while veteran hospitals lacked necessary supplies. By some accounts Forbes may have netted more than $2 million before his malfeasance was brought to Harding's attention by Attorney General Daugherty, who had found out about it from the president's personal physician, Dr. Charles

Sawyer. Having opposed the appointment of Forbes, Daugherty may have been pleased to learn of his dishonesty. But Harding was devastated. After the attorney general briefed him, the president said, "I am heartsick about it."[9]

But heartsickness soon turned to anger. Harding would not take Forbes's larcenies lying down. In an incident documented by a *New York Times* reporter who just happened to be in the White House at the time, the president cornered Forbes in a rage-filled physical confrontation. "You double-crossing bastard!" the president shouted, grabbing Forbes by the throat and shaking him "like a dog would a rat." Harding demanded and got Forbes's resignation. But Harding would not live long enough to see Forbes prosecuted for fraud and bribery, convicted, and sent to federal prison for two years. In addition, the Veterans Bureau attorney, Charles F. Cramer, would commit suicide.[10]

Forbes was treated harshly by the press. As Rosemary Stevens has written, "Allegations became sensations as colorful witnesses described bribes, plots, missing documents, excessive drinking, jumping into a pool fully dressed, greed, revelry run amok." But what Forbes had done was far worse than any other scandal plaguing the Harding administration. Forbes had stolen medicine from wounded soldiers. He was "a man willing to cheat sick and wounded American warriors out of the services they deserved." Such actions do not lend themselves to sympathy and pity in the eyes of most Americans, and it is easy to understand why they provoked Harding's anger.[11]

The scandals in Daugherty's Justice Department involved ole-fashioned political graft and corruption—selling access to the government. Pardons, liquor licenses, offices, judgeships, and other goodies were all for sale. It was so bad that Daugherty's department was mockingly called the "Department of Easy Virtue." Much of the corruption at Justice involved Jesse Smith, whom Agent Starling described as "Daugherty's man Friday, a simple soul with the same friendliness which distinguished Harding but none of the President's grace and polish." Smith was Daugherty's close friend. They came from the same town in Ohio, and they had known each other for many years. It is important to note that Harding had not appointed Smith to his office; Daugherty had. In fact, Smith was never on the government payroll, even though he had an office in the department. So he got no salary. He would make his money in other ways—and a lot of it. He was known to strut around town humming his favorite tune, "My God, How the Money Rolls In."[12]

When Daugherty came to Washington, he rented a house on H Street as his private residence and shared it with Smith. Harding visited on occasion for dinner or poker games. Mrs. Harding was also a guest at the house on H Street. But Daugherty and Smith also rented another house for their clandestine activities, the infamous "Little Green House on K Street," as it was known. Some of Harding's modern detractors fail to take note of this fact, leaving the impression that Harding frequented the house where the nefarious activities took place. Brian Farmer, who ripped Harding in *American Conservatism*, wrote that Harding was at the house on K Street, along with the "Ohio Gang," where they "drank mass quantities of bootleg liquor during Prohibition while they gambled, entertained women, sold government favors, and bribed Congressmen." This is pure fable. According to Agent Edmund Starling, Daugherty did, in fact, rent the house on H Street, and "the President and Mrs. Harding went there to dine with him several times. I mention this only to differentiate the H Street house from the 'Little Green House on K Street,' where the President never went," he wrote. "This latter establishment, so far as I know, was run by lobbyists, and was frequented by people of the same ilk."[13]

The "people of the same ilk" were the so-called Ohio Gang, the name pinned on the powerful Republican political machine that controlled a large faction of state politics. In reality, the Ohio Gang is one of many persistent myths that simply isn't true—at least not in Harding's White House. Harding did appoint a number of people to government positions from his native Ohio, and even from his hometown of Marion, but aside from Daugherty and Smith they were not implicated in wrongdoing. Forbes, Fall, and the others were not from Ohio. This idea that

Harding knowingly appointed a bunch of crooks to office so they could loot the U.S. Treasury is nothing more than a smear.

When Harding found out what Smith was up to, he acted. Smith was scheduled to travel with the president on the trip west, but Harding removed him from the guest list and ordered Daugherty to get him out of Washington. And when he had evidence in hand, the president confronted Smith. Many writers don't give Harding any credit for dealing with the scandals. But in his memoirs, Herbert Hoover, who was close to the president and traveled with him on his western tour, related the story of what Harding did about Jesse Smith. The president called for Smith to meet him at the White House, confronted him about his activities, then told him that he "would be arrested in the morning." But Smith "went home, burned all his papers, and committed suicide."[14]

What exactly Daugherty's role in the scam was is not known. It's a good bet he was neck-deep in it, and after Harding's death Coolidge forced him out of the cabinet. Daugherty was later indicted and tried twice in a court of law. He refused to testify at either trial, taking the Fifth Amendment instead. The results were hung juries. And Daugherty maintained his innocence the rest of his life, although there were very few others willing to do so.

Of all the shenanigans in Harding's administration, the most famous is the Teapot Dome scandal, yet much of the news of this scam broke after Harding's death. Teapot Dome involved oil in the West, specifically two large oil reserves—Teapot Dome, Wyoming, and Elk Hills, California—that had been set aside specifically for use by the U.S. Navy. These naval oil reserves were under the control of the secretary of the navy, at the time a separate cabinet position.

In 1921, Harding's secretary of the interior, Albert Fall, convinced the navy secretary, Edwin Denby, to transfer control of the oil reserves to his department. Harding, trusting Fall's judgment, signed an executive order to officially make the transfer. So, the face of Teapot Dome was Albert Fall. And what a face it was—at least according to Harding's enemies. "The man's face, figure, and mien were a shock to me," wrote

William Allen White. He found it incredible "that such a man could be in a President's Cabinet; a tall gaunt, unkempt, ill visage face that showed a disheveled spirit behind restless eyes." Fall reminded White of the old "patent medicine vendor" who was out "selling Wizard Oil."[15] Not many in Washington had such a negative view of Fall.

A native Kentuckian, Albert Fall had moved west as a young man because of a history of respiratory illnesses, eventually settling in New Mexico, where he became a lawyer. He held a variety of public offices, including in the state house, various territorial positions, and a spot on the state supreme court, before winning a seat in the U.S. Senate after New Mexico became a state. A member of Theodore Roosevelt's Rough Riders, Fall won the abiding affection of his old colonel, who called him "the kind of public servant of whom all Americans should feel proud."[16]

But by the time he entered Harding's cabinet, Fall was experiencing financial hardship involving his New Mexico ranch, and he quietly leased the oil reserves to two private oilmen, Harry Sinclair and Edward Doheny. Sinclair received Teapot Dome and Doheny got Elk Hills. In return, Fall received bribes totaling more than $400,000. The move aroused the suspicions of the nation's leading conservationists and progressive members of Congress, especially when it looked as though Fall's financial fortunes had greatly improved. Fall resigned from the cabinet on March 4, 1923—though likely not because of Teapot Dome, or at least not entirely. It is more likely that Fall, probably confident his scheme would never be found out, saw that he was losing his influence with the president, who was relying more on Hughes, Hoover, and Mellon. The official reason for Fall's departure was so that he could pursue business opportunities back home. The scandal hit the press after Harding's death, and it dragged on in the courts until 1929, when Fall was found guilty and sentenced to a year in jail, the first cabinet officer in American history so punished. The two oilmen were never found guilty of bribery. The secretary of the navy faced the possibility of impeachment and removal from office, but one senator pointed out the flaw in that course of action, saying, "Stupidity is not a ground for impeachment, so far as I can tell."[17]

There was nothing in Fall's background to indicate that he would do what he eventually did as secretary of the interior. Charles Evans Hughes, the secretary of state, wrote of him in his memoirs, remarking about his sometimes distasteful boasting during cabinet meetings: "I had little to do with him, but I did not suspect him of anything worse than vanity and mental indigestion."[18] Fall had won immediate and unanimous Senate approval on March 4, 1921, along with everyone else Harding appointed to the cabinet. No one raised an objection. Fall's successful nomination can be said to be the result of his being a member of the Senate, which also meant that his former colleagues knew him. If there had been something nefarious in his character or background, they would have been in a position to know it. In the Senate, wrote his fellow senator James Watson, Fall "was a man admired by his colleagues for his straightforward manner of dealing with public questions and his acknowledged ability as a lawyer and debater. It was therefore appropriate that Harding, never dreaming of any unfortunate relationship or untoward incident, should put him in his Cabinet."[19] As James Robenalt has written, Albert Fall "was approved unanimously and enthusiastically by the Senate. If Harding misjudged him, so did the entire Senate."[20]

The Teapot Dome revelations, though, only provided more ammunition for Harding's enemies to blast his reputation further. William Allen White jumped on Harding's supposed connections with Big Oil. He believed that Harding's nomination of Fall was the result of a deal struck with "greedy oil," which probably "put Fall in the Cabinet, as Harding's gratitude put Daugherty in the Cabinet." He wrote, "It was field day for Plutocracy when Harding came to the White House. His slogan, 'A Return to Normalcy,' meant, being translated, the return to respectability of those capitalistic forces of greed and cunning in American life which Roosevelt had routed and Wilson civilized. Only in this were they new forces—they stank of oil."[21] Oswald Garrison Villard believed the Harding administration's reputation for corruption to be "entirely true." Teapot Dome "was on the books when Harding was chosen as Presidential candidate by insiders at an early morning hour in one of the rooms of a Chicago hotel;

there is evidence that this robbery was planned well before the convention." But what evidence he had for this, he did not say.[22]

The actual evidence shows something else entirely. As Andrew Sinclair has pointed out, the selection of Herbert Hoover for the cabinet dispels these rumors. It is widely held by Harding's many critics that in exchange for their help with his nomination and his subsequent election, his oil friends wanted control over the Department of the Interior, so as to gain control of the naval oil reserves that would later result in the Teapot Dome scandal. However, the evidence is clear that Hoover, as he said in his memoirs, was given a choice in his cabinet assignments. Harding told Hoover that he could have either Commerce or Interior. The choice was his. "If that is true," Sinclair writes, "then Harding could have made no deal with the oil interests at Chicago to give over control of the Department of the Interior to a representative of the oil interests. Hoover wrote that he *chose* the Department of Commerce." This can only mean that Harding was not in the back pocket of the oil lobby, as is commonly claimed.[23]

Furthermore, Harding did not benefit from any scandal in his administration, and certainly not from Teapot Dome. The scandals were investigated thoroughly by the Senate, and a number of criminal trials were held. Harding's name was never linked to any theft. As Senator Watson wrote in his memoirs, Harding "was in no way responsible for any peculation or fraud that might have been perpetrated by Fall, and of course he had no previous knowledge of any such scheme."[24]

At least a few writers have had the good judgment and courage to resist the temptation to play up the scandals. Writing for the *New York Times* in 2014, Gail Collins noted the unfair treatment that Harding has received. "Most of the chief executives who dwell [at the bottom] came from the Civil War era—like Franklin Pierce and James Buchanan, who sided with the slave owners on the way in, or Andrew Johnson, who screwed things up on the way out," she wrote. "It doesn't seem fair that Warren Harding is stuck with them. His appointees presided over several really juicy political scandals, including Teapot Dome, which was both one of the worst corruption cases in American history as well as the one with the most interesting name. That was definitely bad, but not really in the same ballpark."[25]

According to Jude Wanniski, a Reagan administration official, Teapot Dome was "a rinky-dink scandal by today's standards" and Harding "had nothing to do with the scandal itself." Lew Rockwell of the Ludwig von Mises Institute wrote that the affair that "wrecked his administration was a big nothing compared to the crimes of presidents past and future." Thomas Bailey said Harding knew "what he was doing" when he signed the executive order transferring the oil reserves. "Incredibly enough, what Fall did in making his back-alley deal with Sinclair and Doheny was to some degree in the public interest, for private oilmen were draining adjacent oil pools, the money-pinched Navy needed refined oil, and Doheny did build the enormous storage tanks at Pearl Harbor that were of inestimable value to the Navy during World War II. But the one inescapable fact is that Fall accepted bribes and was jailed." In the end it all worked out for the best, as the U.S. Supreme Court restored the oil fields to the government in 1927.[26]

Harding's administration, generally referred to as "scandal-plagued," is often compared to that of Ulysses S. Grant. Yet there is really no comparison. Unlike Grant, Harding actually did something about the scandals when he found out about them. Harding discovered two scandals and dealt with both of them, which is far more than other scandalous presidents have done. Grant's administration had far more scandals attached to it, yet the old general never fired anyone and only accepted resignations "with great regret." Harding's actions demonstrate that he likely would have reacted against other dishonest employees just as he did against Smith and Forbes, had he not died prematurely.

Yet there are those who contend that Harding simply couldn't say no—couldn't, or more likely wouldn't, tackle the scandal problem in his administration. As the authors of a recent book on the American presidency contend, "Warren G. Harding was an obliging, generous-spirited, amicable man who could not bear to offend anyone." His "chief presidential failure was his unwillingness to root out the corruption, or to offer his country any true moral leadership. Inhabiting an increasingly complex presidency with enormous responsibilities, Harding found himself unable to rise to the challenge," making him "one of the most vilified presidents in American history." The author of a book on "America's Ten Worst Presidents" writes that Harding "did not encourage or condone violations of public trust. He drifted lazily over this bubbling morass of corruption like a hot-air balloon in Macy's Thanksgiving Day Parade." But the way Harding treated Smith and especially Forbes contradicts that claim. It is simply unfair to judge Warren Harding for the troubles that plagued his government after his death, when he had no chance to deal with the problems. We simply do not know what the outcome might have been. We can only look to what he did before his death.[27]

The scandals weighed heavily on the president's mind as his western trip began on June 20, 1923. What was supposed to be a trip of recuperation and relaxation, as well as some good old-fashioned comradery, turned into a nightmare. He must have sensed the end was near, for he drafted a final will before embarking on his westward trip. Harding's health was already in decline. In fact, his health had been a major issue in the run-up to his nomination for president. His heart was weak, and his blood pressure hovered around 175. Not helping matters much were his extremely long workdays as president, sometimes fifteen hours or more. He was having trouble sleeping, couldn't lie down, and had to be propped up in bed with pillows. If not, "he can't get his breath," noted his personal valet. So when Harding saw the killing schedule for his trip, he told Starling to "cut every program" and cut it "to the bone." The First Lady was so worried that she asked Starling to keep the president's doctors close by throughout the trip.[28]

As the trip proceeded, it seems as though Harding found out more of the details of the scams, which didn't help his health. William Allen White, who met with the president during a stop in Kansas City, related the story of Fall's wife visiting Harding while he was in the city. After speaking with the president privately for an hour, Mrs. Fall left abruptly, dodging reporters. What was said is not known, but afterward Harding was "perturbed and anxious."[29]

There are unresolved questions about the meeting, but what is clear is the president's changing demeanor throughout the trip. Hoover took note of Harding's disposition in his memoirs. "I found Harding exceedingly nervous and distraught," he wrote. And the president "grew more nervous as the trip continued. Despite his natural genius for geniality, he was now obviously forcing gaiety." Harding soon took Hoover aside to ask him an important question: "If you knew of a great scandal in our administration, would you for the good of the country and the party expose it publicly or would you bury it?" Hoover replied, "Publish it, and at least get credit for integrity on your side."[30]

After the stop in Alaska, where Harding drove in a ceremonial golden spike to complete the Alaskan railroad, the procession headed down the West Coast at the end of July, where the plan was to stop in Seattle and then go on to Portland and San Francisco. But after his address in Seattle, in which he had some trouble but "managed to get through the speech," Harding became quite ill. Dr. Sawyer, his personal physician, diagnosed a stomach ailment, likely from eating bad seafood, which would require a couple of days of recuperation. Events in Portland were canceled, and the train continued on to San Francisco.[31]

Once in San Francisco, the president checked into the Palace Hotel, and doctors there, including a naval surgeon, Dr. Boone, diagnosed something much worse than mere food poisoning—a heart attack. The situation was serious enough that Hoover called Secretary of State Hughes and told him to get in touch with Vice President Coolidge. But Harding seemed to improve rather quickly the following day. The doctors wanted the president to get complete rest for a period of two months. Hoover called Hughes again to tell him that "the worst seemed to be over." On August 2, newspapers across the country reported that the president had weathered the storm and was on his way to recovery. But that night, President Warren Harding died very suddenly of a stroke, as the First Lady was reading to him. He was fifty-seven years old.[32]

The presidential train on the "Voyage of Understanding" was trans-formed into a funeral train, as it began a four-day trek back to Washington. Millions of Americans stood along the tracks to pay their respects to the fallen president. Many of them openly wept. "Uncovered crowds came silently at every crossroads and filled every station day and night. There was real and touching grief everywhere," wrote Hoover. "At that moment, the affection of the people for Mr. Harding was complete. Had it not been for the continuous exposure of terrible corruption by his playmates, he would have passed into memory with the same aura of affection and respect that attaches to Garfield and McKinley."[33]

Did Harding's weak heart and poor health finally just give out? Or was it something else that killed him? "People do not die from a broken heart," Hoover wrote in his memoirs, "but people with bad hearts may reach the end much sooner from great worries."[34] For Alice Roosevelt Longworth, it was more than his bad health. "He had discovered what was going on around him, and that knowledge, the worry, the thought of the disclosures and shame that were bound to come, undoubtedly undermined his health—one might say actually killed him."[35] Calvin Coolidge agreed. "I do not know what had impaired his health. I do know that the weight of the presidency is very heavy. Later it was disclosed that he had discovered that some whom he had trusted had betrayed him and he had been forced to call them to account. It is known that this discovery was a very heavy grief to him, perhaps more than he could bear."[36]

Contrary to popular myth, Warren Harding did not take his own life, nor did his wife poison him because of his affairs. The basis of the latter story was a man named Gaston Means, a one-time federal agent who authored a book entitled *The Strange Death of President Harding*. Most serious scholars find no truth in these allegations. William Ridings and Stuart McIver, who rated Harding as the nation's worst president, wrote that the poison rumor was a "preposterous suspicion" and that Gaston B. Means was a "con man."[37] Edmund Starling, Harding's Secret Service agent, called Means "a man who would not have been caught dead telling the truth. His engagement as a G-man was a fatal mistake; later he smeared the President and the administration with vicious and scandalous lies which are still quoted as truth by most of the public."[38] Even Alice Roosevelt Longworth bristled with hostility over the allegation. She wrote that, "no matter what Harding's failings may have been, nothing more contemptible and distorted has ever been published about him" as the rumors that he was murdered or committed suicide.[39]

Vice President Calvin Coolidge, informed of Harding's passing while visiting family in Vermont, took the presidential oath of office at 2:47 a.m. on August 3 in the front parlor of his father's house. The senior Coolidge, a justice of the peace, administered the oath—the only time a father has ever sworn in his son as president of the United States. The new president sent a note of condolence to Mrs. Harding. "The world has lost a great and good man. I mourn his loss. He was my Chief and friend," he wrote. "It will be my purpose to carry out the policies which he has begun for the service of the American people and for meeting their responsibilities wherever they may arise."[40]

Eulogies soon poured in from across the country. "Warren Harding was a sensible, hearty, fluent man who was friendly to all. Life repaid him by being extraordinarily friendly to him," the *Commercial Appeal* in Memphis, Tennessee, said. "Mr. Harding was our President. He knew no section over the other. He tried to be fair and he succeeded admirably. He was a good man."[41] The editorial from the *Akron Beacon Journal* was entitled "Ohio's Own Great Son." Harding was "America's best loved president. . . ." He "carried into the greatest office in the world the same gentleness and simplicity that endeared him to every human being that ever met him," the editors wrote. "He was a real man, without pretensions of any kinds. He loved his friends with a devotion that after surpassed wisdom and in his heart there was no room for animosity against enemies. Yet one's heart rebels and even in this hour of sorrow asks whether it was the decree of fate or the foolishness of friends that has sent this great American to an untimely end." Only time "will fix his place in history for the rest of the world."[42]

From the *Los Angeles Times*: "We mourn and the whole world mourns with us the passing of a gentle, kindly soul. Men are great as they are kind. Warren G. Harding was both kind and great. He will go down into the history of this nation as one of the greatest of the Presidents. It is impossible to estimate the debt that the world owes his memory. He came to the White House at a time when the world lay bleeding in the ashes of its agony. And his voice went out to the world, calm and steady, brave and reassuring under his sane, cool, practical guidance." Elected "in the midst of a crisis," he "laid no claim to brilliancy. He was more than brilliant; he was great. Plain people recognized in Warren G. Harding a plain, honest, genuine, square-dealing, simple-spoken man like themselves; they knew his words and they knew him and they believed in him as few public men have been believed before. In Harding the plain virtues of common sense rose to positive genius. He had a level, sane judgment that was a pillar of strength not only to our own nation but to the world."[43]

As these eulogies attest, Harding was a beloved president. People around the country recognized his humility, his honesty, and his kindness toward everyone he met. But the scandals tarnished his reputation. They came out after his death, when he could no longer act or defend himself. And rumors, lies, smears, and innuendo were used to wreck his reputation. The unjust campaign to smear President Harding continues to this day.

RESTORING HARDING'S REPUTATION

*"Warren Harding gave his life in worthy accomplishment
for his country. He was a man of delicate sense of honor,
of sympathetic heart, of transcendent gentleness of soul—
who reached out for friendship, who gave of it loyally
and generously in his every thought and deed. He was a
man of passionate patriotism. He was a man of deep religious feeling. He was devoted to his fellow men."*

—Herbert Hoover

Though he was beloved by the people when he died, Warren Harding's reputation soon plummeted when word began to spread about the scandals embroiling his administration—and about his alleged extra-marital affairs. "Probably no other American President had to run the gauntlet of cruel malice and public odium as Harding ran it during the first four years that followed his death," wrote William Allen White. Because of the onslaught on his reputation, it was not until 1931 that a fitting tribute to his memory was held at his memorial in Marion, Ohio. Florence had passed away in 1924, the year after her husband, and both were initially interred at the Marion Cemetery, then moved to the Harding Tomb when it was completed in 1926. But because of the scandals, which were then roiling Washington, Harding's reputation had been damaged to the point that President Coolidge would not travel to Marion to dedicate the memorial to his predecessor.[1] According to

Herbert Hoover, Coolidge "expressed a furious distaste and avoided it" because it was "a great political liability."[2]

But in the summer of 1931, Hoover, Coolidge's successor as president, a gracious and grateful man who probably realized he would not be in the White House had it not been for Warren Harding, traveled to Marion and delivered a dedication address at the Harding Tomb. "When I became President," wrote Hoover, "I felt that I should return Harding's kindness to me and do it. I eulogized his good qualities and took a slap at the friends who had betrayed him. None of them came to the dedication."[3] His speech in celebration of a man with "a kindly and gentle spirit" who "came from the people" was a testament to all that Warren Harding had accomplished as president.[4]

Hoover first recognized the extraordinary difficulties that had been plaguing the nation when Harding first stepped into the presidential office. "As the aftermath of war our national finances were disorganized, taxes were overwhelming, agriculture and business were prostrate, and unemployment widespread. Our country was torn with injustices to those racial groups of our own citizens descended from the enemy nations. Violent bitterness had arisen over the Treaty of Versailles," he reminded his audience. "These evil spirits aroused by war, augmented by inestimable losses, deep animosities, the dislocations of industry, the vast unemployment in a world still armed and arming confronted Warren G. Harding."

In the immediate aftermath of the war the nation needed healing, and Warren Harding was the perfect man for the job, one who possessed "the healing quality of gentleness and friendliness," Hoover said. "When in 2 years he died, new peace treaties had been made in terms which won the support of our people; tranquility had been restored at home; employment had been renewed and a long period of prosperity had begun." In foreign affairs, the "Washington Arms Conference for the reduction and limitation of battleships identified his administration with the first step in history toward the disarmament of the world. That step was accompanied by the momentous treaties which restored good will among the nations bordering upon the Pacific Ocean and gave to all the world inestimable blessings of peace and security." On the domestic front, Harding's achievements included the "reorganization and reduction of the public debt, the reduction in taxation, the creation of the budget system, the better organization of industry and employment, new services to agriculture, the establishment of a permanent system of care for disabled veterans and their dependents."

Though his administration had been tarred with scandal, that should not tarnish Warren Harding, Hoover said. Of his trip west in 1923, Hoover said, "We saw him gradually weaken not only from physical exhaustion but from mental anxiety. Warren Harding had a dim realization that he had been betrayed by a few of the men whom he had trusted, by men whom he had believed were his devoted friends. It was later proved in the courts of the land that these men had betrayed not alone the friendship and trust of their staunch and loyal friend but they had betrayed their country. That was the tragedy of the life of Warren Harding."[5]

And that tragedy has continued to play out in the assault on Harding's reputation by scholars and historians who seem incapable of considering his real legacy. As Paul Johnson has written, "The deconstruction of the real Harding and his reconstruction as a crook, philanderer, and sleazy no-good was an exemplary exercise in false historiography."[6]

Other scholars have taken note of that falsification of history. Thomas Bailey wrote that the low estimate of Harding's presidency is "based on incomplete evidence," most of it from before the Harding papers became available in 1964, and "badly biased testimony, including the flippant observations of William Allen White and Alice Roosevelt Longworth." And we can add the writings of H. L. Mencken, Charles Thompson, Gaston Means, Nan Britton, and others. Subsequent writers have treated their musings as fact, not mere biased opinion. William J. Ridings and Stuart B. McIver, for example, wrote in *Rating the Presidents* that "Harding was interested mainly in poker, bootleg bourbon, and willing women," rather than "the great domestic and foreign issues of our time. He was, sadly, just a small-town politician, an average man in a job that demanded far more than an average man could deliver."[7]

Such tripe aside, perhaps we can't all agree that Warren Harding was a great president, but who among us that knows the facts can doubt that Warren Harding was at least a good president? Consider Harding's major achievements in just 882 days in office: He revived the American economy and paved the way for the most prosperous decade in U.S. history, an economic expansion that aided every class of citizen. He reduced both taxes and government spending, thereby lessening the burdens on the people. He created the Budget Bureau, which gave the federal government a comprehensive budget for the first time. He restored domestic tranquility, ushering in an era of peace and prosperity. He pardoned war resisters. He pushed for anti-lynching legislation and urged equal rights for black Americans—the first president of the twentieth century to do so. He created the Veterans Bureau to help the hundreds of thousands of wounded American servicemen returning from France. He appointed four justices to the Supreme Court to safeguard the Constitution. He transformed the vice presidency into its modern role in government. He called the Washington Disarmament Conference and achieved reductions in the world's deadliest weapons, receiving the nomination for a Nobel Peace Prize twice. He formally ended World War I. He withdrew American troops from the Caribbean and from the Rhineland in Germany. He improved relations with Mexico and Latin America. He called the World War Foreign Debts Commission to hammer out an agreement on war debt. He provided aid to millions of famine victims in Russia. And all of it in less time than President John F. Kennedy was in office.

Indeed, as James D. Robenalt has written, "John Kennedy was president for almost the same length of time as Warren Harding, but his record was decidedly mixed: Disasters such as the Bay of Pigs and involvement in Vietnam weigh against successes such as the handling of the Cuban missile crisis and the nuclear test ban treaty. Yet history could not have treated these two men more differently. Kennedy became an icon; Harding was deemed a failure."[8]

His accomplishments made Warren Harding an ideal president—certainly not one who fit what Arthur Schlesinger Jr. called "the imperial presidency," but one who fit the mold of what the founding fathers had in mind when they crafted the office, unlike his immediate predecessor, Woodrow Wilson. Harding was open and transparent with the people and the press, deferential to Congress, and respectful of the Constitution. Harding's vision for the nation squared with that of the founding fathers. He believed in their vision, not someone else's.

Harding was also greatly concerned about preserving the Constitution. Though in office just twenty-nine months, Harding appointed four conservative justices to the Supreme Court to ensure that constitutional limitations on the powers and size of government remained in place. In 1921, he appointed former president William Howard Taft to the post of chief justice, fulfilling Taft's lifelong ambition. Taft, the only former president to serve on the high court, would continue in that office until 1930. Harding also appointed George Sutherland, Pierce Butler, and Edward Sanford as associate justices, with Sutherland and Butler becoming part of the famed "Four Horsemen" who led the resistance against FDR's big-government New Deal in the 1930s. But he also helped preserve the Constitution in another way. When told that the original parchment was deteriorating and would soon be lost, Harding initiated the program that restored it and protected it in a safe underground vault to ensure it survives for future generations.

Yet despite his accomplishments, the myths, the lies, the slanders, and the smears persist. Harding's critics say that he accomplished little as president—and little as a United States senator before that. As William Allen White wrote, "Harding in his six years in the Senate talked much but said just nothing. He left in his senatorial record, as he left in his editorial career, no phrase that characterizes a situation, no illuminating comment or convincing argument upon any subject. He was, at the height of his statesmanship, a mere bass drum, beating the time of the hour carrying no tune, making no music, promoting no deep harmony; just a strident, rhythmic noise."[9] And scholars then repeat mere opinions like this as fact. Nathan Miller, for example, has written, "There was no Harding Act or even a Harding Amendment to attract public attention. He introduced little legislation and most of it was petty, designed to provide some advantage for a constituent or campaign contributor."[10] And Jared Cohen has claimed, "While in the Senate, [Harding] made it his business to do nothing."[11]

They neglect to acknowledge the obvious explanation: Out of Harding's six years as a senator, the Democrats were in control for the first four, and by 1920 Harding was deep into a presidential campaign, leaving him only part of one year to get anything accomplished—and that year was taken up by the issue of Wilson's League, which Harding's opposition helped stop. But in his short time in the Senate while Republicans had control, he was a valued member of the Foreign Relations Committee, as well as other committees, and he was given the lead speech in the Senate in the fight against the League of Nations, where he received sustained approval. The party also handed him two very big plums. In 1912, before he was elected to the Senate, he gave the keynote address at the Republican National Convention to renominate Taft for a second term as president, a speech that Nicholas Murray Butler, the president of Columbia University, called "impressive." Four years later, the GOP named him chairman of the national convention, and Butler praised Harding as "a most capable and acceptable officer." Butler was equally captivated by Harding's 1916 convention speech calling for party unity. "The stunning character of his appearance at that time and the effect of his voice and manner, both upon members of the convention and upon the vast audience assembled in the hall, are not likely to be forgotten by those who witnessed them." These facts disprove notions of do-nothingness and show Harding was a well-respected member of the Republican Party.[12]

Harding was not a dumb or an anti-intellectual man, despite snarky comments from scholars who say he was such a hardworking president because he needed more time than others. Anyone who will simply take the time to read through his private letters will see a man who had a grasp of the issues and a knowledge of the inner workings of government. This was especially true of politics. He was a superb politician who understood how the game was played and played it well. As John W. Dean has written, "Harding played politics like he did poker. He was always congenial and enjoyed himself, but he took the game much more seriously than most realized—and he seldom lost. The risks he took were calculated and always conservative; he held his cards close to his chest, and he had a good poker face. The presidency was a high-stakes game and Harding played it with zest, all the while appearing casual and disinterested."[13]

He had worked in politics for years and had been a member of the world's greatest deliberative body, the United States Senate, yet Harding had a low opinion of members of Congress. There are "a good many people in Congress whom my experience has led me to mark down to about ten per cent of their normal appraised value," he wrote to his friend Malcolm Jennings. In a remarkably frank letter, he continued:

> In simple truth, I get discouraged sometimes about the stability of popular government, when I come in contact with the abject surrender of public men to what appears to be about one-half of one per cent of the voters to whom they look for their commission to public service. What the country needs more than anything else is a House and Senate for ten years which gives at least as much thought to the welfare of the Republic as is given to individual candidacies for re-election. Nothing so disheartens me as to have an extended conference with men in responsible places, hear them admit of the correctness of some policy or position and then frankly say it is impossible to go through with the policy or maintain the position and be assured of re-election. I have concluded that I would vastly prefer a limited career with the consciousness of having done the right thing, than to hold on to the constitutional limit by playing to the favor of those who do

the fake work under our political system. My own disappointment with the public estimate of me lies in the fact that so many seem to think I can take a whip and show Congress where to head in. It was possible for my predecessor to follow such a course during the war when men oftentimes put aside their petty interests to perform what was believed to be a patriotic service. Conditions are not quite the same now. Probably I am lacking in the domineering traits which Mr. Wilson possessed and found himself able to exercise for considerable time. In the end he came to failure because of the practices he followed.[14]

Here was a man who understood exactly what was transpiring in Congress—and was as frustrated with it as many Americans are today. Yet, as president, he would not allow himself to fight with Congress as his predecessor had done. He remained true to his understanding of the presidential office under the Constitution.

But what of Harding's admissions that he was unfit for the office? Scholars continually point out Harding's own words and use them against him. "I am unfit for this office," Harding once said, "and should never have been here." In a letter to a close friend in 1919, when he was contemplating a White House run, Harding mentioned his inadequacies, saying, "I have such a sure understanding of my own inefficiency that I should really be ashamed to presume myself fitted to reach out for a place of such responsibility." But is this really a bad mark against the man? Or was it an admirable display of humility? Writes Lew Rockwell, "Of course historians hate him. They say he was a do-nothing president. Harding himself admitted it. He said he was unqualified to be president. Indeed, no man is qualified to be president. Harding was honest enough to say it outright."[15]

Harding understood the burdens of office. In the fall of 1922 he wrote a short note to former president Woodrow Wilson in which he confessed the toll the office takes on the man holding it, something only a former president would understand. "Permit me to express the hope that your own health is mending encouragingly. After an opportunity of eighteen months in which to appraise the weight of burdens which I know to have been yours, there is a sincerity in that kindly wish which could be written by no one without personally knowing something of the task."[16]

Beyond the scandals, Harding has also been grievously slandered on the subject of his extramarital affairs. There is no excuse for running around on a spouse, and Harding had at least two extramarital affairs before he became president, including the infamous tryst with the young Nan Britton, which, we now know through DNA evidence, produced a child. But Harding's detractors have blown his affairs out of proportion and even made up stories to paint him as far worse than he was. One completely made-up story tells of Harding's dalliances with Britton in the Oval Office itself, as well as in a closet nearby. These tales come from Britton's book *The President's Daughter*, published in 1927, which first brought the affair to public light, and from Alice Roosevelt Longworth, who told the fable of the First Lady nearly catching Harding in the act. These myths were later pushed by the likes of Francis Russell, Samuel Hopkins Adams, and others as fact, usually without any attribution.

Yet, interestingly, nothing about these illicit Oval Office trysts leaked in the 882 days Harding was in office, or in the 4 years between his death and the publication of the Britton book, which was so outlandish that no publisher would publish it. It had to be self-published. And not only that, we have reason to doubt these stories because of firsthand accounts from inside the White House. White House doorkeeper Patrick Kenney stated that he "had never heard of Nan Britton," had "never admitted any woman by such a name," and that "*no* strange woman ever came to see President Harding." Ike Hoover, who was the supposed source for Alice Roosevelt Longworth, refuted the whole sordid tale of Oval Office affairs, stating matter-of-factly, "There was never a gadabout by that name or any other name in the White House. Nan Britton is a liar." Secret Service agent Edmund Starling said no such rendezvous with

Britton or any other woman ever happened, "not while he was at the White House. That I know for certain." Beyond what he could speak to from his own direct knowledge, Starling was skeptical that Harding had ever had an affair with Britton, noting in his memoirs that the very idea of the president "pursuing her is something no one who knew him would believe." "If it happened," Starling wrote, "(and I would be foolish to say that I am certain it did, for I am not), [it] began while Harding was in the Senate and ended before he entered the White House. From the moment of his election until the hour of his death he was never free from our surveillance. His acts are things to which I can swear. He never did anything more reprehensible than cuss mildly at a golf ball and play poker with his friends. He was the kindest man I ever knew."[17]

On the subject of the poker games, Alice Roosevelt Longworth described the White House as having "the general atmosphere of a convivial gambling saloon."[18] But Agent Edmund Starling, who "attended all of these gatherings," had a different take.[19] At no time did he ever see "the slightest sign of debauch," he wrote. "The stakes were modest, since these men played purely for the sport of it. How could Andy Mellon, for instance, get a kick out of winning money in a poker game? They played with great zest and good humor, drank moderately and sociably, and smoked—all in the best tradition of the Elks Club."[20]

Yet some historians and scholars, if we can call them that, repeat the most negative, salacious stories, most of which came from Harding's political enemies (in and out of the press), in order to belittle him without ever consulting serious primary sources to corroborate their veracity. Even though Edmund Starling, as a Secret Service agent, was dedicated to the president he was serving at any given time, he maintained a strong personal relationship with Wilson after he left the White House and believed that Harding never should have been president. But he could still be fair-minded. And it was obvious to Starling that Harding had gotten a bad rap. "I think people like to remember the Harding administration as having been abandoned to liquor and sex because the country itself at the time was in such a state. The Roaring Twenties were beginning to howl. There was a mass demonstration of disrespect for the Eighteenth Amendment, and the White House itself joined in this rebellion—plenty of liquor was served there, although the President, as I have said, was a one drink man" who "could not have drunk more if he wanted to. He suffered from stomach trouble, and was allergic to alcohol in any but small doses."[21]

Sure, Warren Harding had personal flaws, but nearly all presidents do. Sure, he made a few choices that turned out to be bad, but he had no way of knowing that at the time. The same could be said of other presidents as well. But Harding did not try to cover anything up. Until his untimely death, he dealt with the problems as they emerged.

But it may be on the roaring twenties, even more than on the scandals, where the gap between the myth and the reality is the biggest. Contrary to popular opinion, it was Warren Harding, not Calvin Coolidge, who was largely responsible for the economic boom of the 1920s. Many historians, though, give credit to Coolidge for the expansion, not Harding. A number of scholars refer to the robust growth era as "Coolidge Prosperity" or even "Coolidge-Hoover Prosperity," leaving Harding out altogether. But this is wrong. Coolidge kept the Harding program in place, even sticking with the indispensable Andrew Mellon, who remained at his post until 1932, when he resigned to become ambassador to Britain. Coolidge took on the fiscal fight personally and won passage of the Revenue Acts of 1924, 1926, and 1928, which brought taxes down further, fueling the economic boom of the roaring twenties.[22] Harding ran the first laps ahead of the other competitors; Coolidge carried the tax baton in the final tough laps to the finish line. This formidable team gave America a formidable economy.

The results of the Harding economic program were staggering, with no equal in all of American history. In our modern era the country is ecstatic over a 4 percent jump in the GDP, but during the 1920s, specifically from 1922 to 1927, the economy averaged 7 percent growth. Manufacturing output climbed 64 percent, while output per worker rose 40 percent. By 1929, the nation's wealth, which had been less than $70 billion in 1921, topped $103 billion (nearly $1 trillion in inflation-adjusted dollars), and the country produced more than 42 percent of the world's manufactured goods. Despite the massive tax cuts, which helped spur the growth, federal revenue increased, and with spending tightly controlled, the government generated a budget surplus every year of the decade and paid off one-third of the national debt, which fell from nearly $26 billion when Harding took office to $17 billion in 1929.[23]

Wages also rose for every class of American worker, and as a result more families found themselves in the middle class. According to Robert Murphy, "Real income per person rose 2.1 percent annually, even though the U.S. population increased from 111.9 million to 121.8 million people."[24] Veronique de Rugy of the Cato Institute notes how the prosperity extended to nearly every American:

> The rising tide of strong economic growth lifted all boats. At the top end, total income grew as a result of many more people becoming prosperous, rather than a fixed number of high earners getting greatly richer. For example, between 1922 and 1928, the average income reported on tax returns of those earning more than $100,000 increased 15 percent, but the number of taxpayers in that group almost quadrupled. During the same period, the number of taxpayers earning between $10,000 and $100,000 increased 84 percent, while the number reporting income of less than $10,000 fell.

America was more prosperous during the roaring twenties than it had been at any time in history. In fact, the unemployment rate reached an unprecedented low of just 1.6 percent in 1926. (And this was before welfare and food stamps, the recipients of which are not counted as unemployed.)[25]

American prosperity was so great and the economy so strong that the United States, unconcerned about the debts America was already owed, began lending money to Germany to make its reparations payments—lifting the German economy out of its morass and helping

marginalize the extremist parties that had arisen as a result of the cata-
clysm of defeat.

The prosperity was also general, boosting the nation as a whole.
And driving the engine was manufacturing. In the 1920 census, for the
first time in American history, more Americans lived in urban areas
than rural ones. Prosperity brought technological advancement to the
cities. Electricity, which was in very few homes before the decade
began, lighted two-thirds of homes by 1929. And with electricity came
the ability to buy new appliances that were being mass produced in
factories across the country—vacuum cleaners, refrigerators, washing
machines, and radios could be found in more American homes. But the
biggest prize of all was the automobile, and with the prosperity of the
1920s more Americans could afford one. In 1914, before the war, there
were 1.2 million cars in America; by 1920, there were 10 million cars;
by the end of the decade 26 million were on the road. By 1929, over 5
million cars were produced per year, compared to fewer than 2 million
in 1920 and just 500,000 in 1914. Harding signed a federal highway
bill to help build new roadways across the country. And new roads and
more cars on those roads led to such innovations as motels and drive-in
restaurants. And the credit for all this tremendous economic growth
belongs to Warren G. Harding.[26]

Nor can it be said that the prosperity—or "excesses"—of the 1920s
led to the Great Depression, despite the apparent consensus among historians and economists that the economic conservatism of the decade is
to blame for creating a great boom and then an even greater bust. In *Bad
Presidents: Failure in the White House*, for example, Philip Abbott lays
the blame squarely at the feet of all three Republican presidents of the
1920s. "Harding, Coolidge, and Hoover together share responsibility
for the Great Depression," he writes, because each one "believed in lower
taxes and less government." Abbott goes on, "For if these Presidents were
responsible for the apparent prosperity of the 1920s, how could they not
be responsible for the 1930s?" Why should they be? For one thing,
Hoover should not be lumped in with Harding and Coolidge. Hoover

was a progressive Republican whose appointment to Harding's cabinet drew the ire of conservatives. He remained as secretary of commerce under Coolidge, but that relationship was not a cordial one. Coolidge, who mockingly referred to Hoover as "Wonder Boy," once remarked, "That man has offered me unsolicited advice every day for six years, all of it bad."[27]

When the depression hit in 1929, President Hoover's policies were not the laissez-faire capitalist policies of Harding, Coolidge, and Mellon, but what has been called the forerunner to Franklin D. Roosevelt's New Deal. In fact, one member of FDR's vaunted "brain trust," Rexford Tugwell, gave credit to Hoover. "The ideas embodied in the New Deal Legislation were a compilation of those which had come to maturity under Herbert Hoover's aegis. We all . . . owed much to Hoover," he said in 1946. Soon after the stock market crash, Hoover raised taxes and spent money on projects designed to "stimulate" the economy. The federal government ran deficits under Hoover, and the national debt was once again on the rise. During the 1932 presidential campaign, FDR even criticized Hoover for spending too much and failing to balance the budget. In short, Hoover departed from the Harding plan, and the depression grew worse as a result.[28]

So if laissez-faire didn't cause the market to crash and the economy to fall into depression, then what did? Simply put, the Federal Reserve's policies. As Ludwig von Mises has argued, almost every economic depression can be blamed on monetary policy. Throughout the 1920s, the Fed lowered interest rates, leading to increased speculation in the stock market, which created a bubble "fueled by the artificially cheap credit." The Fed then began to raise interest rates in 1928 and 1929 in order to slow things down. They slowed them down too much. "In other words," writes Murphy, "when the Fed stopped pumping in gobs of new money that pushed up the stock market, investors came to their senses and asset prices plunged back towards their pre-bubble level." The Great Depression had nothing to do with Warren Harding.[29]

The facts that I have laid out in this book demonstrate the virtues of Warren Harding and the achievements of his presidency. He was not a failure, but a good president with significant accomplishments; the scandals of his administration were not his doing—he had nothing to do with any of them. Though the likelihood of full rehabilitation of Harding's reputation is remote, I do wish the public would take a second look at Warren Harding and view him in the proper light, for they might just see in him at least a bit of themselves: a man who was far from perfect, a mortal sinner like the rest of us, but someone who began life in modesty in small-town America, worked hard, and achieved the American dream, then made it possible, during very trying times, for his "countrymen" to achieve theirs.

NOTES

Introduction: Why Defend Warren G. Harding?

Epigraph: Thomas A. Bailey, *Presidential Greatness: The Image and the Man from George Washington to the Present* (New York: Appleton-Century-Crofts, 1967), 312.

1. Jared Cohen, *Accidental Presidents: Eight Men Who Changed America* (New York: Simon and Schuster, 2019), 232.
2. Bailey, *Presidential Greatness*, 312.
3. Gail Collins, "About Those Presidential Polls," *New York Times*, July 4, 2014.

Prologue: The Most Maligned President in American History

Epigraph: Robert W. Merry, *Where They Stand: The American Presidents in the Eyes of Voters and Historians* (New York: Simon and Schuster, 2012), 90.

1. Margaret Miner and Hugh Rawson, *The Oxford Dictionary of American Quotations* (Oxford: Oxford University Press, 2006), 304.
2. Alice Roosevelt Longworth, *Crowded Hours* (New York: Charles Scribner's Sons, 1932), 325.
3. Rexford G. Tugwell, *The Enlargement of the Presidency* (London: Octagon Books, 1977), 373.

4. William J. Ridings Jr. and Stuart B. McIver, *Rating the Presidents: A Ranking of US Leaders, From the Great and Honorable to the Dishonest and Incompetent* (Citadel Press Book, 1997), 185.
5. Nathan Miller, *Star-Spangled Men: America's Ten Worst Presidents* (New York: A Touchstone Book, 1998), 192–93.
6. Lewis L. Gould, *Grand Old Party: A History of the Republicans* (New York: Random House, 2003), 234.
7. Paula Fass, "Warren Harding," in *The American Presidency: The Authoritative Reference*, ed. Alan Brinkley and Davis Dyer (Boston: Houghton Mifflin Company, 2004), 314.
8. Isaac Chotiner, "How Racism Nearly Derailed Women's Right to Vote," Slate, March 7, 2018, https://slate.com/news-and-politics/2018/03/how-racism-nearly -derailed-womens-right-to-vote.html.
9. Robert E. DiClerico, *The American President* (Englewood Cliffs, New Jersey: Prentice Hall Inc., 1995), 22, 19.
10. Ridings and McIver, *Rating the Presidents*, 183, 185.
11. Ibid., 181.
12. Douglas Alan Cohn, *The President's First Year: None Were Prepared, Some Never Learned: Why the Only School for Presidents Is the Presidency* (Guilford, Connecticut: Lyons Press, 2016), 209.
13. David C. Whitney, *The American Presidents: Biographies of the Chief Executives from Washington through Clinton* (New York: Doubleday, 1993), 238.
14. Kenneth C. Davis, *Don't Know Much About the American Presidents* (New York: Hyperion, 2012), 397–404.
15. Eleanor Herman, *Sex with Presidents: The Ins and Outs of Love and Lust in the White House* (New York: HarperCollins, 2020), 104.
16. Jordan Michael Smith, "America's Horniest President," *Politico*, August 16, 2015, https://www.politico.com/magazine/story/2015/08/warren-harding-child -sex-sandal-121404.
17. Thomas A. Bailey, *Presidential Greatness: The Image and the Man from George Washington to the Present* (New York: Appleton-Century-Crofts, 1967), 312.
18. Robert Spencer, *Rating America's Presidents* (New York: Bombardier Books, 2020), 318.
19. Burton W. Folsom, "The Strange Presidency of Warren G. Harding," Foundation for Economic Education, March 28, 2012, https://fee.org/articles/ the-strange-presidency-of-warren-g-harding/.
20. Robert Murray and Tim Blessing, *Greatness in the White House: Rating the Presidents from George Washington to Ronald Reagan* (University Park: The Pennsylvania State University Press, 1993); Robert Murray and Tim Blessing, "The Presidential Performance Study: A Progress Report," *Journal of American History*, December 1983.

21. Charles F. Faber and Richard B. Faber, *American Presidents Ranked by Performance* (London: McFarland & Company Inc., 2000), 189, 191.
22. Eugene P. Trani, "Warren G. Harding: Life in Brief," Miller Center, University of Virginia, https://millercenter.org/president/harding/life-in-brief.
23. Lewis L. Gould, *The Modern American Presidency* (Lawrence, Kansas: University Press of Kansas, 2003), 56.
24. William E. Leuchtenburg, *The American President: From Teddy Roosevelt to Bill Clinton* (Oxford: Oxford University Press, 2015), 115.
25. Faber and Faber, *American Presidents Ranked by Performance*, 191.
26. Warren Harding, "Back to Normal," Address to the Home Market Club of Boston, May 14, 1920, in *Rededicating America: The Life and Recent Speeches of Warren Harding*, ed. Frederick E. Schortemeier (Indianapolis: Bobbs-Merrill, 1920), 223–29.
27. Jeremy Rabkin, "Warren Gamaliel Harding," in *Presidential Leadership: Ranking the Best and Worst in the White House*, ed. James Taranto and Leonard Leo (New York: A Wall Street Journal Book, 2004), 141–42; DiClerico, *The American President*, 349.
28. Robert F. Martin, "Warren Gamaliel Harding, 1921–1923," in *The American Presidents*, ed. Melvin I. Urofsky (New York: Garland Publishing, Inc., 2000), 305.
29. Steven F. Hayward, *The Politically Incorrect Guide to the Presidents, Part 2: From Wilson to Obama* (Washington, D.C.: Regnery Publishing, 2012), 74.
30. Ivan Eland, *Recarving Rushmore: Ranking the Presidents on Peace, Prosperity, and Liberty* (Oakland, California: The Independent Institute, 2009), 230–35.
31. Merry, *Where They Stand*, 90; Robert W. Merry, "The Worst President Ever? That Title Belongs to Woodrow Wilson," *National Interest*, January 19, 2018, https://nationalinterest.org/blog/the-buzz/the-worst-president-ever-title-belongs-woodrow-wilson-24137.
32. Justin Raimondo, "For a Return to Normalcy," Antiwar.com, January 6, 2016, https://original.antiwar.com/justin/2016/01/05/for-a-return-to-normalcy/.
33. Patrick J. Buchanan, "Rating the Presidents," WND.com, June 16, 2004, https://www.wnd.com/2004/06/25110/.

Chapter 1: The League

Epigraph: David Pietrusza, *1920: The Year of Six Presidents* (New York: Carroll & Graf Publishers, 2007), 41.
1. Evan Thomas, *The War Lovers: Roosevelt, Lodge, Hearst, and the Rush to Empire, 1898* (Boston: Little, Brown and Company, 2010); David Fromkin, *Europe's Last Summer: Who Started the Great War in 1914?* (New York: Vintage Books, 2004), 41.
2. Nell Irvin Painter, *Standing at Armageddon: The United States, 1877–1919* (New York: W. W. Norton & Company, 1987), 344; Rosemary Stevens, *A Time*

of Scandal: Charles R. Forbes, Warren G. Harding and the Making of the Veterans Bureau (Baltimore: Johns Hopkins University Press, 2016), 20.

3. Warren G. Harding to Charles D. Hilles, May 23, 1918, *Selections from the Papers and Speeches of Warren G. Harding, 1918–1923*, ed. Leonard Schlup and John H. Hepp IV (Lewiston, New York: The Edwin Mellen Press, 2008), 26.

4. John M. Barry, *The Great Influenza: The Story of the Deadliest Pandemic in History* (New York: Penguin Books, 2005).

5. George Harvey, "The Truce of Versailles," *Harvey's Weekly*, September 6, 1919.

6. "Wall Street Sees Better Times after Election," *Wall Street Journal*, November 2, 1920.

7. Edward G. Lowry, *Washington Close-Ups: Intimate Views of Some Public Figures* (Boston: Houghton Mifflin Company, 1921), 183.

8. Francis Russell, *The Shadow of Blooming Grove: Warren G. Harding in His Times* (New York: McGraw-Hill Book Company, 1968), 320–21.

9. Pietrusza, *1920*, 11.

10. Ibid., 11, 17, 24–25, 27; Bailey, *Presidential Greatness*, 312.

11. Thomas G. Paterson, et al., *American Foreign Relations: Volume One, A History to 1920* (Boston: Wadsworth, 2010), 294; John Milton Cooper, *Woodrow Wilson: A Biography* (New York: Alfred A. Knopf, 2009), 508; Pietrusza, *1920*, 38.

12. Nathan Miller, *New World Coming: The 1920s and the Making of Modern America* (New York: Scribner, 2003), 23; Pietrusza, 27.

13. David F. Houston, *Eight Years with Wilson's Cabinet, 1913 to 1920*, vol. 2 (New York: Doubleday, 1926) 6, 16–17, 58.

14. Pietrusza, *1920*, 45–47.

15. Ike Hoover, *Forty-Two Years in the White House* (Boston: Houghton Mifflin Company, 1934), 102; Lowry, *Washington Close-Ups*, 124.

16. Hoover, *Forty-Two Years*, 100, 102–3, 107–8; See also William Hazelgrove, *Madam President: The Secret Presidency of Edith Wilson* (Washington: Regnery History, 2016); Pietrusza, *1920*, 51.

17. Warren G. Harding to Frank Scobey, October 25, 1919, *Selections from the Papers and Speeches of Warren G. Harding, 1918–1923*, ed. Leonard Schlup and John H. Hepp IV (Lewiston, New York: The Edwin Mellen Press, 2008), 71.

18. Pietrusza, *1920*, 50.

19. Warren G. Harding to Frank Scobey, May 13, 1919, *Selections from the Papers and Speeches of Warren G. Harding, 1918–1923*, ed. Leonard Schlup and John H. Hepp IV (Lewiston, New York: The Edwin Mellen Press, 2008), 55.

20. John W. Dean, *Warren G. Harding* (New York: Times Books, 2004), 48–49; Harding, "Speech on the League of Nations," U.S. Senate, September 11, 1919, *Congressional Record*, 58, vol. 5, 5219–5225.

21. Pietrusza, *1920*, 49.

Chapter 2: 1919: The Year of Upheaval

Epigraph: Warren G. Harding to Frank Scobey, October 25, 1919, *Selections from the Papers and Speeches of Warren G. Harding, 1918–1923*, ed. Leonard Schlup and John H. Hepp IV (Lewiston, New York: The Edwin Mellen Press, 2008), 70.

1. James Grant, *The Forgotten Depression: 1921: The Crash That Cured Itself* (New York: Simon and Schuster, 2014), 66.
2. Ike Hoover, *Forty-Two Years in the White House* (Boston: Houghton Mifflin Company, 1934), 103.
3. Anthony Read, *The World on Fire: 1919 and the Battle with Bolshevism* (New York: W. W. Norton & Company, 2008), 91–92.
4. I first discovered this poem while reading Donald Rumsfeld's 2018 book on Gerald Ford, *When the Center Held: Gerald Ford and the Rescue of the American Presidency* (New York: Free Press, 2018).
5. Harding to Scobey, January 14, 1919, *Selections*, 49; Read, *The World on Fire*, 51, 92.
6. Read, *The World on Fire*, 53–54.
7. William Allen White, *The Autobiography of William Allen White* (New York: The Macmillan Company, 1946), 611.
8. H. L. Mencken, "The Clowns in the Ring," May 12, 1920; "Who's Loony Now," December 27, 1921, in Malcolm Moos, ed., *A Carnival of Buncombe* (Baltimore: The Johns Hopkins Press, 1956), 12, 47.
9. Ann Hagedorn, *Savage Peace: Hope and Fear in America 1919* (New York: Simon & Schuster, 2007), 184; Robert K. Murray, *Red Scare: A Study in National Hysteria, 1919–1920* (New York: McGraw-Hill Book Company, 1955), 69–70.
10. Hagedorn, *Savage Peace*, 184–85; Murray, *Red Scare*, 71.
11. Hagedorn, *Savage Peace*, 185–86; Murray, *Red Scare*, 73–77.
12. Hagedorn, *Savage Peace*, 221–22.
13. Eric Burns, *1920: The Year That Made the Decade Roar* (New York: Pegasus Books, 2015), 28; Hagedorn, *Savage Peace*, 218.
14. Hagedorn, *Savage Peace*, 218–20.
15. Ibid; Murray, *Red Scare*, 78–79; Burns, *1920*, 27.
16. Burns, *1920*, 27, 30.
17. Ibid., 29–31.
18. William E. Leuchtenburg, *The Perils of Prosperity, 1914–1932* (Chicago: The University of Chicago Press, 1958), 66; Burns, *1920*, 32.
19. Warren G. Harding, "Address Accepting the Republican Presidential Nomination," The American Presidency Project, https://www.presidency.ucsb.edu/documents/address-accepting-the-republican-presidential-nomination-2.
20. Cameron McWhirter, *Red Summer: The Summer of 1919 and the Awakening of Black America* (New York: St. Martin's Griffin, 2011), 13, 56.

21. Warren G. Harding to James R. Sheffield, January 24, 1919, *Selections from the Papers and Speeches of Warren G. Harding, 1918–1923*, ed. Leonard Schlup and John H. Hepp IV (Lewiston, New York: The Edwin Mellen Press, 2008), 51.

22. Isabel Wilkerson, *The Warmth of Other Suns: The Epic Story of America's Great Migration* (New York: Vintage, 2011), 8–11.

23. McWhirter, *Red Summer*, 13.

24. Hagedorn, *Savage Peace*, 312–16; McWhirter, *Red Summer*, 127–48.

25. Hagedorn, *Savage Peace*, 267, 377–78.

26. McWhirter, *Red Summer*, 68–71; Hagedorn, *Savage Peace*, 267–68. As it happens, Ellisville, Mississippi, is my hometown. On occasion my great-grandmother, who was thirteen years old in 1919, talked about the lynching and what townspeople at the time called the "hanging tree," a sweet gum near the railroad tracks running through the middle of town that had been used for that purpose more than once.

27. McWhirter, *Red Summer*, 71.

28. Read, *The World on Fire*, 92–93; Hagedorn, *Savage Peace*, 86–88, 380; Murray, *Red Scare*, 60–61.

29. Amity Shlaes and Matthew Denhart, eds., *The Autobiography of Calvin Coolidge* (Intercollegiate Studies Institute, 2021), 86.

30. Read, *The World on Fire*, 267–72.

31. Grant, *The Forgotten Depression: 1921*, 13–15.

32. Ibid., 17, 20.

33. Ibid., 20, 61.

34. Ibid., 66, 81; Thomas E. Woods Jr., "Warren Harding and the Forgotten Depression of 1920," *The Intercollegiate Review*, Fall 2009, 27.

35. Grant, *The Forgotten Depression: 1921*, 73, 77.

Chapter 3: The Fight for the Republican Presidential Nomination

Epigraph: Warren Harding, "Back to Normal," Address to the Home Market Club of Boston, May 14, 1920, in *Rededicating America: The Life and Recent Speeches of Warren Harding*, ed. Frederick E. Schortemeier (Indianapolis: The Bobbs-Merrill Company Publishers, 1920), 223–29.

1. Warren G. Harding to Malcolm Jennings, March 8, 1919, *Selections from the Papers and Speeches of Warren G. Harding, 1918–1923*, ed. Leonard Schlup and John H. Hepp IV (Lewiston, New York: The Edwin Mellen Press, 2008), 19.

2. David Pietrusza, *1920: The Year of Six Presidents* (New York: Carroll & Graf Publishers, 2007), 78.

3. Francis Russell, *The Shadow of Blooming Grove: Warren G. Harding in His Times* (New York: McGraw-Hill Book Company, 1968), 285–86; Theodore

Roosevelt to Warren Harding, April 30, 1917, *The Letters of Theodore Roosevelt*, ed. Elting E. Morison, vol. 8 (Cambridge: Harvard University Press, 1954), 1185.

4. Warren G. Harding to Theodore Roosevelt, July 18, 1918, *Selections from the Papers and Speeches of Warren G. Harding, 1918–1923*, ed. Leonard Schlup and John H. Hepp IV (Lewiston, New York: The Edwin Mellen Press, 2008), 31.

5. James E. Watson, *As I Knew Them: The Memoirs of James E. Watson* (New York: The Bobbs-Merrill Company Publishers, 1936), 219.

6. Wesley M. Bagby, *The Road to Normalcy: The Presidential Campaign and Election of 1920* (Baltimore: The Johns Hopkins Press, 1968), 25.

7. Alice Roosevelt Longworth, *Crowded Hours* (New York: Charles Scribner's Sons, 1932), 304.

8. Bagby, *The Road to Normalcy*, 26, 29.

9. H. L. Mencken, "The Clowns in the Ring," May 12, 1920, in Malcolm Moos, ed., *A Carnival of Buncombe* (Baltimore: The Johns Hopkins Press, 1956), 13.

10. Edward G. Lowry, *Washington Close-Ups: Intimate Views of Some Public Figures* (Boston: Houghton Mifflin Company, 1921), 93–94.

11. Bagby, *The Road to Normalcy*, 29.

12. Ibid., 31.

13. Mencken, "The Clowns in the Ring," 13–14.

14. Lowry, *Washington Close-Ups*, 50–51; Bagby, *The Road to Normalcy*, 32.

15. Bagby, *The Road to Normalcy*, 33.

16. Watson, *As I Knew Them*, 219; Bagby, *The Road to Normalcy*, 33–35.

17. Robert K. Murray, *The Harding Era: Warren G. Harding and His Administration* (Newtown, Connecticut: American Political Biography Press, 2012), 22.

18. Warren G. Harding to Frank Scobey, April 2, 1918, *Selections from the Papers and Speeches of Warren G. Harding, 1918–1923*, ed. Leonard Schlup and John H. Hepp IV (Lewiston, New York: The Edwin Mellen Press, 2008), 21–24; Pietrusza, *1920*, 81.

19. Warren G. Harding to Frank Scobey, January 14, 1919, and March 10, 1919, *Selections from the Papers and Speeches of Warren G. Harding, 1918–1923*, ed. Leonard Schlup and John H. Hepp IV (Lewiston, New York: The Edwin Mellen Press, 2008), 48, 52.

20. Watson, *As I Knew Them*, 209–10.

21. Warren G. Harding to Frank Scobey, October 25, 1919, *Selections from the Papers and Speeches of Warren G. Harding, 1918–1923*, ed. Leonard Schlup and John H. Hepp IV (Lewiston, New York: The Edwin Mellen Press, 2008), 70.

22. Warren G. Harding to Frank Scobey, November 22, 1919, *Selections from the Papers and Speeches of Warren G. Harding, 1918–1923*, ed. Leonard Schlup and John H. Hepp IV (Lewiston, New York: The Edwin Mellen Press, 2008), 75–76.

23. Warren G. Harding to Clare Hughes, December 16, 1919, and to Frank Scobey, December 16, 1919, *Selections from the Papers and Speeches of Warren G. Harding, 1918–1923*, ed. Leonard Schlup and John H. Hepp IV (Lewiston, New York: The Edwin Mellen Press, 2008), 81, 82.
24. Harry M. Daugherty, *The Inside Story of the Harding Tragedy* (Boston: Western Islands Press, 1975), 19.
25. Thomas A. Bailey, *Presidential Greatness: The Image and the Man from George Washington to the Present* (New York: Appleton-Century-Crofts, 1967), 313.
26. Warren G. Harding to Harry Daugherty, December 20, 1918, *Selections from the Papers and Speeches of Warren G. Harding, 1918–1923*, ed. Leonard Schlup and John H. Hepp IV (Lewiston, New York: The Edwin Mellen Press, 2008), 42.
27. Ibid., 45.
28. Bagby, *The Road to Normalcy*, 39.
29. Warren G. Harding to Charles E. Hard, December 12, 1918, *Selections from the Papers and Speeches of Warren G. Harding, 1918–1923*, ed. Leonard Schlup and John H. Hepp IV (Lewiston, New York: The Edwin Mellen Press, 2008), 39.
30. Warren G. Harding to Frank Scobey, December 16 and December 30, 1919, and November 22, 1919, *Selections from the Papers and Speeches of Warren G. Harding, 1918–1923*, ed. Leonard Schlup and John H. Hepp IV (Lewiston, New York: The Edwin Mellen Press, 2008), 83, 86, 75–76.
31. Bagby, *The Road to Normalcy*, 52–53; "Wood's Indiana Campaign Cost $60,333.78," *Baltimore Evening Sun*, June 3, 1920.
32. Warren G. Harding to Charles Forbes, April 1, 1920, *Selections from the Papers and Speeches of Warren G. Harding, 1918–1923*, ed. Leonard Schlup and John H. Hepp IV (Lewiston, New York: The Edwin Mellen Press, 2008), 96–97.
33. Bagby, *The Road to Normalcy*, 41; Robert K. Murray, *The Politics of Normalcy: Governmental Theory and Practice in the Harding-Coolidge Era* (New York: W. W. Norton & Co., 1973), 8; Harding to Frank Scobey, December 30, 1919, *Selections from the Papers and Speeches of Warren G. Harding, 1918–1923*, ed. Leonard Schlup and John H. Hepp IV (Lewiston, New York: The Edwin Mellen Press, 2008), 86, 88.
34. Bagby, *The Road to Normalcy*, 41; Watson, *As I Knew Them*, 219.
35. William Allen White, *Masks in a Pageant* (New York: Macmillan Company, 1928), 405.
36. Harding, "Back to Normal," in *Rededicating America*, 223–29.
37. Ibid.
38. Robert F. Martin, "Warren Gamaliel Harding, 1921–1923," in Melvin I. Urofsky, ed., *The American Presidents* (New York: Garland Publishing, Inc., 2000), 304; "Did Warren Harding Coin 'Normalcy'? Merriam-Webster, https://www.merriam-webster.com/words-at-play/did-warren-harding-coin-normalcy.
39. Bagby, *The Road to Normalcy*, 83; Daugherty, *The Inside Story*, 37.

40. Bagby, *The Road to Normalcy*, 83; William Allen White, *The Autobiography of William Allen White* (New York: The Macmillan Company, 1946), 585; Charles Willis Thompson, *Presidents I've Known and Two Near Presidents* (Indianapolis: The Bobbs-Merrill Company, 1929), 325.

41. Bagby, *The Road to Normalcy*, 83; Allen White, *The Autobiography of William Allen White*, 585; Willis Thompson, *Presidents I've Known and Two Near Presidents*, 325; Harry Carr, "Republican Nomination Hangs in the Balance," *Los Angeles Times*, June 12, 1920.

42. Bagby, *The Road to Normalcy*, 89.

43. Longworth, *Crowded Hours*, 312.

44. David F. Houston, *Eight Years with Wilson's Cabinet, 1913 to 1920*, vol. 2 (New York: Doubleday, 1926), 93.

45. Carr, "Republican Nomination."

46. E. O. Phillips, "Senators Agree on Harding as Dawn Arrives," *Chicago Daily Tribune*, June 13, 1920.

47. "Deadlock Part of Senate Plan for Dark Horse," *Public Ledger*, June 11, 1920.

48. Mark Sullivan, "Nomination of Harding Due to Senators' Desire to Control Government," *Baltimore Evening Sun*, June 14, 1920.

49. Oswald Garrison Villard, *Fighting Years: Memoirs of a Liberal Editor* (New York: Harcourt, Brace and Company, 1939), 474.

50. Murray, *The Politics of Normalcy*, 8.

51. Bailey, *Presidential Greatness*, 313.

52. Bruce Chadwick, *Lincoln for President: An Unlikely Candidate, An Audacious Strategy, and the Victory No One Saw Coming* (Naperville, Illinois: SourceBooks, Inc., 2009), 82–84.

53. Richard Hofstadter, *American Political Tradition and the Men Who Made It* (New York: Vintage Books, 1989), 223.

54. Watson, *As I Knew Them*, 218, 220.

55. Ibid., 220; Daugherty, *The Inside Story*, 7, 30, 33, 39–40.

56. Murray, *The Politics of Normalcy*, 8–9.

57. Harry Carr, "Country Editor from Ohio Wins Nomination," *Los Angeles Times*, June 13, 1920.

58. "Harding and Coolidge: Typical Republican Team!" *Public Ledger*, June 14, 1920; "Washington Gives Views on Harding," *Public Ledger*, June 13, 1920.

59. H. L. Mencken, "Bayard vs. Lionheart," July 26, 1920, and "In Praise of Gamaliel," October 18, 1920, in Malcolm Moos, ed., *A Carnival of Buncombe* (Baltimore: The Johns Hopkins Press, 1956), 15–16, 30.

60. Thompson, *Presidents I've Known*, 325, 327–28, 330, 332.

Chapter 4: The Election of 1920

Epigraph: Henry L. Stoddard, *As I Knew Them: Presidents and Politics from Grant to Coolidge* (New York: Harper & Brothers Publishers, 1927), 471.

1. William Allen White, *Masks in a Pageant* (New York: Macmillan Company, 1928), 397.
2. Charles Willis Thompson, *Presidents I've Known and Two Near Presidents* (Indianapolis: The Bobbs-Merrill Company, 1929), 341.
3. John W. Dean, *Warren G. Harding* (New York: Times Books, 2004), 14–21.
4. Stoddard, *As I Knew Them*, 473–74.
5. Edmund Starling, *Starling of the White House* (Chicago: People's Club Book, 1946) 169.
6. Warren G. Harding to Albert D. Lasker, May 15, 1922, *Selections from the Papers and Speeches of Warren G. Harding, 1918–1923*, ed. Leonard Schlup and John H. Hepp IV (Lewiston, New York: The Edwin Mellen Press, 2008), 315–16.
7. Charles Evans Hughes, *Autobiographical Notes*, ed. Daniel J. Danelski and Joseph S. Tulchin (Cambridge: Harvard University Press, 1973), 199.
8. James E. Watson, *As I Knew Them: The Memoirs of James E. Watson* (New York: The Bobbs-Merrill Company Publishers, 1936), 228.
9. Nicholas Murray Butler, *Across Busy Years: Recollections and Reflections*, vol. 1 (New York: Charles Scribner's Sons, 1935), 410.
10. Edward G. Lowry, *Washington Close-Ups: Intimate Views of Some Public Figures* (Boston: Houghton Mifflin Company, 1921), 18.
11. William G. McAdoo, *Crowded Years* (Boston: Houghton Mifflin Company, 1931), 388.
12. Oswald Garrison Villard, *Fighting Years: Memoirs of a Liberal Editor* (New York: Harcourt, Brace and Company, 1939), 474, 499.
13. White, *Masks*, 392.
14. Thompson, *Presidents I've Known*, 332–34, 336–37.
15. Warren G. Harding to the *Literary Digest*, November 4, 1920, *Selections from the Papers and Speeches of Warren G. Harding, 1918–1923*, ed. Leonard Schlup and John H. Hepp IV (Lewiston, New York: The Edwin Mellen Press, 2008), 161.
16. Thompson, *Presidents I've Known*, 338–339, 341; Jane and Burt McConnell, *The Presidents of the United States* (New York: Thomas Y. Crowell Company, 1951), 265.
17. Sheryl Smart Hall, *Warren G. Harding and the Marion Star: How Newspapering Shaped a President* (Charleston: The History Press, 2014), 56.
18. Eugene P. Trani and David L. Wilson, *The Presidency of Warren G. Harding* (Lawrence: University Press of Kansas, 1977), 173.
19. Hall, *Warren G. Harding*, 64–65; Brady Carlson, *Dead Presidents: An American Adventure into the Strange Deaths and Surprising Afterlives of Our Nation's Leaders* (New York: W. W. Norton and Company, 2016), 225.
20. Starling, *Starling of the White House*, 165–66.
21. Watson, *As I Knew Them*, 224; "Second Place Not for Hiram Johnson," *Baltimore Evening Sun*, June 2, 1920; Harold L. Ickes, *The Autobiography of a Curmudgeon* (New York: Reynal & Hitchcock, 1943), 235.

22. Stoddard, *As I Knew Them*, 467–68; William Allen White, *The Autobiography of William Allen White* (New York: The Macmillan Company, 1946), 588; Watson, *As I Knew Them*, 225; Calvin Coolidge, *The Autobiography of Calvin Coolidge* (New York: Cosmopolitan Book Corporation, 1929), 148.

23. Coolidge, *The Autobiography*, 141, 143.

24. Robert Sobel, *Coolidge: An American Enigma* (Washington, D.C.: Regnery Publishing, 1998), 236; David Greenberg, *Calvin Coolidge* (New York: Times Books, 2006), 10.

25. Lowry, *Washington Close-Ups*, 27; Edward Connery Lathem, ed., *Meet Calvin Coolidge: The Man Behind the Myth* (Brattleboro, Vermont: The Stephen Greene Press, 1960), 59–60.

26. "Harding and Coolidge: Typical Republican Team!" *Public Ledger*, June 14, 1920.

27. Villard, *Fighting Years*, 474; Claude M. Fuess, *Calvin Coolidge: The Man from Vermont* (Boston: Little, Brown, and Company, 1940), 269, 252.

28. Ickes, *The Autobiography*, 9, 229–34.

29. Alice Roosevelt Longworth, *Crowded Hours* (New York: Charles Scribner's Sons, 1932), 180, 203, 311.

30. Thompson, *Presidents I've Known*, 330–31.

31. White, *The Autobiography*, 586; William Allen White to Warren G. Harding, July 10, 1920, *Selected Letters of William Allen White, 1899-1943*, ed. Walter Johnson (New York: Henry Holt Company, 1947), 206.

32. Warren G. Harding to William Howard Taft, June 30, 1920, *Selections from the Papers and Speeches of Warren G. Harding, 1918–1923*, ed. Leonard Schlup and John H. Hepp IV (Lewiston, New York: The Edwin Mellen Press, 2008), 106; Charles Evans Hughes, *The Autobiographical Notes of Charles Evans Hughes*, ed. David J. Danelski and Joseph S. Tulchin (Cambridge: Harvard University Press, 1973), 196–97; William G. Harding to Henry Cabot Lodge, September 6, 1920, *Selections from the Papers and Speeches of Warren G. Harding, 1918–1923*, ed. Leonard Schlup and John H. Hepp IV (Lewiston, New York: The Edwin Mellen Press, 2008), 142.

33. Harding to Henry Cabot Lodge, July 6, 1920, *Selections from the Papers and Speeches of Warren G. Harding, 1918–1923*, ed. Leonard Schlup and John H. Hepp IV (Lewiston, New York: The Edwin Mellen Press, 2008), 110; Stoddard, *As I Knew Them*, 471.

34. Warren G. Harding, "Address Accepting the Republican Presidential Nomination," The American Presidency Project, https://www.presidency.ucsb.edu/documents/address-accepting-the-republican-presidential-nomination-2.

35. Ike Hoover, *Forty-Two Years in the White House* (Boston: Houghton Mifflin Company, 1934), 106; "Washington Seething with Politics," *The Protectionist*, vol. 32 (May 1920–April 1921), 30.

36. Kenneth Whyte, *Hoover: An Extraordinary Life in Extraordinary Times* (New York: Vintage Books, 2017), 202; Jules Witcover, *Party of the People: A History*

of the Democrats (New York: Random House, 2003), 334; McAdoo, *Crowded Years*, 191.

37. Warren G. Harding to Joe Mitchell Chapple, October 12, 1920, *Selections from the Papers and Speeches of Warren G. Harding, 1918–1923*, ed. Leonard Schlup and John H. Hepp IV (Lewiston, New York: The Edwin Mellen Press, 2008), 152. Chapple was the editor of *National Magazine*.
38. Robert K. Murray, *The Harding Era: Warren G. Harding and His Administration* (Newtown, Connecticut: American Political Biography Press, 2012), 50–51.
39. Wesley M. Bagby, *The Road to Normalcy: The Presidential Campaign and Election of 1920* (Baltimore: The Johns Hopkins Press, 1968), 128–29.
40. Witcover, *Party of the People*, 334.
41. Bagby, *The Road to Normalcy*, 136, 138; Harding to Hiram Johnson, September 6, 1920, *Selections from the Papers and Speeches of Warren G. Harding, 1918–1923*, ed. Leonard Schlup and John H. Hepp IV (Lewiston, New York: The Edwin Mellen Press, 2008), 143.
42. David F. Houston, *Eight Years with Wilson's Cabinet, 1913 to 1920* (New York: Doubleday, 1926), 92–93.
43. "Washington Gives Views on Harding," *Public Ledger*, June 13, 1920.
44. Carlson, *Dead Presidents*, 224; Bagby, *The Road to Normalcy*, 152–53.
45. Bagby, *The Road to Normalcy*, 159.
46. "Tennessee Caught in G.O.P. Cyclone," *Memphis Commercial Appeal*, November 4, 1920.
47. David Pietrusza, *1920: The Year of Six Presidents* (New York: Carroll & Graf Publishers, 2007), 413.
48. Lewis L. Gould, *The Modern American Presidency* (Lawrence, Kansas: University Press of Kansas, 2003), 59.
49. "Eight Years of Democratic Incompetency and Waste are Drawing Rapidly to a Close," *Los Angeles Times*, November 3, 1920.
50. Thompson, *Presidents I've Known*, 329.
51. White, *Masks*, 409; William Allen White, *A Puritan in Babylon: The Story of Calvin Coolidge* (New York: Macmillan Company, 1938), 104; White, *The Autobiography*, 587.
52. H. L. Mencken, "In Praise of Gamaliel," October 18, 1920, in *A Carnival of Buncombe*, ed. Malcolm Moos (Baltimore: The Johns Hopkins Press, 1956), 30–31.
53. *Baltimore Evening Sun*, November 3, 1920.
54. White, *Masks*, 409; H. L. Mencken, "A Carnival of Buncombe," February 9, 1920, in *A Carnival of Buncombe*, ed. Malcolm Moos (Baltimore: The Johns Hopkins Press, 1956), 6.

Chapter 5: The Harding Administration

Epigraph: Warren G. Harding to Louis F. Hart, August 16, 1920, *Selections from the Papers and Speeches of Warren G. Harding, 1918–1923*, ed. Leonard Schlup and John H. Hepp IV (Lewiston, New York: The Edwin Mellen Press, 2008), 135.

1. Bret Hall, "Taking the Presidential Oath: A Look Back at President Harding's Inauguration 96 Years Ago," The Harding Home, January 20, 2017, https://www.hardinghome.org/taking-the-presidential-oath-a-look-back-at-president-hardings-inauguration-96-years-ago/.
2. Warren G. Harding, "Inaugural Address," The American Presidency Project, https://www.presidency.ucsb.edu/documents/inaugural-address-49.
3. Calvin Coolidge, *The Autobiography of Calvin Coolidge* (New York: Cosmopolitan Book Corporation, 1929), 153.
4. "Harding's Advent Means New Prosperity," *Los Angeles Times*, March 5, 1921.
5. "Ave, Harding," *Chicago Daily Tribune*, March 4, 1921.
6. Robert K. Murray, *The Harding Era: Warren G. Harding and His Administration* (Newtown, Connecticut: American Political Biography Press, 2012), 122.
7. H. L. Mencken, "Harding Faces Task with Air of Confidence," *Baltimore Evening Sun*, March 4, 1921, in *A Carnival of Buncombe*, ed. Malcolm Moos (Baltimore: The Johns Hopkins Press, 1956).
8. H. L. Mencken, "Gamalielese," *Baltimore Evening Sun*, March 7, 1921, in *A Carnival of Buncombe*, ed. Malcolm Moos (Baltimore: The Johns Hopkins Press, 1956), 39.
9. Nathan Miller, *Star-Spangled Men: America's Ten Worst Presidents* (New York: A Touchstone Book, 1998), 192.
10. Ibid.
11. Murray, *The Harding Era*, 122.
12. "A Good Official Style," *New York Times*, April 24, 1921.
13. "Ave, Harding."
14. Murray, *The Harding Era*, 92.
15. "Mr. Harding for Simplicity," *The Nation*, January 19, 1921, 72.
16. Lewis L. Gould, *The Modern American Presidency* (Lawrence, Kansas: University Press of Kansas, 2003), 59.
17. Edward G. Lowry, *Washington Close-Ups: Intimate Views of Some Public Figures* (Boston: Houghton Mifflin Company, 1921), 13–14.
18. Eugene P. Trani and David L. Wilson, *The Presidency of Warren G. Harding* (Lawrence: University Press of Kansas, 1977), 36; John W. Dean, *Warren G. Harding* (New York: Times Books, 2004), 97; Andrew Sinclair, *The Available Man: The Life Behind the Masks of Warren G. Harding* (Chicago: Quadrangle Books, 1965), 222; Robert H. Ferrell, *The Strange Deaths of President Harding* (Columbia: University of Missouri Press, 1996), 3.

19. Charles Evans Hughes, *The Autobiographical Notes of Charles Evans Hughes*, ed. David J. Danelski and Joseph S. Tulchin (Cambridge: Harvard University Press, 1973), 200.

20. Lowry, *Washington Close-Ups*, 20.

21. Ronald Radosh and Allis Radosh, "Rethinking Warren Harding," *New York Times*, August 27, 2015.

22. Lowry, *Washington Close-Ups*, 19.

23. Harding to Hart, August 16, 1920, *Selections*, 135; "A Restatement of Senator Harding's Position," *The Outlook*, October 27, 1920, 356.

24. Warren G. Harding to Malcolm Jennings, December 14, 1920, Jennings Papers, as quoted in Sinclair, *The Available Man*; Charles Dawes to Warren G. Harding, January 25, 1921, Harding Papers, as quoted in Sinclair, *The Available Man*.

25. Warren G. Harding to William F. Anderson, February 20, 1921, *Selections from the Papers and Speeches of Warren G. Harding, 1918–1923*, ed. Leonard Schlup and John H. Hepp IV (Lewiston, New York: The Edwin Mellen Press, 2008), 177–78.

26. Dean, *Warren G. Harding*, 82.

27. David S. Barry, *Forty Years in Washington* (Boston: Little, Brown, and Company, 1924), 272.

28. Paul Johnson, *History of the American People* (New York: HarperCollins Publishers, 1997), 708.

29. Miller, *Star-Spangled Men*, 203.

30. Coolidge, *The Autobiography*, 154–55.

31. James E. Watson, *As I Knew Them: The Memoirs of James E. Watson* (New York: The Bobbs-Merrill Company Publishers, 1936), 223.

32. Michael Nelson, ed., *Guide to the Presidency* (London: Routledge Press, 1997), 163.

33. David Pietrusza, *1920: The Year of Six Presidents* (New York: Carroll & Graf Publishers, 2007), 17; Nelson, ed., *Guide*, 163.

34. Thomas Jefferson to Elbridge Gerry, May 13, 1797, *The Papers of Thomas Jefferson*, ed. Barbara B. Oberg, vol. 29 (Princeton: Princeton University Press, 2002), 361–65.

35. Amity Shlaes, *Coolidge* (New York: Harper Collins, 2013), 202; Coolidge, *The Autobiography*, 148.

36. Claude M. Fuess, *Calvin Coolidge: The Man from Vermont* (Boston: Little, Brown, and Company, 1940), 269.

37. Dean, *Warren G. Harding*, 98.

38. David Cannadine, *Mellon: An American Life* (New York: Vintage Books, 2006), 279.

39. Sinclair, *The Available Man*, 185; James Grant, *The Forgotten Depression 1921: The Crash That Cured Itself* (New York: Simon and Schuster, 2014), 136; Cannadine, *Mellon*, 279.

40. Lowry, *Washington Close-Ups*, 154.

41. Gould, *Grand Old Party*, 233.

42. Larry Schweikart and Michael Allen, *A Patriot's History of the United States* (Sentinel, 2004), 536.

43. Cannadine, *Mellon*, 280; Lowry, *Washington Close-Ups*, 212.

44. Kenneth Whyte, *Hoover: An Extraordinary Life in Extraordinary Times* (New York: Vintage Books, 2017), xi, 122.

45. Whyte, *Hoover*, 195, 212.

46. Lowry, *Washington Close-Ups*, 206; Cannadine, *Mellon*, 28.

47. Warren G. Harding to Harry Daugherty, February 9, 1921, *Selections from the Papers and Speeches of Warren G. Harding, 1918–1923*, ed. Leonard Schlup and John H. Hepp IV (Lewiston, New York: The Edwin Mellen Press, 2008), 173.

48. Herbert Hoover, *The Memoirs of Herbert Hoover: The Cabinet and the Presidency, 1920–1933* (New York: The Macmillan Company, 1952), 10, 36.

49. Sinclair, *The Available Man*, 184.

50. Warren G. Harding to Charles Dawes, June 9, 1921, *Selections from the Papers and Speeches of Warren G. Harding, 1918–1923*, ed. Leonard Schlup and John H. Hepp IV (Lewiston, New York: The Edwin Mellen Press, 2008), 204.

51. Annette B. Dunlap, *Charles Gates Dawes: A Life* (Evanston: Northwestern University Press, 2016).

Chapter 6: Rebuilding a Depressed Economy

Epigraph: Warren G. Harding, "Inaugural Address," The American Presidency Project, https://www.presidency.ucsb.edu/documents/inaugural-address-49.

1. David Cannadine, *Mellon: An American Life* (New York: Vintage Books, 2006), 278.

2. James Grant, "How Austerity Cured a Depression," *Washington Post*, January 19, 2012.

3. Ibid., 2–5.

4. Ibid., 136.

5. Harding, "Inaugural Address."

6. Eugene P. Trani, "Warren G. Harding: Life in Brief," University of Virginia Miller Center, https://millercenter.org/president/harding/life-in-brief.

7. Steven R. Weisman, *The Great Tax Wars: Lincoln to Wilson—the Fierce Battles over Money and Power That Transformed the Nation* (New York: Simon & Schuster, 2002), 86–87, 149.

8. "An Unnecessary Amendment," *New York Times*, July 8, 1909.

9. Weisman, *The Great Tax Wars*, 283.

10. Brion McClanahan, *9 Presidents Who Screwed Up America: And Four Who Tried to Save Her* (Washington, D.C.: Regnery History, 2016), 69–72.

11. Robert Higgs, "How War Amplified Federal Power in the Twentieth Century," Foundation for Economic Education, https://fee.org/articles/how-war-amplified-federal-power-in-the-twentieth-century/.

12. John W. Dean, *Warren G. Harding* (New York: Times Books, 2004), 96–97.

13. Warren G. Harding, "Address to a Joint Session of Congress on Urgent National Problems," The American Presidency Project, https://www.presidency.ucsb.edu /documents/address-joint-session-congress-urgent-national-problems.

14. Dean, *Warren G. Harding*, 97.

15. Charles Evans Hughes, *Autobiographical Notes*, ed. Daniel J. Danelski and Joseph S. Tulchin (Cambridge: Harvard University Press, 1973), 201.

16. William Allen White, *Masks in a Pageant* (New York: Macmillan Company, 1928), 413.

17. Henry L. Stoddard, *As I Knew Them: Presidents and Politics from Grant to Coolidge* (New York: Harper & Brothers Publishers, 1927), 475–76.

18. Maury Klein, *Rainbow's End: The Crash of 1929* (Oxford: Oxford University Press, 2001), 67.

19. "Wall Street Sees Better Times after Election," *Wall Street Journal*, November 2, 1920; "Eight Years of Democratic Incompetency and Waste Are Drawing Rapidly to a Close," *Los Angeles Times*, November 3, 1920; "Harding's Advent Means New Prosperity," and "Inauguration 'Let's Go!' Signal to Business," *Los Angeles Times*, March 5, 1921.

20. White, *Masks in a Pageant*, 163–64.

21. Cannadine, *Mellon*, 287; Grant, "How Austerity Cured a Depression," 145; Robert P. Murphy, *The Politically Incorrect Guide to the Great Depression and the New Deal* (Washington: Regnery Publishing, 2009), 85.

22. Grant, "How Austerity Cured a Depression," 147; Cannadine, *Mellon*, 288.

23. Grant, "How Austerity Cured a Depression," 164.

24. Warren G. Harding to M. B. Lamble, June 8, 1923, *Selections from the Papers and Speeches of Warren G. Harding, 1918–1923*, ed. Leonard Schlup and John H. Hepp IV (Lewiston, New York: The Edwin Mellen Press, 2008), 435.

25. James Grant, *The Forgotten Depression: 1921: The Crash That Cured Itself* (New York: Simon and Schuster, 2014), 136; *Historical Tables: Budget of the US Government* (Washington, D.C.: Office of Management and Budget, 2016), 26, https://www.govinfo.gov/content/pkg/BUDGET-2016-TAB/pdf/BUDGET -2016-TAB.pdf.

26. Warren G. Harding to Joseph Medill McCormick, August 29, 1921, *Selections from the Papers and Speeches of Warren G. Harding, 1918–1923*, ed. Leonard Schlup and John H. Hepp IV (Lewiston, New York: The Edwin Mellen Press, 2008), 233.

27. Grant, *The Forgotten Depression*, 164.

28. Edward G. Lowry, *Washington Close-Ups: Intimate Views of Some Public Figures* (Boston: Houghton Mifflin Company, 1921), 153–54.

29. Warren G. Harding to Joseph Medill McCormick, August 29, 1921, *Selections from the Papers and Speeches of Warren G. Harding, 1918–1923*, ed. Leonard Schlup and John H. Hepp IV (Lewiston, New York: The Edwin Mellen Press, 2008), 233.

30. Grant, "How Austerity Cured a Depression," 137.

31. Ibid.

32. John A. Moore, "The Original Supply Siders: Warren Harding and Calvin Coolidge," *The Independent Review* 18, no. 4 (Spring 2014), 604, https://www.independent.org/publications/tir/article.asp?id=991.

33. Ibid.; Carlton Jackson, *Presidential Vetoes, 1792–1945* (Athens, Georgia: University Press of Georgia, 1967), 187–88.

34. Moore, "The Original Supply Siders," 604; Jackson, *Presidential Vetoes,* 187–88; Warren G. Harding, "Address to the Senate Urging Unfavorable Action Upon Bill to Adjust Compensation of Veterans of the World War," The American Presidency Project, https://www.presidency.ucsb.edu/documents/address-the-senate-urging-unfavorable-action-upon-bill-adjust-compensation-veterans-the.

35. Cannadine, *Mellon,* 288.

36. Warren G. Harding to an unknown Congressman, February 7, 1922, *Selections from the Papers and Speeches of Warren G. Harding, 1918–1923,* ed. Leonard Schlup and John H. Hepp IV (Lewiston, New York: The Edwin Mellen Press, 2008), 292.

37. Warren Harding to Joseph W. Fordney, February 16, 1922, *Selections from the Papers and Speeches of Warren G. Harding, 1918–1923,* ed. Leonard Schlup and John H. Hepp IV (Lewiston, New York: The Edwin Mellen Press, 2008), 293–95.

38. Warren G. Harding, "Message to the House of Representatives Returning without Approval a Bill to Provide Adjusted Compensation for World War Veterans," The American Presidency Project, https://www.presidency.ucsb.edu/documents/message-the-house-representatives-returning-without-approval-bill-provide-adjusted.

39. Jackson, *Presidential Vetoes,* 188–89.

40. Warren G. Harding to Charles Dawes, September 26, 1922, *Selections from the Papers and Speeches of Warren G. Harding, 1918–1923,* ed. Leonard Schlup and John H. Hepp IV (Lewiston, New York: The Edwin Mellen Press, 2008), 349.

41. Jackson, *Presidential Vetoes,* 189.

42. "Justice Inevitable," *Chicago Daily Tribune,* September 21, 1922.

43. H. L. Mencken, "Making Ready For 1924," April 2, 1923, in *A Carnival of Buncombe,* ed. Malcolm Moos (Baltimore: The Johns Hopkins Press, 1956), 51–52.

44. Warren G. Harding to Joseph Medill McCormick, August 29, 1921, *Selections from the Papers and Speeches of Warren G. Harding, 1918–1923,* ed. Leonard Schlup and John H. Hepp IV (Lewiston, New York: The Edwin Mellen Press, 2008), 232.

45. Cannadine, *Mellon,* 286–87, 292.

46. Warren G. Harding, "Address Accepting the Republican Presidential Nomination," The American Presidency Project, https://www.presidency.ucsb.edu/documents/address-accepting-the-republican-presidential-nomination-2.

47. Harding, "Inaugural Address."

48. Harding, "Address to a Joint Session of Congress."
49. Trani, "Warren G. Harding," 39; Alfred E. Eckes Jr., *Opening America's Market: U.S. Foreign Trade Policy since 1776* (Chapel Hill: University of North Carolina Press, 1995), 88; Harding, "Address to a Joint Session of Congress."
50. Cannadine, *Mellon*, 310; Susan B. Carter et al., eds., *Historical Statistics of the United States* (Cambridge: Cambridge University Press, 2006), 224. Adjusted for inflation, according to one site, the numbers would be $687.7 billion for 1920, $671.9 billion for 1921, $709.3 billion for 1922, $802.6 billion for 1923, and $977.0 billion for 1929. See Kimberly Amadeo, "1920s Economy," The Balance, May 15, 2018, https://www.thebalance.com/roaring-twenties -4060511.
51. Moore, "The Original Supply Siders," 601.
52. Thomas E. Woods Jr., "Warren Harding and the Forgotten Depression of 1920," *Intercollegiate Review*, Fall 2009, 29.
53. Thomas E. Woods, "The Harding Way," May 4, 2009, *The American Conservative*, https://www.theamericanconservative.com/articles/the-harding -way/.
54. Grant, "How Austerity Cured a Depression."
55. Moore, "The Original Supply Siders," 598.
56. Jim Powell, "America's Greatest Depression Fighter," LewRockwell.com, December 23, 2003, https://www.lewrockwell.com/2003/12/jim-powell/ americas-greatest-depressionfighter-no-it-wasnt-franklin-delano-roosevelt/.
57. Calvin Coolidge, *The Autobiography of Calvin Coolidge* (New York: Cosmopolitan Book Corporation, 1929), 153.

Chapter 7: Putting America First

Epigraph: "January 20, 1920: Americanism," University of Virginia Miller Center, https://millercenter.org/the-presidency/presidential-speeches/january-20-1920 -americanism.
1. Robert K. Murray, *The Harding Era: Warren G. Harding and His Administration* (Newtown, Connecticut: American Political Biography Press, 2012), 265.
2. Warren G. Harding, Address of the Temporary Chairman, Republican National Convention, June 7, 1916, *Official Report of the Proceedings of the Sixteenth Republican National Convention* (New York: The Tenny Press, 1916), 14–28.
3. Chauncey M. Depew, *My Memories of Eighty Years* (New York: Charles Scribner's Sons, 1921), 339–40.
4. Eugene P. Trani and David L. Wilson, *The Presidency of Warren G. Harding* (Lawrence, Kansas: University Press of Kansas, 1977), 109.
5. Ibid., 110–11.
6. Edward G. Lowry, *Washington Close-Ups: Intimate Views of Some Public Figures* (Boston: Houghton Mifflin Company, 1921), 168.

7. Trani and Wilson, *The Presidency of Warren G. Harding*, 109–10; Charles Evans Hughes, *Autobiographical Notes*, ed. Daniel J. Danelski and Joseph S. Tulchin (Cambridge: Harvard University Press, 1973), 199, 202.

8. Charles Evans Hughes, "America First and America Efficient," in Charles Evans Hughes, *Addresses of Charles Evans Hughes* (New York: G. P. Putnam's Sons, 1916), 8–46.

9. Warren G. Harding, "Inaugural Address," The American Presidency Project, https://www.presidency.ucsb.edu/documents/inaugural-address-49.

10. Ibid.

11. "A Restatement of Senator Harding's Position," *The Outlook*, October 27, 1920, 356.

12. Warren G. Harding to Jacob Gould Schurman, September 15, 1920, as quoted in "Mr. Harding Writes A Letter," *Advocate of Peace Through Justice* 82, no. 9 (September/October 1920), 308–9.

13. Ibid.

14. Warren G. Harding to Henry Cabot Lodge, December 29, 1920, *Selections from the Papers and Speeches of Warren G. Harding, 1918–1923*, ed. Leonard Schlup and John H. Hepp IV (Lewiston, New York: The Edwin Mellen Press, 2008), 168.

15. Trani and Wilson, *The Presidency of Warren G. Harding*, 147; Warren G. Harding to Earl D. Bloom, March 4, 1923, *Selections from the Papers and Speeches of Warren G. Harding, 1918–1923*, ed. Leonard Schlup and John H. Hepp IV (Lewiston, New York: The Edwin Mellen Press, 2008), 414.

16. Trani and Wilson, *The Presidency of Warren G. Harding*, 144–45.

17. Ibid., 117–20.

18. Ibid., 122–23.

19. James David Robenalt, *The Harding Affair: Love and Espionage during the Great War* (St. Martin's Press, 2009), 4.

20. Warren G. Harding to Alvaro Obregon, July 21, 1921, *Selections from the Papers and Speeches of Warren G. Harding, 1918–1923*, ed. Leonard Schlup and John H. Hepp IV (Lewiston, New York: The Edwin Mellen Press, 2008), 212.

21. Warren G. Harding to Joseph Medill McCormick, and Harding to Charles Evans Hughes, February 6, 1922, *Selections*, 290–91; Harding to Charles Evans Hughes, May 5, 1922, *Selections from the Papers and Speeches of Warren G. Harding, 1918–1923*, ed. Leonard Schlup and John H. Hepp IV (Lewiston, New York: The Edwin Mellen Press, 2008), 311.

22. Trani and Wilson, *The Presidency of Warren G. Harding*, 236.

23. Murray, *The Harding Era*, 144–45.

24. Trani and Wilson, *The Presidency of Warren G. Harding*, 151.

25. Richard M. Langworth, "Churchill and the Presidents: Warren Harding," The Churchill Project, Hillsdale College, July 30, 2015.

26. Warren G. Harding to Wallace R. Farrington, September 8, 1921, *Selections from the Papers and Speeches of Warren G. Harding, 1918–1923*, ed. Leonard

Schlup and John H. Hepp IV (Lewiston, New York: The Edwin Mellen Press, 2008), 237.

27. Murray, *The Harding Era*, 144.

28. Warren G. Harding, Address at the Opening of the Conference on Limitations of Armaments, November 12, 1921, *Selections from the Papers and Speeches of Warren G. Harding, 1918–1923*, ed. Leonard Schlup and John H. Hepp IV (Lewiston, New York: The Edwin Mellen Press, 2008), 258–61.

29. Trani and Wilson, *The Presidency of Warren G. Harding*, 153–54.

30. Ibid.; Murray, *The Harding Era*, 140.

31. Warren G. Harding to Joseph Medill McCormick, August 29, 1921, *Selections from the Papers and Speeches of Warren G. Harding, 1918–1923*, ed. Leonard Schlup and John H. Hepp IV (Lewiston, New York: The Edwin Mellen Press, 2008), 233.

32. Patrick J. Buchanan, *A Republic, Not an Empire: Reclaiming America's Destiny* (Washington, D.C.: Regnery, 1999), 233.

33. Warren G. Harding to Wallace R. Farrington, September 8, 1921, *Selections from the Papers and Speeches of Warren G. Harding, 1918–1923*, ed. Leonard Schlup and John H. Hepp IV (Lewiston, New York: The Edwin Mellen Press, 2008), 239.

34. Buchanan, *A Republic, Not an Empire*, 234.

35. Warren G. Harding to Jere H. Barr, January 16, 1922, *Selections from the Papers and Speeches of Warren G. Harding, 1918–1923*, ed. Leonard Schlup and John H. Hepp IV (Lewiston, New York: The Edwin Mellen Press, 2008), 277.

36. Alice Roosevelt Longworth, *Crowded Hours* (New York: Charles Scribner's Sons, 1932), 318.

37. Oswald Garrison Villard, *Fighting Years: Memoirs of a Liberal Editor* (New York: Harcourt, Brace and Company, 1939), 497, 500.

38. William Allen White, *The Autobiography of William Allen White* (New York: The Macmillan Company, 1946), 597–98.

39. Edmund Starling, *Starling of the White House* (Chicago: People's Club Book, 1946), 183.

40. Thomas A. Bailey, *Presidential Greatness: The Image and the Man from George Washington to the Present* (New York: Appleton-Century-Crofts, 1967), 280.

41. Maxim Ethan Armbruster, *The Presidents of the United States and Their Administrations, from Washington to Nixon* (New York: Horizon Press, 1969), 280; Bailey, *Presidential Greatness*, 280.

42. William Allen White, *Masks in a Pageant* (New York: Macmillan Company, 1928), 165; David Cannadine, *Mellon: An American Life* (New York: Vintage Books, 2006), 289.

43. Cannadine, *Mellon*, 278.

44. Ibid., 290.

45. Ibid., 290–91.

46. "January 20, 1920: Americanism."
47. Warren G. Harding to Henry C. Wallace, January 24, 1922, *Selections from the Papers and Speeches of Warren G. Harding, 1918–1923*, ed. Leonard Schlup and John H. Hepp IV (Lewiston, New York: The Edwin Mellen Press, 2008), 285.
48. Alfred E. Eckes Jr., *Opening America's Market: U.S. Foreign Trade Policy Since 1776* (Chapel Hill: University of North Carolina Press, 1995), 89.
49. Warren G. Harding to Porter J. McCumber, August 11, 1922, *Selections from the Papers and Speeches of Warren G. Harding, 1918–1923*, ed. Leonard Schlup and John H. Hepp IV (Lewiston, New York: The Edwin Mellen Press, 2008), 331.
50. Eckes, *Opening America's Market*.
51. Bailey, *Presidential Greatness*, 314.
52. Theodore Roosevelt, "First Annual Message to Congress," The American Presidency Project, https://www.presidency.ucsb.edu/documents/first-annual-message-16.
53. Murray, *The Harding Era*, 266–68.
54. Warren G. Harding to Joseph Medill McCormick, August 29, 1921, *Selections*, 234.
55. Murray, *The Harding Era*, 26–68; Trani and Wilson, *The Presidency of Warren G. Harding*, 60–61; Buchanan, *A Republic*, 231.
56. Ibid., 234.

Chapter 8: Harding, National Healer

Epigraph: Warren G. Harding, Speech on Race Relations, Birmingham, Alabama, October 26, 1921, *Selections from the Papers and Speeches of Warren G. Harding, 1918–1923*, ed. Leonard Schlup and John H. Hepp IV (Lewiston, New York: The Edwin Mellen Press, 2008), 248–53.
1. Nick Salvatore, *Eugene V. Debs: Citizen and Socialist* (Urbana: University of Illinois Press, 1984), 225.
2. Ernest Freeberg, *Democracy's Prisoner: Eugene V. Debs, the Great War, and the Right to Dissent* (Cambridge: Harvard University Press, 2008), 13.
3. Ibid., 72.
4. Thomas Fleming, *Illusion of Victory: America in World War I* (New York: Basic Books, 2003), 247; Eugene Debs, "The Subject Class Always Fights the Battles," in *We Who Dared to Say No to War: American Antiwar Writing From 1812 to Now*, ed. Murray Polner and Thomas E. Woods Jr. (New York: Basic Books, 2008), 148–55.
5. Fleming, *Illusion of Victory*, 247.
6. Jonah Goldberg, *Liberal Fascism: The Secret History of the American Left, from Mussolini to the Politics of Meaning* (New York: Doubleday, 2007), 112–13.
7. Fleming, *Illusion of Victory*, 253.

8. H. L. Mencken, "Carnival of Buncombe," February 9, 1920, in *A Carnival of Buncombe*, ed. Malcolm Moos (Baltimore: The Johns Hopkins Press, 1956).

9. Goldberg, *Liberal Fascism*, 114; Robert Higgs, "How War Amplified Federal Power in the Twentieth Century," Foundation for Economic Education, July 1, 1999, https://fee.org/articles/how-war-amplified-federal-power-in-the-twentieth-century/.

10. Warren G. Harding to Malcolm Jennings, January 6, 1922, *Selections from the Papers and Speeches of Warren G. Harding, 1918–1923*, ed. Leonard Schlup and John H. Hepp IV (Lewiston, New York: The Edwin Mellen Press, 2008), 268.

11. John W. Dean, *Warren G. Harding* (New York: Times Books, 2004), 127–28.

12. Robert K. Murray, *The Harding Era: Warren G. Harding and His Administration* (Newtown, Connecticut: American Political Biography Press, 2012), 166–69; Dean, *Warren G. Harding*, 127–29.

13. Oswald Garrison Villard, *Fighting Years: Memoirs of a Liberal Editor* (New York: Harcourt, Brace and Company, 1939), 499; Charles F. Faber and Richard B. Faber, *American Presidents Ranked By Performance* (London: McFarland & Company, Inc., 2000), 189.

14. Bruce Bartlett, *Wrong on Race: The Democratic Party's Buried Past* (New York: Palgrave Macmillan, 2008), 107–10.

15. Carl S. Anthony, "The Most Scandalous President," *American Heritage* 49, no. 4, (August 1998), https://www.americanheritage.com/content/most-scandalous-president.

16. Sheryl Smart Hall, *Warren G. Harding and the Marion Star: How Newspapering Shaped a President* (Charleston: The History Press, 2014), 66.

17. Warren G. Harding to E. J. Miller, January 2, 1920, *Selections from the Papers and Speeches of Warren G. Harding, 1918–1923*, ed. Leonard Schlup and John H. Hepp IV (Lewiston, New York: The Edwin Mellen Press, 2008), 89–92.

18. Dean, *Warren G. Harding*, 124; Randy Krehbiel, *Tulsa 1921: Reporting a Massacre* (Norman: University Press of Oklahoma, 2019), 27.

19. Cameron McWhirter, *Red Summer: The Summer of 1919 and the Awakening of Black America* (New York: St. Martin's Griffin, 2011), 32–35.

20. "The Tulsa Riots," *The Crisis* 22, no. 3 (July 1921), 116; "Whites Advancing Into 'Little Africa'; Negro Death List Is About 15," *Tulsa Daily World*, June 1, 1921; "68 Negros, 9 Whites Dead in Tulsa Race War. Martial Law Is Declared," *Durant Weekly News*, June 3, 1921; "The Tulsa Race Riot: A Report by the Oklahoma Commission to Study the Tulsa Race Riot of 1921," State of Oklahoma, February 28, 2001; Randy Krehbiel, *Tulsa 1921: Reporting a Massacre* (Norman: University Press of Oklahoma, 2019), 116.

21. James D. Robenalt, "The Republican President Who Called for Racial Justice in America after Tulsa Massacre," *Washington Post*, June 21, 2020; "President Harding at Lincoln University," *Lincoln University Herald*, June–August 1921; "Harding Voices Regret over Tulsa Rioting," *New-York Tribune*, June 7, 1921.

22. James David Robenalt, *The Harding Affair: Love and Espionage During the Great War* (New York: Palgrave McMillan, 2009), 3; Harding, Speech on Race Relations, *Selections*, 248–53.

23. "Washington News in Brief," *Chicago Daily Tribune*, October 28, 1921; Villard, *Fighting Years*, 499.

24. Alysa Landry, "Warren Harding: Wanted Assimilation by Way of Citizenship," *Indian Country Today*, July 19, 2016, https://newsmaven.io/indiancountrytoday /archive/warren-harding-wanted-assimilation-by-way-of-citizenship -3QDBS3KfAESGplk9PdIBuQ/.

25. Anthony, "The Most Scandalous President."

26. Warren G. Harding to Gustave Hartman, October 25, 1920, *Selections from the Papers and Speeches of Warren G. Harding, 1918–1923*, ed. Leonard Schlup and John H. Hepp IV (Lewiston, New York: The Edwin Mellen Press, 2008), 156.

27. Anthony, "The Most Scandalous President."

28. Eric Foner, "He's the Worst Ever," *Washington Post*, December 3, 2006.

29. Murray, *The Harding Era*, 229–30; Dean, *Warren G. Harding*, 115.

30. Warren Harding, "Inaugural Address," The American Presidency Project, https://www.presidency.ucsb.edu/documents/inaugural-address-49.

31. Dean, *Warren G. Harding*, 115; Warren G. Harding to Frank Scobey, October 25, 1919, *Selections from the Papers and Speeches of Warren G. Harding, 1918– 1923*, ed. Leonard Schlup and John H. Hepp IV (Lewiston, New York: The Edwin Mellen Press, 2008), 70.

32. Dean, *Warren G. Harding*, 116; Murray, *The Harding Era*, 242; Warren G. Harding to Vorys, Sater, Seymour, and Pease for Consolidated Coal and Coke Company, July 27, 1922, *Selections from the Papers and Speeches of Warren G. Harding, 1918–1923*, ed. Leonard Schlup and John H. Hepp IV (Lewiston, New York: The Edwin Mellen Press, 2008), 325.

33. Dean, *Warren G. Harding*, 117; Murray, *The Harding Era*, 255–56; Herbert Hoover, *The Memoirs of Herbert Hoover: The Cabinet and the Presidency, 1920–1933* (New York: The Macmillan Company, 1952), 47–48; Warren G. Harding to Charles Dawes, September 5, 1922, *Selections from the Papers and Speeches of Warren G. Harding, 1918–1923*, ed. Leonard Schlup and John H. Hepp IV (Lewiston, New York: The Edwin Mellen Press, 2008), 344. For more on the Olney Injunction, see Ryan S. Walters, *Grover Cleveland: The Last Jeffersonian President* (Abbeville, South Carolina: Abbeville Institute, 2021).

34. Warren G. Harding to Elbert H. Gary, April 20, 1922, *Selections from the Papers and Speeches of Warren G. Harding, 1918–1923*, ed. Leonard Schlup and John H. Hepp IV (Lewiston, New York: The Edwin Mellen Press, 2008), 308.

Chapter 9: The Scandals

Epigraph: William Allen White, *Masks in a Pageant* (New York: Macmillan Company, 1928), 619.

1. Herbert Hoover, *The Memoirs of Herbert Hoover: The Cabinet and the Presidency, 1920–1933* (New York: The Macmillan Company, 1952), 48; William J. Ridings Jr. and Stuart B. McIver, *Rating the Presidents: A Ranking of U.S. Leaders, from the Great and Honorable to the Dishonest and Incompetent* (Citadel Press Book, 1997), 184.
2. Edmund Starling, *Starling of the White House* (Chicago: People's Club Book, 1946), 167, 192.
3. Alice Roosevelt Longworth, *Crowded Hours* (New York: Charles Scribner's Sons, 1932), 320–21.
4. Starling, *Starling of the White House*, 171.
5. White, *Masks*, 619.
6. Henry L. Stoddard, *As I Knew Them: Presidents and Politics from Grant to Coolidge* (New York: Harper & Brothers Publishers, 1927), 474.
7. Rosemary Stevens, *A Time of Scandal: Charles R. Forbes, Warren G. Harding and the Making of the Veterans Bureau* (Baltimore: Johns Hopkins University Press, 2016), 36.
8. Ibid., 7–22; John W. Dean, *Warren G. Harding* (New York: Times Books, 2004), 141; Ridings and McIver, *Rating the Presidents*, 139–40.
9. Dean, *Warren G. Harding*, 184; Nathan Miller, *Star-Spangled Men: America's Ten Worst Presidents* (New York: A Touchstone Book, 1998), 207.
10. Dean, *Warren G. Harding*, 141.
11. Stevens, *A Time of Scandal*, viii.
12. Starling, *Starling of the White House*, 172–73, Cohen, 224.
13. Brian R. Farmer, *American Conservatism: History, Theory and Practice* (Cambridge: Cambridge Scholars Press, 2005), 219; Starling, *Starling of the White House*, 172.
14. Hoover, *The Memoirs*, 49.
15. White, *The Autobiography*, 619–20.
16. Stevens, *A Time of Scandal*, 35.
17. Miller, *Star-Spangled Men*, 211.
18. Charles Evans Hughes, *The Autobiographical Notes of Charles Evans Hughes*, ed. David J. Danelski and Joseph S. Tulchin (Cambridge: Harvard University Press, 1973), 201.
19. James E. Watson, *As I Knew Them: The Memoirs of James E. Watson* (New York: The Bobbs-Merrill Company Publishers, 1936), 229.
20. James D. Robenalt, "If We Weren't So Obsessed with Warren G. Harding's Sex Life, We'd Realize He Was a Pretty Good President," *Washington Post*, August 12, 2015.
21. White, *Masks*, 407, 420.

22. Oswald Garrison Villard, *Fighting Years: Memoirs of a Liberal Editor* (New York: Harcourt, Brace and Company, 1939), 497.
23. Andrew Sinclair, *The Available Man: The Life behind the Masks of Warren G. Harding* (Chicago: Quadrangle Books, 1965), 185.
24. Watson, *As I Knew Them*, 229.
25. Gail Collins, "About Those Presidential Polls," *New York Times*, July 4, 2014.
26. Jude Wanniski, "In Defense of President Warren Harding," LewRockwell.com, June 15, 2004, https://www.lewrockwell.com/2004/06/jude-wanniski/in-defense-of-president-warrenharding/; Llewellyn H. Rockwell Jr., "Missing Warren G. Harding," Mises Institute, July 31, 2007, https://mises.org/library/missing-warren-g-harding; Bailey, *Presidential Greatness*, 313–14.
27. Philip B. Kunhardt, Philip B. Kunhardt III, and Peter W. Kunhardt, *The American President* (New York: Riverhead Books, 1999), 69, 73; Miller, *Star-Spangled Men*, 194.
28. Dean, *Warren G. Harding*, 139.
29. William Allen White, *The Autobiography of William Allen White* (New York: The Macmillan Company, 1946), 432.
30. Hoover, *The Memoirs*, 49–52.
31. Ibid, 49.
32. Ibid, 51.
33. Ibid, 52.
34. Ibid, 51.
35. Longworth, *Crowded Hours*, 325.
36. Calvin Coolidge, *The Autobiography of Calvin Coolidge* (New York: Cosmopolitan Book Corporation, 1929), 168.
37. Ridings and McIver, *Rating the Presidents*, 184.
38. Starling, *Starling of the White House*, 182.
39. Longworth, *Crowded Hours*, 325.
40. Claude M. Fuess, *Calvin Coolidge: The Man from Vermont* (Boston: Little, Brown, and Company, 1940), 309.
41. "A Good Man," *Memphis Commercial Appeal*, August 3, 1923.
42. "Ohio's Own Great Son," *Akron Beacon Journal*, August 3, 1923.
43. "The President is Dead," *Los Angeles Times*, August 3, 1923.

Conclusion: Restoring Harding's Reputation

Epigraph: Herbert Hoover, "Address at the Dedication of the Harding Memorial at Marion, Ohio," The American Presidency Project, https://www.presidency.ucsb.edu/documents/address-the-dedication-the-harding-memorial-marion-ohio.
1. William Allen White, *Masks in a Pageant* (New York: Macmillan Company, 1928), 434.
2. Herbert Hoover, *The Memoirs of Herbert Hoover: The Cabinet and the Presidency, 1920–1933* (New York: The Macmillan Company, 1952), 52.
3. Ibid.

4. Hoover, "Address at the Dedication."

5. Ibid.

6. Steven F. Hayward, *The Politically Incorrect Guide to the Presidents, from Wilson to Obama* (Washington, D.C.: Regnery Publishing, 2012), 74.

7. William J. Ridings Jr. and Stuart B. McIver, *Rating the Presidents: A Ranking of U.S. Leaders, from the Great and Honorable to the Dishonest and Incompetent* (Citadel Press Book, 1997), 185.

8. James David Robenalt, *The Harding Affair: Love and Espionage During the Great War* (New York: Palgrave McMillan, 2009), 4.

9. White, *Masks*, 402.

10. Nathan Miller, *New World Coming: The 1920s and the Making of Modern America* (New York: Scribner, 2003), 198.

11. Jared Cohen, *Accidental Presidents: Eight Men Who Changed America* (New York: Simon and Schuster, 2019), 231.

12. White, *Masks*, 402; Nicholas Murray Butler, *Across Busy Years: Recollections and Reflections*, vol. 1 (New York: Charles Scribner's Sons, 1935), 243, 254, 278.

13. Miller, *New World Coming*, 204; Dean, *Warren G. Harding*, 43.

14. Warren G. Harding to Malcolm Jennings, June 6, 1922, *Selections from the Papers and Speeches of Warren G. Harding, 1918–1923*, ed. Leonard Schlup and John H. Hepp IV (Lewiston, New York: The Edwin Mellen Press, 2008), 267–68.

15. Llewellyn H. Rockwell Jr., "Missing Warren G. Harding," Mises Institute, July 31, 2007, https://mises.org/library/missing-warren-g-harding.

16. Warren G. Harding to Woodrow Wilson, October 9, 1922, *Selections from the Papers and Speeches of Warren G. Harding, 1918–1923*, ed. Leonard Schlup and John H. Hepp IV (Lewiston, New York: The Edwin Mellen Press, 2008), 358.

17. Eleanor Herman, *Sex with Presidents: The Ins and Outs of Love and Lust in the White House* (New York: HarperCollins, 2020), 129; Murray, *The Harding Era*, 489; Edmund Starling, *Starling of the White House* (Chicago: People's Club Book, 1946), 170–71.

18. Douglas Alan Cohn, *The President's First Year* (Guilford, Connecticut: Lyons Press, 2016), 210.

19. John W. Dean, *Warren G. Harding* (New York: Times Books, 2004), 165.

20. Starling, 169–70.

21. Ibid., 170, 182–83.

22. David Cannadine, *Mellon: An American Life* (New York: Vintage Books, 2006), 315–18.

23. Patrick J. Buchanan, The *Great Betrayal: How American Sovereignty and Social Justice Are Being Sacrificed to the Gods of Global Economy* (Boston: Little, Brown and Company, 1998), 239–40.

24. Robert P. Murphy, *The Politically Incorrect Guide to the Great Depression and the New Deal* (Washington: Regnery Publishing, 2009), 82.

25. Veronica de Rugy, "1920s Income Tax Cuts Sparked Economic Growth and Raised Federal Revenues," Cato Institute, March 4, 2003, https://www.cato.org/commentary /1920s-income-tax-cuts-sparked-economic-growth-raised-federal-revenues.

26. Larry Schweikart and Michael Allen, *A Patriot's History of the United States* (Sentinel, 2004), 534.

27. Philip Abbott, *Bad Presidents: Failure in the White House* (New York: Palgrave Macmillan, 2013), 133–35.

28. Thomas J. DiLorenzo, *How Capitalism Saved America: The Untold History of Our Country, from the Pilgrims to the Present* (Washington, D.C.: Crown Forum, 2005), 156.

29. Murphy, *The Politically Incorrect Guide*, 13.

INDEX